ANSWERING
JEWISH
OBJECTIONS
JE*to*SUS

Also by Michael L. Brown

Revolution in the Church: Challenging the Religious System with a Call for Radical Change

Answering Jewish Objections to Jesus: Theological Objections

Answering Jewish Objections to Jesus: General and Historical Objections

Revolution! The Call to Holy War

Go and Sin No More: A Call to Holiness

The Revival Answer Book: Rightly Discerning the Contemporary Revival Movements

From Holy Laughter to Holy Fire: America on the Edge of Revival

Israel's Divine Healer

It's Time to Rock the Boat: A Call to God's People to Rise Up and Preach a Confrontational Gospel

Our Hands Are Stained with Blood: The Tragic Story of the "Church" and the Jewish People

Whatever Happened to the Power of God: Is the Charismatic Church Slain in the Spirit or Down for the Count?

How Saved Are We?

The End of the American Gospel Enterprise

Compassionate Father or Consuming Fire: Who Is the God of the Old Testament?

Michael L. Brown is a Jewish believer in Jesus and has a Ph.D. in Near Eastern Languages and Literatures from New York University. He is president of the FIRE School of Ministry and has served as a visiting professor at Trinity Evangelical Divinity School and Fuller Theological Seminary. He has written over fifteen books and is a contributor to the *Oxford Dictionary of Jewish Religion*.

ANSWERING JEWISH OBJECTIONS *to* JESUS

Volume 3

Messianic Prophecy Objections

MICHAEL L. BROWN

Baker Books

A Division of Baker Book House Co
Grand Rapids, Michigan 49516

Published by Baker Books
a division of Baker Book House Company
P.O. Box 6287, Grand Rapids, MI 49516-6287
www.bakerbooks.com

Printed in the United States of America

Library of Congress Cataloging-in-Publication Data
Brown, Michael L., 1955–
    Answering Jewish objections to Jesus : messianic prophecy objections /
    Michael L. Brown.
        p.   cm.
    Includes bibliographical references (p.) and indexes.
    ISBN 0-8010-6423-6 (paper)
    1. Apologetics. 2. Jews—Conversion to Christianity. 3 Jesus Christ—
Messiahship. I. Title.
BV4922.B76 2002
239—dc21   99-046293

To my Jewish people, in Israel,
America, and around the world.
The time of our salvation is at hand!

Contents

Preface

In November of 1971, as a proud, rebellious, heroin-shooting, rock-drumming, Jewish sixteen-year-old, I discovered something I was not looking for, and the course of my life was completely altered. I found out that Jesus was the Jewish Messiah! I learned that he was God's way of salvation for Jew and Gentile alike, and that through faith in him, my life could be transformed—even though I didn't want to be transformed. I loved my sinful ways! But God's goodness overcame my badness, and in a matter of weeks I was a brand-new man.

Of course, it was important to show my caring Jewish parents that Jesus was actually our promised Messiah, the one spoken of in the Hebrew Scriptures, so I handed them a gospel tract with passages from our Jewish Bible that seemed to point to Jesus. The verses really seemed quite clear to me, until a local rabbi began to point out to my father that the verses were actually taken out of context or were misinterpreted or mistranslated. But were they? The rabbi gave me a book written by a Jewish scholar who argued that the prophecies did not point to Jesus at all, and some of the arguments sounded pretty convincing. So I showed my pastor the book, hoping that he could provide answers. Unfortunately, he didn't have much to contribute, despite his sincerity.

This left me in a quandary. If Jesus truly was the prophesied Messiah, then it was right for me as a Jew to put my trust in him. In fact, it was right for me to share this wonderful news with every Jew and Gentile who was open to hearing it. But if Jesus was not the Messiah of the Scriptures, then I had no right believing in him, let alone sharing my beliefs with others.

Certainly, I knew my life had been powerfully changed by Jesus, and some of the prophecies did seem to point to him. But there were other prophecies that didn't seem as clear anymore. What was I to do? There was only one viable option: I needed to continue my prayerful study of the Word of God, and I needed to acquire the necessary scholarly tools to do in-depth analysis of the Messianic prophecies for myself, not relying on other commentaries, dictionaries, opinions, or traditions. By God's grace, that is what I have done for the last thirty years, and this volume represents a distillation of three decades of study of the Messianic prophecies, in particular, as it relates to answering Jewish objections to the application of the Messianic prophecies to Jesus.

Did I study with a closed mind? Absolutely not. To the contrary, I did my best to present myself with question after question, to challenge my beliefs from every angle, to expose myself to the very best arguments I could find, and to try to understand just why so many of my people claimed that Yeshua did not fulfill the Scriptures. I can now say with confidence that I *do* understand the objections, but the objections are certainly wrong. I invite every reader, especially every Jewish reader who does not yet believe in Yeshua as Messiah, to read this volume carefully, with an open heart and mind. I believe each of you will see that the evidence is clear and decisive: Jesus is our Messiah! In fact, countless thousands of Jews have become followers of Yeshua *because of* these very prophecies. Now the faith of these Jewish believers can be strengthened all the more, as objection after objection is dealt with honestly and fairly, while obstacles to faith can be removed from those who have had their share of doubts.

Readers of the first two volumes of the *Answering Jewish Objections to Jesus* series have been expecting the publication of this third volume for some time now. Unfortunately, I fell behind schedule and soon realized that the original plan for volume 3 (which included not only the Messianic prophecies but also two other substantial sections of objections) was becoming unwieldy and that it would be best to focus on the Messianic prophecies alone. You will see that it is still quite a substantial study! The remaining two sections of objections—namely, objections to the New Testament (thirty-four total) and objections arising from Jewish tradition (eighteen total)—will be presented in a fourth volume. I apologize for the delays and appreciate the patience of the many readers who have been asking, "When is the Messianic prophecy volume coming out?" At last, it is done. Included in this volume is a short appendix that presents seven principles of interpreting Messianic prophecy. As simple as these principles are, they too are the reflection of many years of study and, I trust, will be of genuine help to serious students of the Scriptures.

To recap what has been published in this series to date: Volume 1 deals with general and historical objections to Jesus (thirty-five objections in all, numbered 1.1–1.19 and 2.1–2.16 respectively). Volume 2 deals with theological objections (twenty-eight in all, numbered 3.1–3.28). The present volume deals with major objections to the Messianic prophecies (thirty-nine in all, numbered 4.1–4.39). Volume 4, yet to be published, will deal with objections to the New Testament and objections arising from Jewish tradition. The table of contents in each volume lists the specific objections covered, enabling the reader to get an overview of the material at a glance and making it easy to locate each individual objection. If there is sufficient reader interest, these four volumes will eventually be combined into a one-volume reference edition, with some special studies and further notes added.

The *general objections*, addressed in volume 1, can be boiled down to the perception, "Jesus is not for Jews! Our religion is Judaism, not Christianity. No true Jew would ever believe in Jesus." The *historical objections*, also in volume 1, tend to be more substantial, having to do with the very purpose of the Messiah (in other words, the claim that the role of the Messiah was to bring peace to the world) or the alleged failure of the church ("Christian" anti-Semitism and the divisions and scandals of the "church" worldwide). At the heart of these objections is the statement, "Jesus cannot be the Messiah because we are obviously not in the Messianic age."

Theological objections, treated at length in volume 2, cut to the heart of the differences between traditional Judaism and the Messianic Jewish/Christian faith. These differences revolve around the nature of God (the Trinity, the deity of Jesus, the person of the Holy Spirit), the nature of man and the need for salvation, and sin and the means of atonement. In sum, these objections claim, "The religion of the New Testament is a completely foreign religion that is not only un-Jewish but is also unfaithful to the Hebrew Bible."

Messianic prophecy objections, addressed in the present volume, arise from traditional Judaism's rejection of our standard Messianic prophetic "proof texts." These objections either deny that the prophecies in question have anything to do with Jesus, claiming that they have been mistranslated, misquoted, or taken out of context by the New Testament authors or traditional Christian apologists, or argue that none of the *real* Messianic prophecies—the so-called provable prophecies—were ever fulfilled by Jesus. In short, these objections say, "We don't believe Jesus is the Messiah because he didn't come close to living up to the biblical description of the Messiah."

Jewish *objections to the New Testament,* to be dealt with in volume 4, can be boiled down to several statements: The New Testament misquotes and misinterprets the Old Testament, at times manufacturing verses to suit its purposes; the genealogies of Jesus given by Matthew and Luke are hopelessly contradictory at best and entirely irrelevant anyway; the New Testament is filled with historical and factual errors (especially Stephen's speech!); the teachings of Jesus are impossible, dangerous, and un-Jewish (and Jesus as a person was not so great either); the New Testament is self-contradictory. To sum up these objections rather bluntly, "Only a fool would believe in the divine inspiration of the New Testament."

Finally, *objections based on traditional Judaism* are founded on two key points: (1) "Judaism is a wonderful, fulfilling, and self-sufficient religion. There is no need to look elsewhere." (2) "God gave us a written and an oral tradition. We interpret *everything* by means of that oral tradition, without which the Bible makes no sense."

Each of the volumes in this series follows a similar format. I begin with a concise statement of the objection, followed by a concise answer to the objection, which is then followed by an in-depth answer, which considers possible objections to the answer and includes citation of important sources as needed. For those interested in more detailed discussion and study, substantial endnotes have been provided. Other readers may choose to skip the notes and concentrate on the main text.

I have dedicated this study to my Jewish people everywhere in the world, with the fervent hope that in this generation more and more Jews will turn to God and put their faith in Yeshua the Messiah. I believe it's time! The Messianic prophecies are our sure, reliable guide, a bedrock of our faith, and the written assurance that Jesus indeed is the one. I pray that every seeking soul will find him, and I thank the Lord for the privilege of finally putting these precious scriptural truths into print. May he alone be honored and exalted.

Michael L. Brown
September 16, 2002
the evening after Yom Kippur, the Day of Atonement

Note on citations and sources: Rabbinic literature is cited using standard conventions (e.g., the letter "m." before a rabbinic source means "Mishnah" while "b."

stands for "Babylonian Talmud"). When there was a difference in the numbering of biblical verses between some Christian and Jewish versions, the Jewish numbering was put in brackets (e.g., Isa. 9:6[5]). Bear in mind, however, that the actual verses are identical; only the numbering is different. Also, in keeping with the stylistic conventions of the publisher, all pronouns referring to deity are lowercase. However, in keeping with traditional Jewish conventions, other words (such as Rabbinic, Temple, and Messianic) have been capitalized. Unless otherwise noted, all emphasis in Scripture quotations is my own.

PART 4

MESSIANIC
PROPHECY
OBJECTIONS

כָּל הַנְּבִיאִים כּוּלָם לֹא נִתְנַבְּאוּ אֶלָּא לִימוֹת הַמָּשִׁיחַ
All the prophets, all of them, did not prophesy
except of the days of the Messiah.
Babylonian Talmud, Sanhedrin 99a

4.1. If Jesus is really the Messiah, and if he is so important, why doesn't the Torah speak of him at all?

> You would be surprised to see how many passages and concepts actually point to Jesus the Messiah in the Torah. But before you question my beliefs, are you aware that the Torah doesn't say much about the "traditional" Jewish Messiah? Does this mean the Messiah is unimportant to traditional Judaism? And the Torah says nothing about the oral law. What does this imply? You might want to think twice about your argument.

In the Torah (i.e., the Five Books of Moses), the four times the word *mashiach* is found (Lev. 4:3, 5, 16; 6:15), it refers to the anointed high priest *(hakohen hamashiach),* not the Messiah. In fact, with few possible exceptions, the term *mashiach* is almost never used with reference to the Messiah in the Hebrew Scriptures. Also, there is no concept of the Messiah as the son of David in the Torah, since David was not born until many years later. So, we are not looking primarily for direct references to "the Messiah" (and certainly not to the "son of David") as such in the Torah.[1] Rather, we are looking for foreshadowings, general predictions, and "pre-illustrations" of the Messiah in the Torah. Here are just a few.

The Akedah (also known as the binding of Isaac), the story of Abraham's willingness to sacrifice his own son in obedience to God (Genesis 22), points to the Messiah in several ways, particularly as this story was developed in Rabbinic tradition. You will remember from our earlier discussion (vol. 2, 3.15) that in the Akedah, the rabbis stressed both Abraham's obedience and Isaac's willing participation, also teaching that although Isaac was not actually sacrificed, it was counted as if he were. So, for the rabbis, the actions of both the father and the son were of great significance in this biblical account, an account referred to daily in the traditional Jewish prayer service. As we look back at Genesis 22, bearing in mind the importance of the Akedah in Rabbinic thought, we can draw a few parallels between the Akedah and the Messiah.[2]

1. We see that Abraham proved his total dedication to God through his sacrificial actions: "Now I know that you fear God, because you have not withheld from me your son, your only son" (Gen. 22:12). In the same way, God demonstrated his love and commitment to us by giving us his own Son: "He who did not spare his own Son, but gave him up for us all—how will he not also, along with him, graciously give us all things?" (Rom. 8:32).

2. Isaac is referred to in Genesis 22 as Abraham's *only* son *(yachid):* "Take your son, your only son, Isaac, whom you love, and go to the region of Moriah. Sacrifice him there as a burnt offering on one of the mountains I will tell you about" (Gen. 22:2; see also 22:12, just cited).[3] In the same way, the New Testament describes Jesus in his sacrificial death as God's *only* Son: "For God so loved the world that he gave his one and only Son, that whoever believes in him shall not perish but have eternal life" (John 3:16).

3. Isaac's willingness to be sacrificed illustrates the Messiah's obedience, even to the point of death. (The difference, of course, is clear: Isaac died only in the mind of Rabbinic tradition; the Messiah literally gave his life. For more on this, see vol. 2, 3.15.)

4. Abraham was confident that even though he was about to sacrifice his son on the mountain, he would somehow return from the mountain *with* his son: "He said to his servants, 'Stay here with the donkey while I and the boy go over there. We will worship and then we will come back to you'" (Gen. 22:5). The writer to the Hebrews comments: "By faith Abraham, when God tested him, offered Isaac as a sacrifice. He who had received the promises was about to sacrifice his one and only son, even though God had said to him, 'It is through Isaac that your offspring will be reckoned.' Abraham reasoned that God could raise the dead, and figuratively speaking, he did receive Isaac back from death"

(Heb. 11:17–19). Thus, Isaac's return from virtual death pre-figures the Messiah's return from literal death.

Genesis records, "As the two of them went on together, Isaac spoke up and said to his father Abraham, 'Father?' 'Yes, my son?' Abraham replied. 'The fire and wood are here,' Isaac said, 'but where is the lamb for the burnt offering?'"(Gen. 22:6–8).

Yes, God himself *did* provide the lamb for the burnt offering to take Isaac's place on that fateful day on Mount Moriah. Centuries later, God provided the final sacrificial Lamb, when the Messiah took our place on Mount Calvary. As John the Immerser (known to Christians as John the Baptist) said, "Look, the Lamb of God, who takes away the sin of the world!" (John 1:29). You can see that the account of the binding of Isaac is rich with Messianic imagery![4]

Moving to another prefigurement of the Messiah in the Torah, we see that the life of Joseph also points to several unique aspects of the ministry of Jesus. (Remember that events and people that foreshadow the Messiah are not meant to be specific in every detail but rather illustrative in broad, sweeping ways. The parallels in the lives of Jesus and Joseph, however, are really quite striking.) Joseph was rejected by his own brothers (Genesis 37), suffered because of false accusations and slander even though he himself was righteous (Genesis 39), but was then exalted to become the savior of Egypt and the world (Genesis 41). And during the entire time that he was respected and revered by these Gentiles, he was unknown to his own brothers, considered as good as dead. In fact, the first time they saw him in his exalted position in Egypt, they did not recognize him (Gen. 42:7–8). It was only the *second time* that he revealed himself to them: "So there was no one with Joseph when he made himself known to his brothers" (Gen. 45:1). Ironically, it was his brothers' betrayal of him when he was only a teenager that caused Joseph to go to Egypt, resulting in the saving of the lives of many Gentiles and then, ultimately, of his own flesh-and-blood family: "God sent me ahead of you to preserve for you a remnant on earth and to save your lives by a great deliverance" (Gen. 45:7).

So also, Yeshua was betrayed by his own people, slandered and falsely accused (though he was perfectly righteous), delivered over to death, and then exalted to be the Savior of the Gentile world—precisely because his own nation rejected him. In the end, in what is commonly called his *second coming,* he will make himself known to his brothers, and the weeping will be great (Zech. 12:10–14; note also

Gen. 45:2). Even traditional Jewish scholars have noted the pattern of a rejected, then hidden, then revealed, Messiah.[5] It is certainly apt!

Let's turn now to the sacrificial system, a subject that receives far more emphasis in the Torah than the dietary laws or even the laws governing human relationships and conduct (see vol. 2, 3.9). This sacrificial system was undeniably important to the biblical Jew, and it points to the ultimate sacrifice for our sins, Yeshua the Messiah. It was Rashi who said the heart of the sacrificial system was "life for life," an innocent victim taking the place of the guilty party. That's why it was the blood that made atonement, since the life of the flesh is in the blood (Lev. 17:11; for more on this, see vol. 2, 3.10). But was God primarily interested in the blood of bulls and goats? Could their blood really take away sins? Certainly not. Rather, the rivers of blood that flowed from the countless thousands of sacrificial animals served to point the way to the truly innocent one who would lay down his life on our behalf.

These truths are most fully spelled out in the Day of Atonement (Yom Kippur) rituals, as outlined in Leviticus 16. Two goats played a central role in these rituals. One was slain, and its blood was brought into the Most Holy Place to cleanse it from the defiling sins of the nation.

> In this way [the high priest] will make atonement *[kipper]* for the Most Holy Place because of the uncleanness and rebellion of the Israelites, whatever their sins have been. He is to do the same for the Tent of Meeting, which is among them in the midst of their uncleanness.
>
> Leviticus 16:16

The other goat, commonly known as the "scapegoat,"[6] was to be kept alive, and the high priest was to

> lay both hands on the head of the live goat and confess over it all the wickedness and rebellion of the Israelites—all their sins—and put them on the goat's head. He shall send the goat away into the desert in the care of a man appointed for the task. The goat will carry on itself all their sins to a solitary place; and the man shall release it in the desert.
>
> Leviticus 16:21–22

These two goats, the sacrificial center of the central day of Israel's calendar, ultimately point to the twofold role of the Messiah: (1) His blood makes atonement for our sins, breaking down the barrier of defilement that stood between us and God, and (2) as we confess our sins, he carries away all our rebellion and wickedness.

These insights lead to an important observation. The anti-missionaries (see vol. 1, xvi) claim that Christianity overemphasizes the issue of atonement for sin, arguing that the Rabbinic approach is better, which emphasizes study of the law and observance of the law. Yet the fact of the matter is that Christianity derives its theology of atonement *from the law*. Therefore, because the New Testament faith recognized the centrality of the sacrificial system in the Bible, it also built its Messianic beliefs on that very foundation. It's hard to get more Torah-centered than that! Yes, belief in Jesus the Messiah is *totally* grounded in the Torah, even more so than the traditional Jewish beliefs about the Messiah.

Even the high priest points to the Messiah, since his main role—a tremendously important, God-ordained role in ancient Israel—was to make intercession and atonement for the nation. Indeed, as he wore his priestly garments, whenever he would enter the Holy Place, he would "bear the names of the sons of Israel over his heart," and the turban on his head signified that he would "bear the guilt involved in the sacred gifts the Israelites consecrate, whatever their gifts may be" (Exod. 28:29, 38). So important was his role as mediator of the people that his very death brought atonement (see vol. 2, 3.15 for this crucial topic). Later Rabbinic tradition even taught that the *garments* of the high priest atoned (see b. Zevahim 68b; cf. also b. Moed Katan 28a).[7] How powerfully this points to the high-priestly role of Yeshua our Messiah!

Here is just a sample of this rich teaching as found in the Letter to the Hebrews. Jesus became like one of us so as to atone for our sins (see below, 4.35), and he was (and is) the greatest high priest we have ever had:

> Now there have been many of those [earthly] priests, since death prevented them from continuing in office; but because Jesus lives forever, he has a permanent priesthood. Therefore he is able to save completely those who come to God through him, because he always lives to intercede for them.
>
> Such a high priest meets our need—one who is holy, blameless, pure, set apart from sinners, exalted above the heavens. Unlike the other high priests, he does not need to offer sacrifices day after day, first for his own sins, and then for the sins of the people. He sacrificed for their sins once for all when he offered himself. For the law appoints as high

priests men who are weak; but the oath, which came after the law, appointed the Son, who has been made perfect forever.

Hebrews 7:23–28

When [Messiah] came as high priest of the good things that are already here, he went through the greater and more perfect tabernacle that is not man-made, that is to say, not a part of this creation. He did not enter by means of the blood of goats and calves; but he entered the Most Holy Place once for all by his own blood, having obtained eternal redemption. The blood of goats and bulls and the ashes of a heifer sprinkled on those who are ceremonially unclean sanctify them so that they are outwardly clean. How much more, then, will the blood of [Messiah], who through the eternal Spirit offered himself unblemished to God, cleanse our consciences from acts that lead to death, so that we may serve the living God!

For this reason [Messiah] is the mediator of a new covenant, that those who are called may receive the promised eternal inheritance— now that he has died as a ransom to set them free from the sins committed under the first covenant.

Hebrews 9:11–15

What a high priest we now have! In every way, through his life and death, he fulfilled that which the biblical high priests could only point toward. They were the shadow; he is the very substance. In fact, he fulfills the images of both the sacrifice of atonement and the priest who offers that atoning sacrifice to God. The Torah *does* point to Yeshua, without doubt. He even pointed this out himself, informing his disciples after his resurrection: "This is what I told you while I was still with you: Everything must be fulfilled that is *written about me* in the Law of Moses, the Prophets and the Psalms" (Luke 24:44).[8]

The New Covenant Scriptures record a conversation between Jesus and a member of the Sanhedrin named Nicodemus in which our righteous Messiah pointed to the Torah to explain his impending death for the sins of his people, saying, "Just as Moses lifted up the snake in the desert, so the Son of Man must be lifted up [meaning, in crucifixion], that everyone who believes in him may have eternal life" (John 3:14–15). Yeshua was referring to the account in Numbers 21:4–9, when the Israelites who sinned against God were bitten by poisonous snakes and then found healing and relief when they looked to the bronze snake Moses erected on a pole (in obedience to divine command). In similar fashion, all humanity, guilty of sin and smitten with deadly spiritual poison, has only one antidote for this mortal condition: the cross of the Messiah. As one commentator pointed out, in both cases "the object elevated before them was the emblem of their judgment,"[9] the snake being a symbol of the judgment that came against the Israelites for their sin in Numbers 21, and the cross being the symbol of terrible judgment and death in Jesus' day. What a fitting analogy![10]

But Jesus was not the first to draw attention to the symbolism of the lifted-up snake in the desert. In the intertestamental work known as The Wisdom of Solomon (probably composed between 120–100 B.C.E.), it is written:

> For when the terrible rage of wild animals came upon your people
> and they were being destroyed by the bites of writhing serpents,
> your wrath did not continue to the end;
> they were troubled for a little while as a warning,
> and received a symbol of deliverance to remind them of your law's
> command.
> For the one who turned toward it was saved, not by the thing that was
> beheld,
> but by you, the Savior of all.
> And by this also you convinced our enemies
> that it is you who deliver from every evil.
>
> The Wisdom of Solomon 16:5–8 NRSV[11]

So, by looking at the symbol of deliverance—the snake raised up on a pole—the people of Israel put their hope in God their Savior and were healed and set free. How much more can this be said of Yeshua, the Savior himself, the fullness of God incarnate!

The Book of Acts also records a sermon by Peter—one of Yeshua's first twelve disciples and therefore a man taught by the Messiah himself—in which he too claims that Moses pointed to Jesus, specifically as the divinely sent prophet par excellence (see Acts 3:22–23). Although the passage to which Peter referred (Deut. 18:15) is not exclusively a Messianic prophecy, Peter was right on target in applying it to Yeshua. We read in Deuteronomy 18:9–22 that God promised his people he would raise up for them a prophet like Moses, someone who would hear God's words and declare them to the people so that they would not be dependent on the superstitious practices of the surrounding nations (the ancient equivalents of things like astrology, sorcery, and séances). This prophet was to be of great importance, and God strictly warned Israel, "If anyone does not listen to my words that the prophet speaks in my name, I myself will call him to account" (Deut. 18:19).

You might say, "But doesn't this refer to a key prophet being raised up in every generation in Israel?" I believe so. And Jesus was the last and greatest national prophet among our people, the preeminent prophet of his generation or of any other generation, the Prophet with a capital *P*. He predicted the terrible destruction of Jerusalem and the Temple, warning of the consequences of rejecting his words. Also, because there was a conspicuous lack of prophetic voices in the centuries immediately preceding the coming of the Messiah into the world,[12] the people began to look more and more for a great end-time prophet, a forerunner of the Messianic kingdom they were expecting. We know this from the Dead Sea Scrolls (4QTestimonia; cf. also 1QS 9:1) as well as from the New Testament (e.g., John 1:19–21; 7:40; see also Luke 7:16; Acts 7:37).[13]

When Jesus ministered on the earth, people recognized him to be a great prophet (see Luke 7:16, "'A great prophet has appeared among us,' they said. 'God has come to help his people.'"). After his death and resurrection—there was no arguing with the resurrection!—Peter did not hesitate to proclaim that Yeshua was the ultimate prophet spoken of by Moses (see Acts 3:22–23). To this day, we still have not fully recovered from the destruction of the Temple and the devastation of Jerusalem, which Yeshua foretold in graphic detail (see esp. Luke 19:41–44; see also vol. 4, 5.22). And he was the prophet who foretold his own death, resurrection, and ultimate return, also assuring his followers that his message (called "the good news of the kingdom") would spread throughout the whole world before his return, something that is being rapidly and remarkably fulfilled (see vol. 1, 2.2). We would do well to heed that prophet's words![14]

But the story doesn't end there. Let's take a closer look at the passage in Deuteronomy 18. Moses said to the people, "The LORD your God will raise up for you a prophet like me from among your own brothers. . . . The LORD said to me: '. . . I will raise up for them a prophet like you from among their brothers'" (Deut. 18:15a, 17a–18a). The meaning, it seems, is fairly straightforward: Just as God raised up Moses to hear God's words and declare them to the people of Israel, so also in the future (or in every generation), God would raise up a prophet like Moses who would also hear God's words and declare them to the people. The problem is that according to Deuteronomy 34:10–11, "*. . . no prophet has risen in Israel like Moses*, whom the LORD knew face to face, who did all those miraculous signs and wonders the LORD sent him to do in Egypt—to Pharaoh and to all his officials and to his whole land." The identical phrase is used in both passages (namely, raising up a prophet like Moses), but we are told explicitly that no such prophet arose again in Israel's history.[15]

So, Deuteronomy 18 tells us that the Lord would raise up such a prophet for his people, but Deuteronomy 34 tells us that, in the fullest sense, no such prophet arose. It is quite natural, then, that Jewish people reflecting on these Torah passages would begin to ask, "Where, then, is that prophet like Moses? Where is that leader to whom the Lord will speak face-to-face, who will work signs and wonders and deliver us from bondage?" And this passage helps to explain why there is clear evidence that the Jewish people in the first century of this era expected that there would be a great prophet associated with the Messiah or identical to the Messiah. This hope is grounded in the Torah of Moses itself.[16]

Finally, we should look at Genesis 49:10, a prophetic promise to Judah, often pointed to as a key Messianic prediction.[17] Before examining this specific passage, however, some background from the Torah is necessary. When God called Abram in Genesis 12, he promised him that through his offspring the entire world would be blessed (Gen. 12:1–3).[18] This promise was reiterated several times in Genesis, to Abram/Abraham himself, as well as to his son Isaac and to his son Jacob (see Gen. 18:18; 22:18; 26:4). Over the course of these generations, there was a process of selection: Abraham had two sons—Ishmael and Isaac—but the promise of worldwide blessing came through Isaac. Isaac in turn had two sons (twins)—Esau and Jacob—but the promise of worldwide blessing came through Jacob (later called Israel). Jacob had twelve sons, all of whom, as descendants and then tribes of Israel, would be heir to the promise in a limited sense. But the specific Messianic promise would come through only one son. Which son would that be?

All of us know the Tanakh teaches that the Messiah will be a descendant of King David, who was a descendant of Judah (1 Chron. 2:3–15). But Genesis 49:10 indicates that the kingship coming to Judah was actually prophesied by Jacob on his deathbed, hundreds of years before David was ever born. This important verse has been translated several different ways, in both Jewish and Christian versions. The overall meaning is clear, however, as will be seen by comparing a number of key modern translations (the first two quotations are from Christian translations, the second two, Jewish):

The scepter shall not depart from Judah,
Nor a lawgiver from between his feet,
Until Shiloh comes;
And to Him shall be the obedience of the people. (NASB)

The scepter will not depart from Judah,
nor the ruler's staff from between his feet,
until he comes to whom it belongs
and the obedience of the nations is his. (NIV)[19]

The scepter shall not depart from Judah,
Nor the ruler's staff from between his feet;
So that tribute shall come to him
And the homage of peoples be his. (NJPSV)[20]

The scepter shall not depart from Judah nor a scholar from among his descendants until Shiloh arrives and his will be the assemblage of nations. *(Stone)*[21]

The differences in translation arise primarily because of the Hebrew word *shiloh* in the second half of the verse. Is it a person's name or title (Shiloh), perhaps meaning "man of rest"? If so, to whom does it refer? The Messiah? Is it the name of a place (again, Shiloh), mentioned elsewhere in the Bible (e.g., Josh. 18:1; Judg. 18:31; Jer. 7:12)? If so, it is difficult to understand exactly what the prophecy means. Should the Hebrew be divided into two words, *shai lo,* meaning "tribute to him," in which case the translation would be "until tribute comes to him" (from the nations of the world, cf. Ps. 72:10), or should it be read as *she-lo,* meaning "to whom it belongs"? Both of these renderings could well refer to the Messiah.

Is Genesis 49:10 a Messianic prophecy? I believe a good case can be made for this, since (1) it points to Israel's legitimate kingship coming through Judah; (2) David, the first king in the Judean dynasty, became the prototype of the Messiah; and (3) the obedience of the nations is promised to that royal leader.

Does this verse, then, point specifically to Jesus? If the passage clearly indicates that the Messiah had to come before a certain time in history—namely, before the scepter departed from Judah and the ruler's staff from between his feet—and if that time in history ended shortly after Yeshua's death and resurrection, then we could say the passage pointed specifically to him. However, as Dr. Walter Riggans has explained, it is difficult to be dogmatic about this, since the

Hebrew can legitimately be translated in several different ways. His conclusion is that "although there must be a genuine modesty about the presentation of the Messianic interpretation of this verse *vis-à-vis* Jesus, nevertheless, Christians can be confident that their reading of it has integrity and perhaps even probability."[22]

This much is sure: (1) There is nothing in Genesis 49:10 that would rule out Yeshua from being the one who fulfilled the prophecy, especially since hundreds of millions of people around the world obey him and follow him (see below, 4.32–4.33). (2) If it is Messianic and points to a king who had come more than nineteen hundred years ago, then it *must* be Yeshua, in which case the day will come when his Jewish people will also acknowledge him as king. (3) If it is not Messianic, then quite obviously it does not apply to the "traditional" Jewish Messiah either.

This leads to an important closing observation: While our traditional Jewish friends challenge us and question why the Torah doesn't speak of Jesus, it is really the Messiah of Jewish tradition who is hardly mentioned at all,[23] while Yeshua is pointed to in many different ways— as the promised seed through whom the entire world would be blessed by the God of Israel; in the binding of Isaac; in the figure of Joseph; in the sacrificial system; in the priestly order; as the prophet greater than Moses. Yeshua is there! I encourage you to pray as the psalmist did in Psalm 119:18: "Uncover my eyes, and I will behold wonders in your Torah."[24]

4.2. Nowhere in the Hebrew Bible are we told that we must "believe in the Messiah."

> This is hardly an accurate statement, and it is not even in harmony with Jewish tradition. Believing in God, his prophets, and his Messiah is basic to the biblical faith, while one of the thirteen principles of the Jewish faith as articulated by Maimonides (Rambam), is that we must believe in the coming of the Messiah, awaiting him every day with unwavering faith.

This objection is really quite odd. (It may also be quite new; I first heard it from anti-missionaries in the late 1980s.) Apparently, it is a reaction to the New Testament emphasis on putting one's faith in the Messiah, on "believing in Jesus." The argument runs something like this: "There will be no need to believe in the Messiah, because when he comes, there will be peace on earth. You will be able to look out the window and see that the Messiah has come. There will be no war, no hatred, no strife."

Of course, this distorts even *traditional* Jewish thinking about the Messiah and the Messianic age, let alone biblical thinking, both of which point to a clear human response to the Messiah and his kingdom. Further, the kind of logic used here works against Rabbinic Judaism as well, since nowhere in the entire Hebrew Bible does it say, "Believe in the oral law," yet the oral law forms the very substance of traditional Judaism. Nonetheless, answering this particular objection gives us the opportunity to discuss some important Messianic truths, so I'll take a little time to explain the reasons for my belief more fully.

First, however, to demonstrate just how "un-Jewish" the objection is—and by that I mean un-Jewish in a traditional sense—I quote here the words of Rabbi Shmuley Boteach from his book on the Messiah in Hasidic thought. He claims that "the belief in the coming of the Messiah is more central to Judaism than even the observance of the Sabbath or Yom Kippur,"[25] even referring to the belief in the coming of the Messiah as "the cardinal principle of Jewish faith," and noting that "one is required not only to *believe* in the coming of the Messiah, but to actually *await* his arrival."[26] Similarly, Rabbi Shmuel Butman, a Lubavitcher leader in "the Rebbe is the Moshiach" movement,[27] answered the question, "Why must we look forward to the coming of the Moshiach?" as follows:

> . . . In the opening paragraph of his laws about the Moshiach (Hilchos Melachim 11:1), Rambam states:
>
> > ". . . Whoever does not believe in him [the Moshiach], or does not look forward to his coming, denies not only the other prophets but the Torah and Moshe, our Teacher, for the Torah attested concerning him [the Moshiach] . . ." (and he goes on to quote verses in the Torah that refer to the Moshiach).
>
> This is a remarkable halachic ruling. Even one who firmly believes in the coming of the Moshiach, yet his belief is no more than a dispassionate agreement that Moshiach eventually will come, not only does not fulfill his obligation; the Rambam rules that he actually denies the entire Torah and the authority of Moshe Rabbeinu, through whom G-d gave the Torah![28]

So, one Orthodox rabbi states that "the belief in the coming of the Messiah is more central to Judaism than even the observance of the Sabbath or Yom Kippur"(!), while another Orthodox rabbi emphatically teaches that Jews must *fervently believe* in the coming of the Messiah—otherwise they deny the entire Torah![29] And when Messiah comes, what then? Does the Jew then *cease* to believe in the Messiah, or does he joyfully embrace his arrival? The answer is self-evident, and it is exactly what we mean when we say, "Believe in Jesus the Messiah." In other words, Messiah has come! Your sins can be forgiven, as Jeremiah promised (Jer. 31:31–34), and you can receive a new heart and a new spirit, as Ezekiel declared (Ezek. 11:19; 18:31; 36:26). What could be more basic than that? In fact, it is more important to "believe in the Messiah" *after* his arrival than before his arrival.[30] Otherwise, we would be like a young man who believes passionately that God will send him a bride, and then when that God-sent woman of his dreams finally arrives, he says, "She's not the one!" What a pity that would be.

For many years prior to Yeshua's birth, our people longed for the coming of the Messiah, believing that his arrival was at hand. When at last he came into this world and revealed himself, his emissaries went everywhere, announcing the good news. "Messiah is here! Messiah has come!" The faith and expectancy of the people then rose to a fever pitch. But when he died, many were disillusioned: "We thought he was the Messiah. What happened? We had hoped he was the one who was going to redeem Israel." (See Luke 24:13–21 for a good example of the psychological state of the Messiah's followers immediately after his death.)

But then he rose from the dead, and his followers began to spread the word: It is true! He is risen, just as he said. Messiah lives! Redemption has come! Believe in him and be reconciled to God. Turn from your sins today. (See, e.g., Acts 2:22–40; 3:17–26; 16:1–34.) What a shame that so many of our people did not—and still do not—believe in him, our true Messiah and Redeemer. That's why his emissaries gave such strong warnings: "Take care that what the prophets have said does not happen to you: 'Look, you scoffers, wonder and perish, for I am going to do something in your days that you would never believe, even if someone told you'" (Acts 13:40–41, quoting Hab. 1:5).

In speaking such words, exhorting their people to believe in God and his servant, the Messiah, Yeshua's followers were following in the footsteps of the Torah and the Prophets. Such belief was absolutely fundamental. (See vol. 2, 3.7, for more on this.) When God sent Moses and Aaron to deliver their people, it was essential that the people believed in him *and them*. (See Exod. 4:1–31 and throughout the Torah. By the way, should Jews now *stop* believing in Moses since he lived and died more than three thousand years ago? I think you get the point! Not surprisingly, this ongoing call to believe Moses formed Rambam's seventh fundamental principle of belief: "The prophecy of Moses our Teacher has priority.") After Moses' death, it was crucial that the people then believed in Joshua, their new leader. (See Josh. 4:14; to believe means to reverently and explicitly trust.)

Not to believe in God and his servants meant certain destruction. To give just a few examples, Lot's sons-in-law refused to believe Lot or the angels, so they were destroyed with the city of Sodom (Gen. 19:14); the Israelites refused to believe in God's words spoken through Moses and Aaron, so they died in the wilderness (see Numbers 14, esp. v. 31); Moses and Aaron themselves were banned from the Promised Land for lack of faith in the Lord's command (Num. 20:1–12); our people were led into the Babylonian captivity because "they mocked God's messengers, despised his words and scoffed at his prophets until the wrath of the Lord was aroused against his people and there was no remedy" (2 Chron. 36:16).

How different things could have been if they had only heeded King Jehoshaphat's exhortation spoken many decades earlier: "Listen to me, Judah and people of Jerusalem! *Have faith* in the Lord your God and you will be upheld; *have faith* in his prophets and you will be successful" (2 Chron. 20:20). If only they had listened to Isaiah's words of warning: "If you do not stand firm in your faith, you will not stand at all." (Isa. 7:9; the English translation reflects a word play in the Hebrew: *'im lo' ta'aminu ki lo' te'amenu*.) But we did not believe.

It is sad to say, but *one of our people's greatest sins has been chronic unbelief*—toward the Lord and the servants he sends to us. To this day, the vast majority of Jews around the world (especially in Israel) do not actively believe in God or his Word. History is repeating itself:

> When the Lord heard [his people's complaints in the wilderness], he was very angry; his fire broke out against Jacob, and his wrath rose against Israel, for they did not believe in God or trust in his deliverance. . . . In spite of all this, they kept on sinning; in spite of his wonders, they did not believe.
>
> Psalm 78:21–22, 32

And though the LORD has sent all his servants the prophets to you again and again, you have not listened or paid any attention.

Jeremiah 25:4

It was no different with the coming of the Messiah into the world. Only a minority of our people believed (or believes) in him. And although the crowds once followed Jesus because of his many miracles—just as our people all believed in Moses when they saw the miracles he performed—they soon turned against him, with some even clamoring for his death, just as they once clamored for Moses' death. According to Numbers 14:10, *the whole assembly* [of Israel] talked about stoning" Moses and Aaron; according to Matthew 27:22, an angry Jewish crowd called for Jesus' crucifixion. I take no pleasure in recounting this, but we cannot ignore the facts.

In light of all this, it makes perfect sense that Isaiah 52:13–53:12, the most famous Messianic prophecy in the Bible (see objections 4.5–4.17) begins with the words, "See, my servant will act wisely; he will be raised and lifted up and highly exalted," but then asks immediately (53:1), *Who has believed our message* and to whom has the arm of the LORD been revealed?" That is the million-dollar question—to put it lightly.

Have *you* believed our message? Our Messiah has come, paying the price for our sins, rising from the dead, opening the way for us to have an intimate relationship with God, and providing for our eternal salvation. Believe in him and you too can be "saved"—meaning forgiven, cleansed, transformed, and empowered to live a holy life. What are you waiting for?

4.3. Isaiah 7:14 does not prophesy a virgin birth! And it has nothing whatsoever to do with Jesus, since it dealt with a crisis seven hundred years before he was born.

Although biblical scholars of varied religious backgrounds continue to debate the precise significance of Isaiah 7:14 (Jewish scholars disagree among themselves, as do Christian scholars), the overall meaning is clear: The prophet speaks of a supernatural event of great importance to the house of David, apparently the birth of a royal child. When read in the larger context of Isaiah 7–11, it is not difficult to see how Isaiah 7:14 was taken to be Messianic. Matthew therefore had good reason to cite this passage with reference to the birth of Jesus the Messiah. But you have raised some fair questions, so let's look at them in a little more detail.

Isaiah 7:14 is often attacked by the anti-missionaries as a "central" prophecy of the New Testament, as if it were quoted dozens of times by the New Testament authors and as if it were grossly misinterpreted there. In fact, it is quoted only *once* in the entire New Testament, and when understood properly—in terms of Isaiah's original prophecy and Matthew's quotation—you will see that the Messianic interpretation makes good scriptural sense.

Let's begin by looking back to the original context, dating to more than seven hundred years before the birth of Jesus. The people of Judah had a crisis on their hands. They were being attacked by their brothers in the north, the Israelites, who were joined by the Arameans. These enemy armies were heading toward Jerusalem, and their goal was to take the city, remove the reigning king (remember that in Judah, the king was always a descendant of David), and place their own man on the throne.

How real was the threat? So real that it is the "house of David" that is addressed twice in Isaiah 7 (vv. 2 and 13), something that takes on real significance when we realize that outside of this chapter of Isaiah, the phrase occurs only *three other times* in the remaining 165 chapters of the Major Prophets (two other times in Isaiah, namely, 16:5; 22:22; once in Jeremiah, namely, 21:12; not at all in Ezekiel). This attack was nothing less than a frontal assault on God's established dynasty, the dynasty from which the Messiah would come. Unfortunately, the current king in David's line, Ahaz, was a faithless man who was more prepared to hire a foreign army to help him fight than to rely on God. And so it was that the Lord sent the prophet Isaiah to speak to this weak Davidic king, urging him to put his trust in Yahweh alone and assuring him that Judah's enemies would be defeated:

> Yet this is what the Sovereign Lord says:
> "It will not take place,
>   it will not happen,
> for the head of Aram is Damascus,
>   and the head of Damascus is only Rezin.
> Within sixty-five years

Ephraim will be too shattered to be a people.
The head of Ephraim is Samaria,
    and the head of Samaria is only Remaliah's son.
If you do not stand firm in your faith,
    you will not stand at all."

Isaiah 7:7–9

But Ahaz refused to stand firm in his faith, even when the Lord offered to give him a sign of supernatural proportions: "Ask the LORD your God for a sign, whether in the deepest depths or in the highest heights" (Isa. 7:11). Faithless Ahaz wanted nothing to do with this. So the Lord rebuked him with these words: "Hear now, you house of David! [Notice that Ahaz is not simply addressed as the king, but rather as the representative of the house of David; the Hebrew here and in the next verse is in the plural, so Ahaz is not being addressed alone.] Is it not enough to try the patience of men? Will you try the patience of my God also? Therefore the Lord himself will give you a sign: The virgin *('almah)* will be with child [or "is with child"] and will give birth to a son, and will call him Immanuel" (Isa. 7:13–14).[31]

That is the famous prophecy! The following verses, which clearly contain elements of *judgment* as well as deliverance, are not quoted as often but are certainly relevant:

He [namely, Immanuel] will eat curds and honey when he knows enough to reject the wrong and choose the right. But before the boy knows enough to reject the wrong and choose the right, the land of the two kings you dread will be laid waste. The LORD will bring on you and on your people and on the house of your father a time unlike any since Ephraim broke away from Judah—he will bring the king of Assyria. [Bear in mind that Ahaz was looking to this very same Assyria, rather than to the Lord, to deliver him from the present military threat; how ironic!]

Isaiah 7:15–17

Who is this Immanuel? Some say a child to be born to Isaiah; some say a child to be born to Ahaz; some say a child to be born to one particular Judean woman at that time, although she is not specifically named in the context; some say a child to be born to an unidentified Judean woman at that time. The context does not make this matter clear (in spite of Isaiah 8:8; cf. also 8:10; both verses have the words *'immanu 'el* in the Hebrew text).[32] It would be fair to say, however, that the birth of the child has something to do with the future of the house of David, since (1) the main threat of Israel and Aram, Judah's enemies in this chapter, was that they would oust the Davidic king and put their own man on the throne; (2) the Lord specifically says he will give a sign to the unbelieving house of David, and that sign has to do with the birth of a son; and (3) the following chapters, especially 9 and 11, contain some of the most significant Messianic prophecies in the Bible, focusing on the birth and supernatural reign of a new Davidic king. We will return to the larger context of this passage after addressing several more questions.[33]

What is the supernatural sign given by God?[34] Some say Isaiah is simply predicting that the child born will be a boy (not the most supernatural sign, since the chances of being right are fifty-fifty); some say the sign is to be found in the name Immanuel, which means "God is with us" (and will deliver us); some say the sign is that the mother would prophesy for the first time (giving her son the name Immanuel by divine inspiration, which, of course, is hardly a sign if she already knew about this prophecy!); some say the nature of the sign is found in verses 14 to 17—in other words, a child will be born soon, bearing a significant name, and before he reaches a certain age, God will defeat Judah's enemies; some say the nature of the sign is exactly the opposite, namely, that before the promised child reaches a certain age, Judah will be devastated; some say the sign consists in the supernatural nature of the birth, since the woman who will conceive Immanuel will be a virgin.[35] This much is obvious from the context: The sign must clearly bear the marks of divine activity and intervention, since Ahaz grieved the Lord by refusing to ask for a sign, "whether in the deepest depths or in the highest heights," as a result of which the Lord said that *he himself* would give Ahaz a sign. What a sign it needed to be![36]

This leads to a question that has received almost endless discussion for close to twenty centuries: Does the word 'almah mean "virgin"? My answer—as a committed believer in Yeshua the Messiah—may surprise you: While the word 'almah can refer to a virgin, it does not specifically mean "virgin." Its basic meaning is primarily related to adolescence, not sexual chastity.[37] The evidence is actually fairly clear: (1) There is a masculine equivalent to 'almah, namely, 'elem, occurring twice in the Hebrew Scriptures (1 Sam. 17:56; 20:22). It simply means "youth, young man," with no reference to virginity at all. Just substitute "male virgin" in either of these two passages, and the absurdity of such a translation will be seen at once. (Cf., e.g., 1 Sam. 17:56, where Saul wants to learn more about David after he killed Goliath. Did Saul say, "Find out whose son this male virgin is"? Hardly! He simply said, "Find out whose son this young man is"—because *'elem* meant "young man," not "male virgin.")[38] (2) The words *'elem* (masc.) and *'almah* (fem.) should be derived from a Semitic root meaning "to come into puberty, to come into heat (for an animal)," *not* from a Semitic root meaning, "to hide, be hidden" (with a supposed reference to virginity).[39] (3) In the other Semitic languages, *'almah* does not specifically mean "virgin."[40] (4) Within the Tanakh, *'almah* does not, in and of itself, clearly and unambiguously mean "virgin." Outside of Isaiah 7:14, *'almah* occurs six times in the Old Testament, and in four of these cases, the NIV—a conservative Christian translation—does *not* render the word as "virgin." Why? Because that is not the primary meaning of the word.[41] (5) The related noun *'alumim*, occurring in Isaiah 54:4 and Psalm 89:45[46], is correctly translated as "youth" (not "virginity") in the KJV, the NKJV, the NASB, and the NIV, all of which translate *'almah* in Isaiah 7:14 as "virgin."[42] Again, youthfulness, not sexual chastity, is the basic meaning of the word. (6) In Aramaic, *'almah* (i.e., *'ulemta'*) sometimes refers to women who have been sexually active.[43]

To put it simply, there are women who are fifty years old and have never been with a man, making them fifty-year-old virgins, and this is perfectly acceptable English usage, since virginity has to do with sexual chastity, not age. But it would be incorrect to speak of a fifty-year-old *'almah* in biblical Hebrew usage, since the root *'-l-m* has more to do with age and sexual development (i.e., adolescence) than with sexual chastity.[44]

"Exactly!" you say. "If Isaiah wanted to speak of a virgin birth, he would have used the Hebrew word *betulah,* a word that clearly and unequivocally means 'virgin.'"[45]

Not at all! Actually, there is no single word in biblical Hebrew that always and only means "virgin" (called in Latin *virgo intacta*).[46] As for the Hebrew word *betulah,* while it often refers to a virgin in the Hebrew Scriptures, more often than not it has no reference to virginity but simply means "young woman, maiden."[47] In fact, out of the fifty times the word *betulah* occurs in the Tanakh, the NJPSV translates it as "maiden"—rather than "virgin"—thirty-one times![48] This means that more than three out of every five times that *betulah* occurs in the Hebrew Bible, it is translated as "maiden" rather than "virgin" by the most widely used Jewish translation of our day.[49] Not only so, but the Stone edition of the Tanakh, reflecting traditional Orthodox scholarship, frequently translates *betulah* as "maiden" as well.[50] Even in verses where the translation of "virgin" is appropriate for *betulah*, a qualifying phrase is sometimes added, as in Genesis 24:16: "The maiden *(na'arah)* was very beautiful, a virgin *(betulah)* whom no man had known." Obviously, if *betulah* clearly and unequivocally meant "virgin" here, there would be no need to explain that this *betulah* never had intercourse with a man.[51] Just think of normal English usage; we would never say, "The young woman was a virgin, and she never had sexual intercourse in her life." How redundant![52] What other kind of virgin is there?

Just consider the absurdity of translating *betulah* with the word "virgin" instead of "maiden" in some of the following verses. (Note that all of the verses cited here use "maiden" or the like—rather than "virgin"—in both the NJPSV and the Stone edition, which are leading Jewish, not Christian, translations.)

- "Be ashamed, O Sidon, for the sea has spoken, the fortress of the sea, saying: 'I have neither labored nor given birth, I have neither reared young men nor brought up young women'" (Isa. 23:4 NRSV). Could you imagine translating this with "brought up virgins"? What parent says, "I've raised young men and virgins"?)

- "'Slaughter old men, young men and maidens, women and children, but do not touch anyone who has the mark. Begin at my sanctuary.' So they began with the elders who were in front of the temple" (Ezek. 9:6; cf. 2 Chron. 36:17. It is very common for *betulah* to be parallel with *bahur*, "young man"—not young male virgin—as it is in this verse. There is no thought here about virgins being a special category of those who would be slain. Rather, the command is comprehensive: Slay the old men, the young men and young women, the mothers and children. Virginity is not an issue here.)

- "I made a covenant with my eyes not to look lustfully at a girl" (Job 31:1; this was Job's personal pledge of piety. Obviously, he was not promising never to look lustfully at a virgin. How could he know which attractive young lady was a virgin and which was not? Rather, he had promised not to lust after a young woman.).[53]

- In Joel 1:8 *betulah* refers to a widow: "Lament—like a maiden girt with sackcloth for the husband of her youth" (NJPSV). A widow is hardly a virgin![54]

- Even more clear is Isaiah 47:1, rendered in the NIV as, "Go down, sit in the dust, Virgin Daughter of Babylon; sit on the ground without a throne, Daughter of the Babylonians. No more will you be called tender or delicate." Yet a few verses later we read that this "Virgin" will lose *her husband* and *her children* on the very same day! "Now then, listen, you wanton creature, lounging in your security and saying to yourself, 'I am, and there is none besides me. I will never be a widow or suffer the loss of children.' Both of these will overtake you in a moment, on a single day: loss of children and widowhood. They will come upon you in full measure, in spite of your many sorceries and all your potent spells" (Isa. 47:8–9).

Of course, Israel, Zion, or the surrounding nations could be referred to as a *betulah*, always translated as "Maiden" in such contexts by the NJPSV (see n. 55).[55] The point, however, is clear: *Betulah* did not immediately convey the image or meaning of "virgin." Otherwise, the usage would be totally inappropriate in these verses in which the *betulah* is married and with children. Once again, virginity was not the issue.[56] In fact, an ancient Aramaic text even makes reference to a *betulah* who is pregnant but cannot bear![57]

All this is of great importance when we remember that anti-missionaries commonly tell us that if Isaiah had intended to prophesy a virgin birth clearly, he would have used *betulah* rather than *'almah*.[58] Not so! Rather, neither word in and of itself would clearly and unequivocally convey the meaning of virgin.[59]

"Well then," you say, "you've shot yourself in the foot with your own argument! Even if you're right about *betulah* not always meaning 'virgin,' you've said that *'almah* doesn't necessarily mean 'virgin' either. What then has happened to your major Messianic prophecy? What has become of the prophecy of the virgin birth of Jesus?"

That's a very good question, and it leads me to explain the real meaning of Isaiah's prophecy, especially as Matthew looked back at it more than seven hundred years later. It's a lot deeper and more profound than you may have realized! In reality, it is the very fact that the original prophecy is so obscure and difficult that provides the key to understand the depth of Matthew's insight. Let me take a few minutes and explain all of this to you.

For almost thirty years now, I have been reading commentaries on the Book of Isaiah, often with the goal of seeking to understand the meaning of this famous prophecy found in chapter 7. At this very moment, as I write these words in my office, I am surrounded by commentaries and special studies dealing with Isaiah 7:14, including the classic Jewish commentaries in Hebrew (Rashi, Ibn Ezra, Radak, Metsudat David, Metsudat Zion, among others, along with the later commentary of Samuel David Luzzatto, known as Shadal, and also Targum Jonathan in Aramaic) and Christian commentaries from every perspective, both conservative and liberal (J. A. Alexander, F. Delitzsch, B. Duhm, G. A. Smith, G. B. Gray, G. Fohrer, O. Kaiser, H. W. Wildberger, J. W. Watts, J. N. Oswalt, E. J. Young, B. S. Childs, J. Blenkinsopp, and others); studies on Messianic prophecy (including E. W. Hengstenberg, C. A. Briggs, E. Riehm, F. Delitzsch, F. F. Bruce, J. Smith, A. W. Kac, R. Santala, G. Van Groningen, W. Riggans, A. Fruchtenbaum, and others); and whole books or articles written just on this subject (E. A. Hinson, A. H. Bartlett, J. B. Payne, J. H. Walton, G. Miller, R. Niessen, and many others)—not to mention the treatment of this passage in biblical dictionaries and encyclopedias. I have really thought about this prophecy and considered carefully what others have written.[60]

What is my conclusion? Simply this: From our current vantage point, it is impossible to determine exactly what the prophecy meant to the original hearers when it was delivered, other than that it was a promise of a supernatural sign, a birth of great importance to the house of David, a token of divine intervention and deliverance, and a rebuke to unbelief and apostasy.[61] Many commentators also point out that the wording of the birth announcement in Isaiah 7:14 follows the pattern of several other major birth announcements in the Hebrew Bible, underscoring the importance of the announcement here:

- To Hagar, Abram's concubine: "The angel of the LORD also said to her: 'You are now with child and you will have a son. You shall name him Ishmael, for the LORD has heard of your misery'" (Gen. 16:11).
- Regarding the birth of Samson: "The angel of the LORD appeared to her and said, 'You are sterile and childless, but you are going to conceive and have a son.' . . . 'you will conceive and give birth to a son.' . . . He said to me, 'You will conceive and give birth to a son'" (Judg. 13:3, 5, 7).

All three of these birth announcements—concerning Ishmael, Samson, and Immanuel—are of great significance in the Hebrew Bible, and all three are introduced with similar words and phrases. Also relevant is an ancient pagan text from the city of Ugarit (north of Israel, in modern-day Syria), written roughly five hundred years before Isaiah and announcing the birth of a god to a goddess in words very similar to those used in Isaiah 7:14: "Behold, the maiden [Ugaritic *ġal-matu*, the equivalent of Hebrew *'almah*] will bear a son."[62]

All this points to the fact that a birth of great importance was being announced by the prophet, especially for David's house. It was God's answer to the attack on the Davidic dynasty, and it was meant as a demonstration of his power and reality. As Matthew looked back at this prophecy in context, this is what he saw: The birth of Immanuel is highly significant in Isaiah 7–8; there are two major Messianic prophecies found in Isaiah 9 and 11;[63] Yeshua's birth truly was a supernatural sign (part of the sign being that the *'almah* was in fact a virgin, yet she gave birth to a son); and Yeshua *was* Immanuel—a name found nowhere else in the Bible or the Ancient Near East (see n. 32)—in the literal sense of the name (God is with us!), as seen clearly in Isaiah 9:5–6[6–7] (see below, 4.4).[64] Therefore Matthew could say that this prophecy reached its "fulfillment" with the birth of Jesus the Messiah since (1) the meaning of the text in its original historical context is somewhat veiled from our eyes, and not enough is said in the context to interpret the verses in a definite and dogmatic way; and (2) as a prophecy regarding the line of David and the coming Davidic king, and as part of Israel's ongoing sacred Scriptures, we can see that its full and complete meaning was reached with the birth of the Messiah.[65]

But this is not only true of Isaiah 7:14. This is also true of other Messianic prophecies that were originally spoken regarding the birth or reign of Davidic kings who lived at those times—in other words, contemporaries of the prophets who were delivering the messages. It was only decades or even centuries later, when the writings were recognized as Holy Scripture, that these prophecies were understood to be still unfulfilled Messianic prophecies (see principles 2 and 4 in the appendix for further explanation).

Put another way, Isaiah 7:14, when read in the context of Isaiah 7–11—one of the key Messianic sections in the prophetic books—ultimately pointed to Jesus/Yeshua, our Messiah and King. In Isaiah 7 he is about to be born; in Isaiah 9 he is already born and declared to be the divine king (see below, 4.5, and see also vol. 2, 3.3); in Isaiah 11 he is ruling and reigning (in the supernatural power of the Spirit, at that). As Matthew looked back at these prophecies hundreds of years later, it would have been apparent to him that (1) these chapters were clearly linked together, and (2) the promises of a worldwide, glorious reign of the promised Davidic king were not yet realized. Something must have happened in Isaiah's day relative to the birth of an Immanuel figure, but its greater promise—elaborated more fully in chapters 9 and 11—did not reach fulfillment in any sense of the word.[66]

And how do we know that Matthew had these other chapters of Isaiah in mind? He cited them or made reference to them elsewhere in the first four chapters of his book! So, in Matthew 1:23 he quotes Isaiah 7:14; in 4:15–16 he quotes Isaiah 9:1–2[8:23–9:1]; and in 2:23 he makes reference to Isaiah 11:1 (see vol. 4, 5.3). This means Matthew was not looking at Isaiah 7:14 in isolation, but rather in the larger context of the Messianic prophecies of Isaiah 7–11 (some would also include chapter 12 in this Messianic section).

We ask again, Who was this Immanuel? He was a king promised to the line of David—with an important, symbolic name—whose birth would serve as a divine sign. And if Immanuel is also the king spoken of in Isaiah 9 and 11, he was to be the Messiah, seen prophetically as emerging on the immediate horizon of history (see again principle 4 in the appendix). In that light, it is interesting to note that the promise of yet another child of promise, Maher-Shalal-Hash-Baz in chapter 8, seems to take the place of the Immanuel prophecy in chapter 7 in terms of the immediate historical context spoken of there. In other words, Isaiah declares that before Immanuel reaches a certain age, Judah's enemies would be destroyed, and then God would bring judgment on Judah as well. But the birth in Isaiah 8 seems to repeat this very same promise, with one important exception: The text indicates the child was actually born, whereas there is no record of Immanuel being born in Isaiah's day.

The Catholic Old Testament scholar, Joseph Blenkinsopp, even suggested that

> the very close structural parallel between 7:10–17 and 8:1–4 would suggest the hypothesis . . . of *alternative accounts of one sign-act*, the first addressed to the dynasty, the second to the Judean public. The parallelism may be set out as follows:

• Immanuel	• Maher-shalal-hash-baz (8:1, 3)
• The Young Woman	• The Prophetess (8:3)
• "the young woman is pregnant and about to give birth to a son"	• "she became pregnant and bore a son"
• "she will give him the name Immanuel"	• "call him Maher-shalal-hash-baz"
• "before the child knows how to reject what is bad and choose what is . . . good"	• "before the child is able to say, 'my father' or 'my mother' . . .'"
• "the king of Assyria" (7:17)	• "the king of Assyria" (8:4)

To round it off, the declaration of the meaning of the sign-act is followed in both cases by a threat of punishment for Judah to be administered by the Assyrians as agents of Yahveh (7:18–25; 8:5–10). I conclude, then, that within the prophetic world view, Immanuel and Maher-shalal-hash-baz represent different aspects of the divine intervention in human affairs at that critical juncture. They are, so to speak, the recto and verso of the same coin.[67]

How interesting! Two birth prophecies with similar subject matter and similar time frames following one after the other, but with different names for the boys to be born (Immanuel and Maher-Shalal-Hash-Baz) and with the birth of the latter actually described (as would be expected), while the birth of the former is not. It seems, then, that for Isaiah's contemporaries, the birth of Maher-Shalal-Hash-Baz virtually took the place of the birth of Immanuel, leaving this important prophetic announcement without any record of fulfillment for more than seven hundred years.

I am fully aware of the standard, quite logical, Jewish argument against any fulfillment of the Immanuel prophecy hundreds of years after Isaiah's day. As summarized in the *Encyclopedia Judaica:*

> The medieval Jewish commentator David Kimḥi (on Isa. 7:14) comments that the sign was to strengthen Ahaz's conviction in the truth of the prophet's message. This would imply that the sign be contemporary with Ahaz and not a symbol for a future occurrence. The birth of Immanuel therefore could not take place, as Christianity has it, in the distant future after the period of Isaiah.[68]

However, this argument fails to take into account that (1) it was a promise to the house of David as a whole (addressed, significantly, in the plural in verses 13–14), and the promises to the Davidic kings often had meaning beyond their own generations (see appendix); (2) the Maher-Shalal-Hash-Baz prophecy becomes the more prominent in terms of Isaiah's own day, serving as the time setter; (3) the prophecy is shrouded in some degree of obscurity, allowing Matthew to look at it afresh and inquire as to its deeper meaning.[69]

It is also fair to point out that Matthew's interpretive method, throughout his writings, is quite typical of the best of ancient Jewish interpretation, reflecting literal interpretations, allegorical interpretations, plays on words, and midrashic allusions.[70] Thus, in the first two chapters alone, he cites Micah 5:1–2 (in Matt. 2:5–6), interpreted as a direct prophecy of the birth of the Messiah in Bethlehem; Hosea

11:1 (in Matt. 2:15), interpreted as a prophetic parallel (in other words, as it happened to Israel in its infancy, so also did it happen to Yeshua in his infancy; see vol. 4, 5.2); Jeremiah 31:15 (in Matt. 2:18), where Rachel is heard allegorically and poetically weeping for her children once again; and then, in all probability, Isaiah 11:1 and several other prophetic passages (in Matt. 2:23) as a play on words related to a title of the Messiah in the Tanakh (see vol. 4, 5.3).

For Matthew—rightly so—the Hebrew Bible was the Messiah's Bible, and therefore, given that (1) Yeshua was literally Immanuel, God with us, (2) the Immanuel prophecy was clearly directed to the house of David, (3) Miriam, Yeshua's mother was an 'almah who had never known a man, and (4) the surrounding context in Isaiah contained highly significant Messianic prophecies, it is no wonder that Matthew pointed to Isaiah 7:14 as being "fulfilled" in the birth of Jesus the Messiah.[71] Who else fulfilled it? Or put another way, since Matthew knew beyond a doubt that Jesus was the Messiah and since he knew that Yeshua was born of a virgin, was he wrong to quote Isaiah 7:14 in reference to Yeshua's miraculous birth? Was it not another important link in the chain of promises and prophecies given to David and his line?

It is also interesting (and extremely well known) that the Septuagint translated the Hebrew 'almah with the Greek parthenos (normally rendered "virgin") more than two hundred years before the time of Jesus. This has been cited for the last two millennia as a further proof that 'almah really meant "virgin." Otherwise, why would the Jewish translators of the Septuagint render the Hebrew in that way before Jesus was born? Anti-missionaries have recently countered by pointing out that parthenos does not always mean "virgin" either, as evidenced by the Septuagint's rendering of Genesis 34:3, where Dinah is still called a parthenos even after being raped.[72]

Actually, I agree in part with this anti-missionary argument. While it is not absolutely decisive (for a number of reasons), we cannot, as I have stated, argue that Hebrew 'almah would have clearly and unequivocally conveyed the meaning of "virgin" to Isaiah's hearers and (later) readers.[73] Yet I believe there is something of importance in the Septuagint's rendering, leading me to the fascinating comment on this passage made by none other than Rashi himself.

Am I saying that Rashi claimed that 'almah meant "virgin"? Actually, he has been misquoted to this effect, as Rabbi Tovia Singer points out quite passionately:

One of the most well known missionary books to flagrantly misquote Rashi in this manner is David Stern's *Jewish New Testament Commentary*. On pages six and seven of his book, Stern writes,

> The most famous medieval Jewish Bible commentator, Rabbi Shlomo Yitzchaki ("Rashi," 1040–1105), who determinedly opposed christological interpretation of the *Tanakh*, nevertheless wrote on Isaiah 7:14, "Behold, the *'almah* shall conceive and bear a son and shall call his name *Immanu'el*." This means that our Creator will be with us. This is the sign: The one who will conceive is a girl *(na'arah)* who never in her life has had intercourse with any man. Upon this one shall the Holy Spirit have power." *(Mikra'ot G'dolot, ad loc.)*

The fact is Stern's quote of Rashi simply does not exist. What Stern has done is deliberately change the words of Rashi in order to provide his readers with a completely distorted, christological version of Rashi's commentary. In essence, these missionaries are walking in the path of Matthew who tampered with the text of Isaiah 7:14 in order to present his readers with a christological rendition of the prophet's words.

Here is what Rashi actually says on this verse.

> **Immanuel . . .** Meaning, that our Rock will be with us, and this is the sign: She is a young girl and has never **prophesied** *(nitneviet)*, yet in this instance, Divine inspiration shall rest upon her. . . .

Missionaries have mistranslated the Hebrew word *nitneviet* in Rashi's commentary to mean "sex" or "intercourse." This is a preposterous translation. This Hebrew word means "prophesied," not "intercourse." The Hebrew word *nitneviet* is a common word in the Hebrew language. It is related to the Hebrew word *navie* which means "a prophet," a word with which most students of the Bible are familiar.

It is unfortunate, yet predictable, that missionaries do to the words of Rashi what Matthew did to the words of Isaiah. [74]

Now, Rabbi Singer is completely right to point out the serious error in Dr. Stern's extremely valuable commentary, although Stern did *not* deliberately alter a single word of Rashi's commentary. (He would no more deliberately mistranslate a text than he would bow down to Buddha.) Rather, the source that he used in this one particular case was not accurate, and Dr. Stern, being a serious scholar and a man of the highest integrity, promptly corrected this error when it was brought to his attention. Thus, beginning with the 1996 printing, his commentary reads:

> Victor Buksbazen, a Hebrew Christian, in his commentary *The Prophet Isaiah*, quoted Rashi as writing that in Isa 7:14 "*'almah*" means "virgin." In the first four editions of the *Jewish New Testament Commentary* I cited this Rashi. It has been pointed out to me that Rashi did not write what I represented him as having written, so I have removed the citation from the main body of the *JNTC* and herewith apologize for not checking the original source.[75]

To his credit, Stern not only corrected this erroneous citation, but he actually added an appendix in which he translated Rashi's commentary to Isaiah 7:14 in full, even stating candidly, "I am embarrassed by a mistake uncorrected in the first four editions of this Commentary, in which I misquoted Rashi. . . . I regret misrepresenting Rashi."[76]

There is, however, something Rabbi Singer failed to tell his readers. It is he who has not been totally forthcoming. He actually *left out* Rashi's closing comments on verse 14, in which that illustrious Jewish commentator said something of great interest to Christians. As rendered by Rashi's "official" English translator, Rabbi A. J. Rosenberg: *"And some interpret that this is the sign, that she was a young girl ['almah] and incapable of giving birth."* So the birth itself was unusual and perhaps even supernatural![77]

Does Rashi say that *'almah* means "virgin" here? Absolutely not. Does he say that Isaiah prophesied a virgin birth? Not at all. Does he apply the text to Jesus? Of course not. Yet despite his strong dislike for Christian interpretation of Messianic prophecy, he acknowledges that some Jewish commentators interpret the text to indicate that God's sign to Ahaz had to do with the highly unusual nature of the birth: She would be only an *'almah*—a young girl!—and for such a woman to give birth would not be normal.[78] How interesting! Not only so, he also notes that the plural *'alamot* in Song of Solomon 1:3 means "virgins" *(betulot)*.

With this in mind, we return to the Septuagint's rendering of Isaiah 7:14, where no less an authoritative source than the *Theological Dictionary of the New Testament* states that

> on purely lexical grounds it is impossible to say whether the translator is expressing true virginity when he uses *parthenos* at Is. 7:14. The total picture of LXX usage demands no more than the sense of a "woman

untouched by man up to the moment of the conception (of Immanuel)."
. . . [However o]n the basis of LXX usage it is also possible that the
translator of Is. 7:14 envisaged a non-sexual origin of the virgin's son.[79]

In other words, while the evidence is not entirely clear, it is possible that the Septuagint rendering indicated an expectation that the birth spoken of in Isaiah 7:14 would be virginal (and, hence, supernatural), just as the Hebrew could point to the unusual nature of the birth. *In the fullness of time*—to use a New Testament expression (see Gal. 4:4)—it became apparent that the *'almah* of whom the prophet spoke, this unnamed maiden, was in fact a *parthenos*—a virgin—bearing the very Son of God. If a different word had been used (e.g., a specifically designated woman/wife, rather than just "the *'almah*"), then a later virginal conception would have been impossible. The miraculous nature of the sign ultimately becomes clear in light of its fulfillment, whatever the original expectations and overall understanding might have been.[80]

To reiterate: Rashi's closing comment is of importance, since some Jewish interpreters felt that it was striking to read of an *'almah* being pregnant and soon to bear a child. Centuries after Isaiah's day, this uniqueness came to the fore, quite possibly reflected in the Septuagint's *parthenos*, and then certainly reflected in Matthew's Greek text. So, the deepest meaning of the prophecy became apparent as the fullness of time dawned. This is the kind of thing where you look back at the Word and say, "This is amazing. It was hidden in the Scriptures all along."

There are some who still claim that Yeshua did not fulfill the prophecy because he was never called Immanuel (in particular, by his mother, as spelled out in Isaiah 7:14). But this objection can be easily refuted: (1) According to 2 Samuel 12:24–25, Solomon was to be called Jedidiah, but he was never referred to by this name once in the Tanakh.[81] (2) The Talmud and a number of Rabbinic commentaries claim that the birth of Hezekiah fulfilled Isaiah 9:6, referring all the names of the child to him (see below, 4.4). But when was he ever called by any of these names, let alone called by all of them? Yet that did not stop these traditional Jewish sources from claiming that this passage referred to him. How then can the argument be made that Isaiah 7:14 cannot refer to Jesus because he was not called Immanuel in the New Testament? (3) The fact is that Yeshua the Lord is praised and adored *as Immanuel* by millions of his followers around the world. Many of the great hymns of the church center in on that one key name, including the medieval classic beginning with the words, "O come, O come, Emmanuel, and ransom captive Israel."[82]

To conclude, then, there is no substance to the argument that Matthew misinterpreted Isaiah 7:14 when he claimed that the prophecy was fulfilled in Yeshua's virgin birth. To the contrary, his interpretation reflects genuine insight into a difficult passage of Scripture, an insight that bears the mark of the inspiration of the Holy Spirit.[83]

4.4. Isaiah 9:6[5] does not speak of a divine king (or Messiah).

> The most natural, logical, and grammatically sound translation of Isaiah 9:6[5] is: "For a child has been born to us, a son has been given to us, and the government shall be on his shoulder, and his name is called Wonderful Counselor, Mighty God, Father Forever, Prince of Peace" (my translation). This is in harmony with other verses in our Hebrew Scriptures that point toward the divine nature of the Messiah, and the names of the child should be taken as descriptive of the Messiah himself.

Since we have already dealt at length with the subject of the divine nature of the Messiah, including specific discussion of Isaiah 9:6[5] (see vol. 2, 3.1–3.4), we will look at two questions here, returning to the question of the Messiah's divinity at the end of our discussion. First, What is the proper translation and meaning of the verse? And second, Is it a Messianic prophecy?

The oldest Jewish translation of Isaiah 9:6[5], found in the Septuagint, understands all the names as referring to the king, rendering this verse into Greek as follows: "For a child is born to us, and a son is given to us, whose government is upon his shoulder: and his name is called the Messenger of great counsel *[Megalē hē archē]*: for I will bring peace upon the princes, and health to him."[84] The Targum, while explicitly identifying this as a Messianic prophecy, renders the verse in Aramaic with an interesting twist, ". . . and his name will be called from before the One who is wonderful in counsel, the mighty God who exists forever, Messiah, because there will be abundant peace upon us in his days" (translated literally). The problem with this translation, aside from the fact that it is grammatically strained, is that almost all the names are heaped upon God, and only the last two are given to the son—although it is the naming of this royal child that is central to the verse. How odd! Clearly, the names refer to the son, not to the Lord who gave them. In other words, the Targumic rendering would be like saying, "And God—the great, glorious, holy, wonderful, eternal, unchangeable Redeemer and King and Lord—calls his name Joe." There is no precedent or parallel to this anywhere in the Bible and no logical explanation for this rendering, nor is it even a natural, grammatical rendering of the Hebrew. The characteristics of the royal child are central—highlighted here by his names—not the characteristics of the Lord. As the brilliant Hebrew and Rabbinic scholar Franz Delitzsch noted, even Samuel David Luzzatto, one of the greatest of the Italian rabbis, rightly observed that "you do not expect to find attributes of God here, but such as would be characteristic of the child."[85] This agrees with statements in the Talmudic and midrashic writings, along with the comments of Abraham Ibn Ezra, all of which state that the names refer to the child.[86]

Contemporary Jewish translations have done their best to come up with another solution, but none of the translations improves on the straightforward, obvious rendering found in most Christian versions. The JPSV of 1917 avoids the whole issue, simply transliterating (rather than translating) the Hebrew words.[87] The translation in the Stone edition follows the Targum and reads, "For a child [explained in the footnote to be Hezekiah] has been born to us, a son has been given to us, and the dominion will rest on his shoulder; the Wondrous Adviser, Mighty God, Eternal Father, called his name Sar-Shalom [Prince of Peace]." But none of these translations does justice to the clear meaning of the original text, and one could easily argue that once the clear meaning is avoided, the verse becomes difficult to translate.

The most imaginative translation is that of the NJPSV, rendering the whole name as a sentence: "The Mighty God is planning grace; The Eternal Father, a peaceable ruler."[88] This would be similar to—but substantially longer than—the name of Isaiah's son in Isaiah 8:1–4, "Maher-Shalal-Hash-Baz," which means "hasten prey, speed plunder." The problems with the rendering of the NJPSV are: (1) This is the very first time in the recorded history of the translation and interpretation of Isaiah that anyone has ever come up with this rendering. If the NJPSV is right, that would mean that in more than twenty-five hundred years of reading and studying the text, no one else ever got it right.[89] From the viewpoint of Jewish tradition, that would be almost unfathomable, since traditional Jews believe that the ancient rabbis were far closer to the original meaning of the biblical text, passing down their traditions and interpretations to the later generations who were more removed from the original. How then could a traditional Jew believe that the Targum was wrong, the Talmud was wrong, the medieval commentaries were wrong, all other Jewish interpreters and translators were wrong, while a translation composed in the last third of the twentieth century was right?[90] (2) It eliminates the possibility of these four pairs of names being throne names, similar to the custom in ancient Egypt in which the new pharaoh would receive four royal names at his coronation—something many scholars believe to be the case here.[91] (3) The length of the name for the child seems completely unwieldy, even compared to the name Maher-Shalal-Hash-Baz in the next chapter.[92]

For all these reasons, the rendering of the NJPSV should also be rejected, despite its ingenuity, whereas there is no good reason to reject the rendering found in many Christian translations, which gives four double names to the royal child.[93] That is why the translations of this passage in two recent commentaries by two highly respected, nonfundamentalist scholars—Brevard S. Childs, long-time professor at Yale University, and the Catholic scholar Joseph Blenkinsopp, a professor at the University of Notre Dame for over thirty years—follow this pattern (respectively): "For a child has been born for us, a son has been given to us, and the government will be on his shoulders, and his name will be called: 'Wonderful Counselor, Mighty God, Everlasting Father, Prince of Peace.'"[94]; "For a child has been born for us, a son has been given to us, the emblems of sovereignty rest on his shoulders. His titles will be: Marvelous Counselor, Hero Warrior, Eternal Father, Prince of Peace."[95] As we noted above, these translations are in keeping with some important Rabbinic traditions that also understand all the names to be those of the (Messianic) child.

Still, it is fair to ask how a prophecy delivered about a child to be born in the eighth century b.c.e. can be applied to the Messiah. The answer is simple, however, based on widely accepted principles of Messianic prophecy that explain why both Christian sources and a number of traditional Jewish sources also interpret this passage Messianically. First, we must recognize that every prophecy regarding a Davidic king is a potential Messianic prophecy (see vol. 2, 3.3). The glorious promises spoken at the birth or coronation of a king in the line of David may have been *partially* fulfilled by a given ruler like David or Solomon or Hezekiah, but they reach their complete goal

(= "fulfillment") in the Messiah, both the son of David and the one greater than David (see below, 4.22 and 4.29, which refer to Psalm 2 and Psalm 110, respectively). Second, as a well-educated, Conservative Jewish rabbi once emphasized to me, the prophets saw the Messiah coming on the immediate horizon of history. (For details on this, see the appendix.) Third, it is clear that the prophecy was not fulfilled by Hezekiah or any other Judean king (and therefore, by definition, by any other son of David) until the time of Yeshua. Therefore, it is either a false prophecy or a Messianic prophecy.

We can get greater clarity on all these issues by considering Hezekiah as the possible subject of Isaiah's prophecy, remembering that it is the birth of the royal son that prompts great joy and celebration and guarantees the defeat of Judah's oppressive enemies. Beginning in Isaiah 9:1[8:23], the prophet declares:

> Nevertheless, there will be no more gloom for those who were in distress. In the past he humbled the land of Zebulun and the land of Naphtali, but in the future he will honor Galilee of the Gentiles, by the way of the sea, along the Jordan—
>
>> The people walking in darkness
>>> have seen a great light;
>> on those living in the land of the shadow of death
>>> a light has dawned.
>> You have enlarged the nation
>>> and increased their joy;
>> they rejoice before you
>>> as people rejoice at the harvest,
>> as men rejoice
>>> when dividing the plunder.
>> For as in the day of Midian's defeat,
>>> you have shattered
>> the yoke that burdens them,
>>> the bar across their shoulders,
>>> the rod of their oppressor.
>> Every warrior's boot used in battle
>>> and every garment rolled in blood
>> will be destined for burning,
>>> will be fuel for the fire.
>> For to us a child is born,
>>> to us a son is given,
>>> and the government will be on his shoulders.
>> And he will be called

> Wonderful Counselor, Mighty God,
> Everlasting Father, Prince of Peace.
> Of the increase of his government and peace
>   there will be no end.
> He will reign on David's throne
>   and over his kingdom,
> establishing and upholding it
>   with justice and righteousness
>   from that time on and forever.
> The zeal of the LORD Almighty
>   will accomplish this.
>
> Isaiah 9:1–7

On a certain level, the meaning of these verses is clear: Great deliverance was about to come to the people of God because the glorious son of David was born. The promised child was here! It was this royal son who would establish the worldwide dominion of the Lord, reigning on the throne of his father, David.

Putting aside for a moment the name of the child in 9:6[5], Delitzsch is right in stating that it is understandable if Isaiah's contemporaries thought for a time that Hezekiah might indeed be this promised son of David. The Talmud even states that God wanted to make Hezekiah the Messiah and make Sennacherib, the Assyrian king, Gog and Magog—but Hezekiah was unworthy.[96] In reality, it would seem that his birth was heralded with great excitement and anticipation, with a lofty prophetic oracle of glorious proportions. And Hezekiah *was* mightily used by the Lord, cleansing the Temple, restoring the holy days and feasts, and experiencing God's supernatural deliverance from the Assyrians (see 2 Kings 18–20; 2 Chron. 29–32). This was quite an impressive résumé, but not impressive enough, since (1) Hezekiah's reign came nowhere near fulfilling the prophetic word; (2) his son, Manasseh, was the most wicked king in Judah's history; and (3) within four generations, the nation was in exile in Babylon. Yet Isaiah declared that "of the increase of his government and peace *there will be no end. He will reign on David's throne and over his kingdom, establishing and upholding it with justice and righteousness *from that time on and forever.*"

The only way the famous medieval refutationist Isaac Troki could argue against this was to claim that the words don't really mean what they say. He writes first that the words "without end" are "a mere figure of speech," and then continues:

We find, similarly, in Isaiah ii. 7, "And his land was full of silver and gold, and there was *no end* to his treasures; and his land was full of horses, and there was *no end* to his chariots." Thus we also find in Ecclesiastes iv. 8, "There is One, and no second, and he has neither son nor brother; and there is *no end* to all his troubles."[97]

Then, concerning the promise that through this royal son the kingdom of David would be established "with justice and righteousness from that time on and forever," Troki states that this expression "shows that his dominion—that is the dynasty of David—will never perish. And though an interruption occurred during the time of the captivity, the government, nonetheless, will, in the days of the Messiah, return to the scion of David."[98]

But neither of Troki's arguments is compelling in the least. Regarding the expression "without end, no end" (Hebrew, *eyn kets*), it is clear from the examples he cites that these words refer to something that can hardly be counted or measured because it is so vast and boundless, like the riches of Solomon or the troubles of an afflicted man. How then can this prophecy that states "of the increase of his government and peace there will be no end" apply to Hezekiah? Even granting that the words "without end" do not have to be taken literally in terms of an eternal kingdom—although this would be a perfectly good way of expressing that concept in Hebrew—they simply do not describe Hezekiah's reign, which was quite limited in international scope and influence. As for Troki's contention that Isaiah's prophecy need not refer to an uninterrupted reign of David's son, I can only ask in reply, How could Isaiah have been more clear? Is there no significance to the words "from that time on and forever"?

Putting all this together, and taking the words at their face value, it would seem that an unbiased reading of the text points to an everlasting, worldwide reign for this son of David, a king whose nature transcended human bounds. We explored this deep, biblical truth in volume 2, 3.2–3.3, discussing at some length the divine nature of the Messiah, explaining how God made himself fully known to man through Yeshua, literally pitching his tent among us and walking in our midst.[99] This is a rich scriptural concept that opens up passages such as Zechariah 12–14, beginning with Zechariah 12:10. In this verse God himself says, "They will look on me, the one they have pierced," although the context makes it clear that it isn't God himself who was pierced but rather his servant (see below, 4.31), pointing to a deep identification between the two. This is followed by Zechariah

13:7, where the Messiah is called *geber amiti,* literally, "the man that is God's fellow" (or "God's colleague"; the word is always used in the Tanakh with reference to a close companion or neighbor).[100] All this culminates with Zechariah 14:3–5, where the text states that the LORD (meaning Yahweh) will go forth and fight against all the nations that come against Jerusalem, and "on that day his feet [meaning Yahweh's!] will stand on the Mount of Olives, east of Jerusalem, and the Mount of Olives will be split in two from east to west, forming a great valley, with half of the mountain moving north and half moving south. . . . Then the LORD my God will come, and all the holy ones with him." Verses such as these present only two choices: Either Yahweh himself—visibly and physically—will descend onto the Mount of Olives, or else Yeshua the Messiah—the very image of God and the fullness of God in bodily form—will come in the clouds with his holy ones and put his feet on the Mount of Olives.[101]

What about Micah 5:2[1]? Does this text also point to the divine nature and eternal origin of the Messiah? The classic language of the King James Version, reflected in many subsequent Christian versions, affirms the divinity of the Messiah: "But thou, Bethlehem Ephratah, though thou be little among the thousands of Judah, yet out of thee shall he come forth unto me that is to be ruler in Israel; whose goings forth have been from of old, from everlasting." This rendering is normally interpreted to mean that the Messiah, who is an uncreated, eternal being, would be physically born in the obscure little town of Bethlehem. Most Jewish translations, however, (and a number of Christian translations) read the text very differently. For example, the NJPSV translates, "And you, Bethlehem of Ephrath, least among the clans of Judah, from you shall one come forth to rule Israel for Me—one whose origin is from old, from ancient times." This would mean the Davidic king (the Messiah?) had his origins in the obscure town of Bethlehem many years ago, back in the ancient time of David (who lived three centuries prior to Micah).

Which translation is right? It comes down to the rendering of the Hebrew phrase describing the nature of the Messiah's origins, *miqedem mi-yemey 'olam.* The first word simply means "from of old" and is used elsewhere in Micah to refer back to God's promises to the patriarchs, which he made "from days of *qedem*" (Micah 7:20, rendered in the King James with "from the days of old"). The next two words, however, would most naturally be translated "from eternity" (literally, from "days of eternity"), unless context indicated a translation of "from ancient days" (in other words, way back in the very distant past). In most cases in the Scriptures, *'olam* clearly means eternity, as in Psalm 90:2, where God's existence is described as *me'olam we'ad'olam*, "from eternity to eternity" (cf. njpsv).[102] There are, however, some cases where *'olam* cannot mean "eternal" but rather "for a long time" (either past or present). How then does Micah use the word?

In Micah 2:9; 4:5, 7, *'olam* clearly means "forever," as commonly rendered in both Jewish and Christian versions. This would point clearly to a similar rendering just a few verses later in 5:2[1]. In Micah 7:14, however, the expression "as in the days of *'olam*" is used in a non-eternal sense, the whole verse being translated in the King James with, "Feed thy people with thy rod, the flock of thine heritage, which dwell solitarily in the wood, in the midst of Carmel: let them feed in Bashan and Gilead, as in the days of old." This indicates we cannot be dogmatic about the translation of Micah 5:2[1], since the context allows for an "eternal" or merely "ancient" meaning.

In this light, the commentary of Rashi on Micah 5:2[1] takes on added significance, since (1) he reads it as a clear Messianic prophecy; (2) he makes reference to Psalm 118:22, which says that the stone rejected by the builders has become the chief cornerstone (a verse quoted several times in the New Testament with reference to Yeshua, who was rejected by the leaders of his people but chosen by God); and (3) he interprets the end of the verse as pointing to the preexistence of the Messiah (or, at the least, of his name) rather than as pointing only to Bethlehem as the ancient city of David (which is made clear at the beginning of the verse). Here is Rashi's commentary (words in bold indicate Scripture text):

> **1 And you Bethlehem Ephrathah** whence David emanated, as it is stated (I Sam. 17:58): "The son of your bondsman, Jesse the Bethlehemite." And Bethlehem is called Ephrath, as it is said (Gen. 48:7): "On the road to Ephrath, that is Bethlehem." **you should have been the lowest of the clans of Judah** You should have been the lowest of the clans of Judah because of the stigma of Ruth the Moabitess in you. **from you shall emerge for Me** the Messiah, son of David, and so Scripture says (Ps. 118:22): "The stone the builders had rejected became a cornerstone." **and his origin is from of old** "Before the sun his name is Yinnon" (Ps. 72:17).[103]

This is certainly a noteworthy interpretation. Also noteworthy is the commentary on this verse by two of the most respected contemporary scholars of the Hebrew Bible, David Noel Freedman and Francis Anderson:

> . . . the person spoken of here has some connection with the remote past. "One whose origin is from of old, from ancient times" (NJPS). A legitimate *sensus plenior* [i.e., fuller meaning in the light of unfolding scriptural revelation] is that this Ruler will be a superhuman being, associated with God from the beginning of time. Psalm 2:7 speaks of the king as the one whom God "sired" (by adoption). Psalm 110 places the king on God's right hand. At the least the language suggests that the birth of the Messiah has been determined, or predicted in the divine council, in primal days. Micah 4–5 thus has time points in the Beginning and End as well as the Now. Even if *mōṣā'ôt* means no more than an oracle expressing the divine determination, it does not require a great shift in conceptuality to move to the Son of Man figure of the later apocalypses—the *Urmensch*—and to the classical Christology of the ecumenical creeds or the heaven-created Adam of the Quran or the Metatron of the Jewish mystics. So Christians did not abuse the text when they found Jesus in it. Or to put it more cautiously in a negative way, this mysterious language relates the *mōšēl* whose outgoings have been from of the olden days to God (*lî*) in a special way. He will rule "for" Yahweh. [104]

So then, Micah 5:2(1) can also be understood as pointing to the Messiah's eternal nature, undergirding our reading of Isaiah 9:6[5] as pointing to the Messiah's divinity.

4.5. If you want to know what Isaiah 53 is talking about, just read Isaiah 52 and 54. The context is the return of the Jewish people from Babylonian exile, 550 years before Jesus.

> There is some truth to what you are saying. The prophet saw the future glory of Israel and the work of the Messiah against the backdrop of the end of the exile. But the context is larger—beginning in Isaiah 40. It spells a new beginning for Israel, a new creation and a new exodus, a time when all the world will ultimately see the glory of the Lord. The events predicted in Isaiah 53 are far greater than the return of about forty-five thousand Jews from Babylon in the sixth century B.C.E. Rather, in these passages in Isaiah,

> the exile serves as a symbol of the spiritual bondage of the
> Jewish people, while the return from exile serves as a fig-
> ure of their redemption. These prophecies of redemption
> culminate in the glorious Messianic prophecy found in Isa-
> iah 52:13–53:12.

Isaiah 52:13–53:12 is one of the most important Messianic prophecies in the entire Hebrew Bible, and I would not be exaggerating to say
that more Jews have put their faith in Jesus as Messiah after reading
this passage of Scripture than after reading any other passage in the
Tanakh. To the unbiased reader, it clearly speaks about the death and
resurrection of the righteous servant of the Lord on behalf of his sinful people. It speaks of Yeshua! Not surprisingly, anti-missionaries have
raised numerous arguments to this interpretation, frequently claiming
that the passage speaks of the *people of Israel* as opposed to *the Messiah* (that is to say, they argue for a national interpretation rather than
an individual interpretation).

Interestingly, the national interpretation is not found once in the
Talmuds, the Targums, or the midrashim (in other words, not once
in all the classical, foundational, authoritative Jewish writings). In
fact, it is not found in any traditional Jewish source until the time of
Rashi, who lived in the eleventh century c.e.[105] That is saying something! For almost one thousand years after the birth of Yeshua, not
one rabbi, not one Talmudic teacher, not one Jewish sage, left us an
interpretation showing that Isaiah 53 should be interpreted with reference to the nation of Israel (as opposed to a righteous individual,
or righteous individuals, within Israel), despite the fact that these
verses from Isaiah are quoted in the New Testament and were often
used in Jewish-Christian debate.

We will take up the subject of the national interpretation of this
passage more fully when we deal with the next objection, below, 4.6.
For now, we will answer two important questions: (1) In the preceding chapters of Isaiah (namely, 40–51), is "the servant of the Lord"
always speaking of *the nation* of Israel as opposed to *an individual*
who represents Israel? (2) Does the surrounding context speak only
of the exile of the Jewish people from Babylon?

The servant of the Lord (Hebrew, *'ebed*) is mentioned a total of sev-
enteen times in Isaiah 40–51, sometimes with reference to the nation
of Israel as a whole (41:8–9; twice in 42:19; 43:10; twice in 44:21; 45:4;
48:20), and sometimes with reference to a righteous individual within
the nation (49:3, 5–7; 50:10). In several verses, it is not clear whether

an individual or the nation (or a righteous remnant within the nation) is referred to, although a good case can be made for the individual interpretation (42:1; 44:1–2).[106] Significantly, the most personal, specific, individual language is found in Isaiah 52:13 and 53:11, roughly the beginning and the end of this glorious prophetic passage. Reviewing the data just presented, we can see something very important: The references to the servant *as a people* actually *end* with Isaiah 48:20, while the references to the servant *as an individual* come into indisputable focus *beginning* with Isaiah 49 and continuing through the end of chapter 53. Thus, by the time we reach Isaiah 52:13, the spotlight is on a person, not a people. The picture is becoming clearer! (We will take up this discussion again in the next objection.)

Let's look at the evidence in a little more depth. There are some unmistakable *national* references to the servant in Isaiah 41–48. In the following verses, the "servant" refers to the Jewish people:

- "But you, O Israel, my servant, Jacob, whom I have chosen, you descendants of Abraham my friend, I took you from the ends of the earth, from its farthest corners I called you. I said, 'You are my servant'; I have chosen you and have not rejected you" (Isa. 41:8–9). Notice that here the servant consists of the *descendants* (plural) of Abraham.
- "'You are my witnesses,' declares the Lord, 'and my servant whom I have chosen, so that you may know and believe me and understand that I am he. Before me no god was formed, nor will there be one after me'" (Isa. 43:10). God clearly identifies his servant as his *witnesses* (plural).

At times, however, this servant is nonresponsive to the purposes of God:

- "Hear, you deaf; look, you blind, and see! Who is blind but my servant, and deaf like the messenger I send? Who is blind like the one committed to me, blind like the servant of the Lord? You have seen many things, but have paid no attention; your ears are open, but you hear nothing" (Isa. 42:18–20).

In fact, even as God's servant—the Jewish people—is being led out of Babylonian exile, the servant is *still* deaf and blind: "Lead out those who have eyes but are blind, who have ears but are deaf" (Isa. 43:8).

This hardly sounds like the righteous servant of the Lord who else-where *opens the eyes of the blind*. The contrast is quite stark:

- "Here is my servant, whom I uphold, my chosen one in whom I delight; I will put my Spirit on him and he will bring justice to the nations. . . . I, the Lord, have called you in righteousness; I will take hold of your hand. I will keep you and will make you to be a covenant for the people and a light for the Gentiles, to open eyes that are blind, to free captives from prison and to release from the dungeon those who sit in darkness" (Isa. 42:1, 6–7).

This servant is obedient and righteous, setting captives free, and according to the Targum, this servant is none other than the Messiah.[107] This is confirmed by Rabbi David Kimchi—one of the so-called "big three" medieval Rabbinic commentators—who also interpreted the words "Behold my servant" in Isaiah 42:1 with specific reference to "King Messiah."[108] And this image occurs even more plainly in Isaiah 49, where the servant is *called Israel* and yet is sent on a mission to *redeem Israel*. The servant is a righteous individual who represents the nation.[109] The servant, as in Isaiah 42, is the Messiah![110]

> Listen to me, you islands; hear this, you distant nations: Before I was born the Lord called me; from my birth he has made mention of my name. He made my mouth like a sharpened sword, in the shadow of his hand he hid me; he made me into a polished arrow and concealed me in his quiver. He said to me, "You are my servant, Israel, in whom I will display my splendor." But I said, "I have labored to no purpose; I have spent my strength in vain and for nothing. Yet what is due me is in the Lord's hand, and my reward is with my God." And now the Lord says—he who formed me in the womb to be his servant to bring Jacob back to him and gather Israel to himself, for I am honored in the eyes of the Lord and my God has been my strength—he says: "It is too small a thing for you to be my servant to restore the tribes of Jacob and bring back those of Israel I have kept. I will also make you a light for the Gentiles, that you may bring my salvation to the ends of the earth." This is what the Lord says—the Redeemer and Holy One of Israel—to him who was despised and abhorred by the nation, to the servant of rulers: "Kings will see you and rise up, princes will see and bow down, because of the Lord, who is faithful, the Holy One of Israel, who has chosen you."[111]

> Isaiah 49:1–7

According to the next verses, it is the servant who actually leads the people out of captivity—quite supernaturally. This is because the Babylonian captivity is a type and symbol of the nation's spiritual captivity and exile from God. Their return from exile typifies their deliverance from all bondage, a time of new creation, a new—and in some ways, greater—exodus, and the servant who leads the way functions in some ways as a new Moses.[112]

How do we explain the fact that the servant is called *Israel* in Isaiah 49:3 if, in fact, the text is speaking of an individual rather than the nation? This is actually not just a "Christian" problem, since (as stated in n. 110) the three leading medieval Jewish commentators interpret the servant of Isaiah 49 as referring to an individual (namely, the prophet) rather than to the nation. Thus, they too must explain why the servant (a person) is called Israel. But this is really not an obstacle at all, as indicated by the interpretation offered by Metsudat David, another leading medieval Jewish commentator: "Behold, before Me, you [meaning the prophet] are like the entire multitude of Israel *[hamon yisra'el]*, and I glory in you as in all of them." If this could be said about a prophet of Israel (as interpreted by these medieval rabbis), how much more could it be said about the Messiah of Israel, who both represents and fulfills the destiny of the people of Israel? It simply means that Israel realizes its goals through her greatest King and Leader, the Messiah; therefore it should come as no surprise to us if, at times, the Messiah is referred to as "Israel." This presents no problem at all. In fact, it reinforces the connection between the Messiah and his people.

How then do we put this all together in the immediate scriptural context, which constantly refers to the Babylonian exile? If the prophet was announcing the end of the exile and the release of the Jewish people from bondage, then in some of these passages the national interpretation makes good sense, as if to say, "Behold God's servant, Israel, marching out of exile and back to the Promised Land." But if the prophet was only speaking of an individual—either himself or the Messiah—in some passages, the reference to the exile seems to make less sense. Yet this is clearly the backdrop to several of the chapters in Isaiah under discussion here (e.g., Isa. 48:20).

This also seems to be the context in the verses immediately preceding Isaiah 52:13, namely, 52:11–12: "Depart, depart, go out from there! Touch no unclean thing! Come out from it and be pure, you who carry the vessels of the LORD. But you will not leave in haste or go in flight; for the LORD will go before you, the God of Israel will be your rear guard." Wouldn't this suggest that *the very next verse* would be speaking about the same time frame, namely, the deliverance of the Jewish people from Babylonian exile more than five hundred years before the time of Jesus? Not necessarily!

First, we must remember that many traditional Jewish interpreters—from the Targum until today—had no problem reading Isaiah 52:13–53:12 with reference to the Messiah, thus reading this section of Isaiah as a distinct passage in its own right. In other words, the passage was interpreted independent of the preceding context of the return from the Babylonian exile. Otherwise, how could followers of the Lubavitcher Rebbe in our day interpret this passage with reference to their leader who lived and died twenty-five hundred years *after* the return from exile? Or how could the Targum paraphrase this passage to reflect the events of the Bar Kochba War, which took place more than six hundred years after the return of the exiles?[113] And why did Rashi begin his comments on Isaiah 52:13 by stating that the passage applied to the righteous remnant within Jacob who would prosper *at the end of days?*[114]

Second, those traditional Jewish commentators—from Rashi, Ibn Ezra, and Radak to contemporary Orthodox commentators—who interpret the passage with reference to Israel as a whole (as opposed to the Messiah as the chief representative of Israel) generally do so with reference to Israel's sufferings through the ages, right up to the Holocaust in the twentieth century. Therefore, the context of the exile from Babylon has long since been forgotten.

Third, the universal glory that was to follow Israel's release from Babylonian captivity simply *did not take place* as a result of Israel coming out of captivity. Consider what Isaiah prophesied:

> A voice of one calling:
> "In the desert prepare
>   the way for the Lord;
>   make straight in the wilderness
>   a highway for our God.
> Every valley shall be raised up,
>   every mountain and hill made low;
>   the rough ground shall become level,
>   the rugged places a plain.
> And the glory of the Lord will be revealed,
>   and all mankind together will see it.
> For the mouth of the Lord has spoken."
>
> Isaiah 40:3–5

The LORD will lay bare his holy arm
in the sight of all the nations,
and all the ends of the earth will see
the salvation of our God.

Isaiah 52:10

Many similar verses in Isaiah could be cited (see, e.g., Isa. 41:17–20; 43:16–21; 51:9–11), but there is no avoiding the obvious conclusion: The return from exile of less than forty-five thousand Jews (see Nehemiah 7) was hardly an earth-shattering, heaven-opening, miraculous event of cosmic proportions. It did *not* reveal the glory of the Lord and all the earth did *not* witness his salvation. Therefore, being true to the larger context and carefully interpreting the specific verses, the following picture emerges with clarity: It is the Messiah as the servant of the Lord who leads the way for his people, the Messiah as the new Moses who liberates them in a new exodus, but this time it is not from Egypt or even from Babylon. Rather, he leads his people out of spiritual bondage—symbolized here by the Babylonian exile—and into the fulfillment of their spiritual destiny. As stated above, the exile serves as the backdrop for these Messianic prophecies, and marching out of the exile, fulfilling the mission of God's servant Israel, is God's servant the Messiah, the ideal representative of the people, setting the captives free and bringing salvation to the ends of the earth.

It is with good reason, therefore, that the New Testament authors cited Isaiah 40 with reference to John the Immerser, who came to prepare the way for the Messiah (see Matt. 3:1–3). This means that *the Lord himself* in the person of Yeshua the Messiah would come to Zion, as Isaiah also prophesied in chapter 52: "Listen! Your watchmen lift up their voices; together they shout for joy. When the LORD returns to Zion, they will see it with their own eyes" (Isa. 52:8)—and this would be the cause of great rejoicing and victory. God would come to deliver his people!

You could picture it like this: Out of the Babylonian exile the prophet sees a mighty deliverance, as Yahweh makes a way in the desert, a highway for the redeemed (Isaiah 35), a new exodus. In prophetic vision, a people marches out from the exile, and as this people draws closer, it becomes clear that it is actually a person, not a nation; an ideal Israelite, not the people as a whole; the Messiah and true Redeemer, not a sinful brood who always falls short of the mark (Isa. 57:3–13a; 59:1–8). Out of the shadows of the exile, the light of God's redemption begins to dawn, and as the sun reaches its zenith, we can see clearly that Israel's salvation does not center on a partial, national deliverance from exile but on a true and lasting deliverance from sin. The Messianic interpretation makes perfect sense!

The Messiah, the righteous servant of the Lord, fulfills the destiny of his people and nation. In his triumph, Israel triumphs; in his obedience, Israel—along with the nations—becomes obedient. In fact, this is the only fair, logical, and consistent way to interpret Isaiah 52:13–53:12 in context.[115] If it is not Messianic, then Isaiah prophesied falsely, since the glorious salvation and deliverance he prophesied did not come to pass. If it is Messianic, then we see how the Messiah—a Jew, an Israelite, one of his own people—enables Israel to fulfill its calling. Just consider how literally these verses have come to pass (or continue in their process of coming to pass):

- According to Isaiah 42:4, "he will not falter or be discouraged till he establishes justice on earth. In his law *[torah]* the islands will put their hope." We can watch this progressive prophecy being fulfilled before our eyes, as Yeshua the Messiah, through his followers on earth and by the power of the Spirit, continues to bring justice and liberty and equality to more and more peoples of the earth (see vol. 1, 2.1). And at this very hour, in the most distant, formerly godforsaken places on the earth, on scattered islands in the middle of vast oceans, multitudes of people eagerly await and embrace Yeshua's teaching, revealing the one true God, the God of Israel.

- According to Isaiah 49:1–7, the servant of the Lord would first be rejected by his own people, Israel, before bringing salvation to the nations. As proclaimed by the Lord himself in verse 6: "It is too small a thing for you to be my servant to restore the tribes of Jacob and bring back those of Israel I have kept. I will also make you a light for the Gentiles, that you may bring my salvation to the ends of the earth." How perfectly this speaks of Jesus!

- According to Isaiah 50:4–10, the servant of the Lord, most definitely an individual,[116] would suffer rejection and beating. This is how the servant described his sufferings (because of his obedience to God): "I offered my back to those who beat me, my cheeks to those who pulled out my beard; I did not hide my face from mocking and spitting" (v. 6). This accurately describes some of the sufferings endured by Jesus because of his obedience to God.

- Finally, Isaiah 52:13–53:12 describes in great detail the glorious exaltation of the servant of the Lord after suffering rejection and death at the hands of his people. Yet his very death provided atonement and redemption for the world! (Because of the importance of this passage, the next twelve objections will deal with specific points raised against the standard Christian and Messianic Jewish interpretation, which applies the prophecy to Yeshua.)

Israel, as the national servant of the Lord, failed in its mission, often being unrighteous. But through the Messiah—the ideal Israelite and the righteous servant of the Lord—the servant's mission was fulfilled, culminating in the grand announcement of Isaiah 53:12, where God says: "Therefore I will give him a portion among the great, and he will divide the spoils with the strong, because he poured out his life unto death, and was numbered with the transgressors. For he bore the sin of many, and made intercession for the transgressors." What a wonderful Savior! And this leads right into the joyful proclamation of Isaiah 54, where the salvation and blessing and prosperity of Jerusalem are announced.

If Isaiah 54 was interpreted in terms of Israel's coming out of exile (as claimed in this objection), we can safely say that the prophecies of this chapter of Isaiah were *not* fulfilled. Many of the Jewish people did indeed return from exile, but Jerusalem was not gloriously rebuilt (see vv. 11–12), nor was it established in righteousness and peace (vv. 13–14), nor was it supernaturally protected from its enemies (see vv. 15–17 in light of the wars with Rome in 67–70 and 132–135 c.e. that devastated Jerusalem, just to mention two major examples of bloody conflicts endured by the city and its people). Once again, the salvation and glory depicted here are far greater than that which the exiles experienced when they returned to their land more than twenty-five hundred years ago. There really is no comparison. But when we read the text rightly—in other words, in light of the Messianic prophecies of the preceding chapters—everything becomes clear: Salvation has come! For a time, Israel has rejected her Messiah, but soon her day will come and Jerusalem will be delivered and established as the praise of all the earth (see Isa. 62:1–7), the center of God's kingdom (see Isa. 2:1–4), the place of Messiah's return (see Zech. 14:1–4).

We can see, then, that it is the Messianic interpretation of these critically important "servant of the Lord" passages that is in harmony with the larger context and true to both the letter and spirit of the words. Those interpreting these prophecies with reference to Jesus have every reason to be totally confident in the soundness of their interpretation.

4.6. Isaiah 53 speaks of the people of Israel, not Jesus (or any Messiah).

> It is impossible, both contextually and logically, for Isaiah 53 to be speaking of the people of Israel. Rather, the text clearly speaks of one individual, and as many rabbis recognized through the ages, that individual was the Messiah.

For the last thousand years, religious Jews have often interpreted Isaiah 53 with reference to the people of Israel, but that has by no means been the consensus interpretation, and it is not the interpretation of the Talmudic rabbis. So, for example, the Targum interprets the passage with reference to the Messiah—as a warring, victorious king, even to the point of completely twisting the meaning of key verses[117]—while the Talmud generally interprets the passage with reference to the Messiah, or key individuals (like Moses or Phineas), or the righteous (for details on this, see 4.8). Note also that Sa'adiah Gaon, the influential ninth-century Rabbinic leader, interpreted Isaiah 53 with reference to Jeremiah. This means that virtually without exception, the earliest traditional Jewish sources—and therefore the most authoritative Jewish sources—interpret Isaiah 52:13–53:12 with reference to an individual, and in some cases, with reference to the Messiah. As stated above (4.5), this is highly significant.

While it is true that Rashi, Ibn Ezra, and Radak all interpreted the passage with reference to Israel, other equally prominent leaders, such as Moses ben Nachman (called Nachmanides or the Ramban), felt compelled to follow the weight of ancient tradition and embrace the individual, Messianic interpretation of the Talmudic rabbis (found in the Midrash, despite his belief that the plain sense of the text supported the national interpretation). Noteworthy also is the oft-quoted comment of Rabbi Moshe Alshech, writing in the sixteenth century, "Our rabbis with one voice accept and affirm the opinion that the prophet is speaking of the Messiah, and we shall ourselves also adhere to the same view." This too is highly significant, since Alshech claims that *all his contemporaries* agreed with the Messianic reading of the text, despite the fact that Rashi, Ibn Ezra, and Radak had all come out against that reading. Could it be that Rabbi Alshech and his contemporaries came to their conclusions because the text clearly pointed in that direction? The Messianic interpretation is also found in the Zohar as well as in some later midrashic works (for references, see below, 4.8). Thus, it is clear that there is substantial *Jewish tradition*— spanning a period of up to two thousand years—that differs with your objection.

Most recently—really, from the early 1990s and right up to this day—Isaiah 53 has been applied to Menachem Schneerson (1902–1994), the Grand Rabbi of the Lubavitcher Hasidic movement. Obviously, his followers had no problem applying the prophecy to him as an individual (as opposed to the people of Israel as a whole), in keeping with the most ancient Jewish traditions.

All this is especially important when you realize that sections from Isaiah 52:13–53:12 are quoted several times in the New Testament, and the passage as a whole can arguably be called *the* clearest prophecy of Jesus in the entire Tanakh. Yet many traditional Jewish commentators and teachers have *still* interpreted the prophecy as Messianic. How tempting it would have been for the Talmudic rabbis and their successors to interpret this passage with reference to Israel—rather than to the Messiah or any other individual—seeing that it played such an important role in Christian interpretation and polemics. Yet they did not interpret the passage with reference to the nation of Israel in any recorded traditional source for almost one thousand years, nor did they interpret it with reference to national Israel with unanimity thereafter.

This is all the more striking when you consider that there is a tradition dating back to Origen, a scholarly Christian leader in the second century, who stated that some Jewish leaders in his day interpreted the passage with reference to Israel, not the Messiah.[118] In other words, the national, non-Messianic interpretation was apparently used in some Jewish circles more than three centuries before the completion of the Talmud, yet it simply didn't stick. It was known, it seems, but it didn't take root in any Rabbinic source of any kind until the eleventh century. This is saying something!

Still, the bottom line is the scriptural text itself, and a careful examination of the evidence makes it clear that Isaiah 52:13–53:12 cannot refer to Israel as a whole for the following reasons.

1. Throughout Isaiah 52:13–53:12, the servant is depicted as completely righteous yet lowly and afflicted, despised and rejected (before

his final exaltation). This cannot possibly apply to the people of Israel as a nation; otherwise, the Torah cannot be true. For the Torah plainly promises, again and again, that if, *as a nation,* we live righteously before God, we will be the head and not the tail, lifted high and not brought low, blessed and not afflicted, revered and not rejected. This is indisputably clear, as Leviticus 26 and Deuteronomy 28 explain in great detail. Really, I see no way that an honest reading of these lengthy Torah passages (which do not stand alone but rather summarize what is taught throughout the Torah) can differ with this conclusion: If the people of Israel were righteous, as described in Isaiah 53, then they would be blessed and not cursed. (See vol. 1, 2.4.)

It was only when our nation as a whole (or as the clear majority) was sinful (and therefore hostile to God and his servants) that *a righteous individual* (like Jeremiah or one of the prophets) or *a righteous remnant* (like the few godly believers in Elijah's day) could *suffer for their righteousness,* since they would be going against the grain of a society that had rejected God and his laws. But the thought of *the people of Israel, as a whole, being righteous* and yet *suffering for their righteousness* is totally unthinkable from a Torah perspective.[119] For *righteous Israel* to suffer humiliation, shame, and death at the hands of her enemies—going like sheep to the slaughter—would be a complete breach of the national covenant, since the Torah explicitly taught that Israel's blessings and curses would first be experienced *in this world* as opposed to the world to come (see again vol. 1, 2.4). In Christian terms, such a reversal of the covenant promises would be similar to Jesus condemning a true Christian to hell. Yet according to your interpretation, God himself (see Isa. 53:10) would cause totally righteous and obedient Israel to be slaughtered by the Gentiles to the point of total, national disfigurement (interpreting Isaiah 52:14 according to your viewpoint, with reference to the nation, not an individual). Quite simply, this cannot be.

2. According to Isaiah 52:13–15, the servant of the Lord would not only suffer terrible disfigurement and suffering but would then be highly exalted, to the point that kings would stand in awe of him and bow down to him. While this applies perfectly to Jesus the Messiah, who is adored and venerated by kings and leaders around the world, no such exaltation has taken place for our people Israel. So, not only do the verses referred to *not* fit the corporate Israel interpretation, but the verses that follow can hardly be understood to be the words of the kings! How could these kings confess their wonder and amazement at Israel's exaltation if such exaltation has never occurred?[120]

3. Isaiah presents a picture of a totally righteous, guileless servant of the Lord. According to the anti-missionaries, this is a picture of Israel. But when did our nation ever live like this? When do the Scriptures, or even our own history books, record a time when *as a nation*, there was no deceit on our lips or violence in our midst (Isa. 53:9), when we were as silent as lambs going to the slaughter before our oppressors (v. 7)? What generation could be called God's "righteous servant" (v. 11)? Yet if the national interpretation were true, Israel would have to be a righteous nation. At no point in our history has this been true. Is that the reason that the closest the Talmud comes to a national interpretation of Isaiah 53 is in b. Berakhot 5a, where verse 10 is applied to righteous individuals within the nation?

Note carefully that the servant was *not* smitten by God because of his guilt but rather because of the guilt of others (Isa. 53:4, 8). The servant was not guilty! The others transgressed, committed iniquity, and went astray (vv. 5–6). Not so the servant of the Lord! He bore the sin of many, but he himself did not sin (v. 12). This description fits Yeshua perfectly. In no way does it describe the people of Israel (or any other people for that matter).

4. According to Isaiah 53:4–6 and 12, the servant's suffering brought healing to the people. We sinned, he suffered, and his suffering brought us redemption and forgiveness and mercy and healing. This cannot possibly apply to the sufferings of Israel. Our people's terrible suffering did not bring healing to the nations who afflicted us. To the contrary, the nations who attacked us and punished us and abused us were judged by God for their deeds! (We will return to this shortly, when we deal with Isaiah 52:3–5, below.) In complete contrast with this, when our Messiah died on the cross, he prayed for those crucifying him, saying, "Father, forgive them, for they do not know what they are doing" (Luke 23:34), and he explained to his disciples prior to his death that his body was being broken and his blood was being shed as a ransom for many (Mark 10:45). He died for a sinning world. He died that we might live. All who have truly put their trust in him have found forgiveness of sin and transformation of life by the power of his death and resurrection.

Once again, it is only fair to ask, When can these truths be applied to the people of Israel? How is it right to apply Isaiah 53 to the nation as a whole? The answer by now should be obvious: Isaiah 53 does not apply to the nation but to a righteous individual who represents the nation—Yeshua, our Messiah and King.

"There's still one problem with your argument," you say. "You neglected to factor in Psalm 44, a lengthy passage of Scripture that demonstrates that even *righteous Israel* sometimes suffered terribly at the hands of its enemies. This undermines one of your main points and backs up my position that Isaiah 53 is speaking of righteous Israel suffering humiliation and pain at the hands of its oppressors."

At first glance, Psalm 44 seems to back up your thesis, describing in detail the terrible sufferings that the nation was experiencing—rejected by God; plundered by their enemies; given up to be devoured by the nations; disgraced, taunted, and shamed; brought down to the dust—and then stating explicitly:

> All this happened to us,
> > though we had not forgotten you
> > or been false to your covenant.
> Our hearts had not turned back;
> > our feet had not strayed from your path.
> But you crushed us and made us a haunt for jackals
> > and covered us over with deep darkness.
>
> If we had forgotten the name of our God
> > or spread out our hands to a foreign god,
> would not God have discovered it,
> > since he knows the secrets of the heart?
> Yet for your sake we face death all day long;
> > we are considered as sheep to be slaughtered.

Psalm 44:17–22

Indeed, some of these very verses have been quoted at the beginning of deeply moving studies on the Holocaust, especially verse 17, "All this happened to us though we had not forgotten you or been false to your covenant." Doesn't this mean, then, that the Jewish people *as a nation* could be godly and righteous and yet be judged by God and defeated and destroyed by their enemies? Certainly not! As previously emphasized, that would make void the whole theology of the Torah and completely contradict fundamental passages in God's covenant with our people (in particular, Leviticus 26 and Deuteronomy 28) stating that national obedience would bring blessing, while national disobedience would bring judgment. Yet if your reading of Psalm 44 were correct, it would mean that national obedience brought judgment. This simply cannot be.

"But what about Isaiah 52:3–5, where the text explicitly states that the Jewish people were sold into captivity although they had done nothing wrong. And this is the very text that precedes Isaiah 53!"

As rendered in the NJPSV, Isaiah 52:3–5 reads:

> For thus said the LORD:
> You were sold for no price,
> And shall be redeemed without money.
> For thus said the Lord GOD:
> Of old, My people went down
> To Egypt to sojourn there;
> But Assyria has robbed them,
> Giving nothing in return.
> What therefore do I gain here?
>   —declares the LORD—
> For My people have been carried off for nothing,
> Their mockers howl
>   —declares the LORD—
> And constantly, unceasingly,
> My name is reviled.

Does this text indicate that Israel suffered without cause? Obviously not. Rather, the Hebrew words *hinam* (vv. 3 and 5, translated here as "no price" and "for nothing") and *'ephes* (v. 4, rendered here as "nothing") simply compliment the words "without money" in verse 3. It is true that *hinam* can sometimes mean "without cause" (as in Job 9:17; Ps. 35:7), but it can also mean "in vain" (as in Prov. 1:17) or "without compensation" (as in Gen. 29:15). As for *'ephes*, it simply means "nothing, none" and has no moral connotations in the Scriptures (see, e.g., Isa. 5:8, where *'ephes maqom* means "no place").[121] How then can we be sure how these words should be rendered here? The context makes it obvious: As stated, the issue is one of "no money, no compensation," as introduced in verse 3, "You were sold for nothing, and without money you will be redeemed," and that is the theme of verses 4–5, as quoted above. Also, Isaiah elsewhere states that Israel was "sold" because of its sins! *This* is the prophet's theology of why his people suffered: "*Because of your sins you were sold; because of your transgressions your mother was sent away*" (Isa. 50:1b; the Hebrew verb for "sold" is identical in form to that found in 52:3).[122] There is even a Talmudic interpretation of Isaiah 52:3 that states that the phrase "for nothing were you sold" means "[you were exiled] because you worshipped idols [which have no value]," while the phrase "and without money you will be redeemed" means "even without repentance and good deeds" (b. Sanhedrin 98a).[123] So the Talmud states that the people of Israel were exiled because of their sins rather than without cause. Note also that Isaiah 52:4 specifically mentions *Assyria's* treatment of the Jewish people. But in Isaiah 10:6b, God said of this same Assyria, "I send him against a *godless* nation, I dispatch him against *a people who anger me.*" Thus, our people's suffering and exile were hardly *without cause;* rather, it was *without compensation.* This agrees with the consistent teaching of the Scriptures.[124]

How then should Psalm 44 be understood? Very simply, it is the *prayer of the righteous remnant on behalf of the sinning nation.* It is the godly "standing in the gap" for the godless, the righteous making intercession on behalf of the unrighteous.[125] You see, when the nation as a whole persisted in sin, it brought divine judgment down on everyone, and even the righteous suffered in the midst of their guilty brothers and sisters (cf. Lam. 2:1–12). National sin made life miserable for one and all alike. Thus, in Psalm 44, the godly, suffering minority intercedes for the ungodly, suffering majority. Also, because of Israel's sense of corporate solidarity—they were one body, one community, and one member was intertwined with another member, for better or for worse—as the righteous Israelites watched their sinning brethren being destroyed, they prayed for the others as if they were praying for themselves.

Normally, in the Tanakh the righteous intercessors would take on the guilt of the nation, as Daniel did in his prayer recorded in Daniel 9. Verses 5–8 express this clearly:

> . . . *we* have sinned and done wrong. *We* have been wicked and have rebelled; *we* have turned away from your commands and laws. *We* have not listened to your servants the prophets. . . . Lord, you are righteous, but this day *we* are covered with shame—the men of Judah and people of Jerusalem and all Israel, both near and far, in all the countries where you have scattered us because of *our* unfaithfulness to you. O LORD, we and our kings, our princes and our fathers are covered with shame because *we* have sinned against you.

Daniel himself was righteous, but he freely and fully confessed the sins of his people as his own as well, including himself by saying "we" and "our" instead of "they" and "their" (cf. also Neh. 1:4–7; Ezra 9:1–15).

In Psalm 44 the godly remnant makes an appeal to the Lord based on their innocence, crying out for mercy on the nation as a whole because of their devotion to him (or at the least, crying out for mercy on *themselves* because of their devotion). This is the only interpretation that makes sense in light of the explicit teaching of the Torah and the consistent historical testimony of the entire Hebrew Bible, both of which testify to the fact that obedient Israel was blessed by God, while disobedient Israel was judged by him. Moreover, this sheds light on the intercessory power of the Messiah, described in Isaiah 53 and further explained in the New Testament writings: Through his perfect righteousness, the Messiah was able to make multitudes of sinners righteous too (Isa. 53:11b; Rom. 5:15–21).

None of this can be said about the so-called righteous remnant of Israel. Certainly, the Hebrew Scriptures indicate that in every generation in Israel's history there were righteous individuals—never the majority of the people but always the decided minority—and these individuals often went against the grain of the sinful society and corrupt religious establishment. I have no problem with the concept of a righteous remnant.[126] The problem arises when we try to make them into a distinct entity, as required by the text of Isaiah 53. In reality, this "remnant" has no history and cannot possibly be described with words such as, "He grew up before him like a tender shoot, and like a root out of dry ground" (Isa. 53:2a), since the righteous remnant does not have a specific origin or upbringing. Nor do verses such as Isaiah 53:7, speaking of the servant's lamblike silence and submission in the midst of his suffering, apply to the remnant, which was sometimes actively opposed to the sinful majority and even led resistance movements to overthrow their oppressors (as the Maccabees did in the second century B.C.E.). Nor was the righteous remnant ever highly exalted to the point that kings bowed down before it/them, as stated explicitly in the end of Isaiah 52. Quite simply, a concrete person, not an abstract group of hardly identifiable individuals, is described by the prophet in Isaiah 53.

This is driven home by reading some of Rashi's comments to Isaiah 53, all of which make far more sense when applied to Jesus, our Messiah, than when applied to the righteous remnant. As you read, ask yourself, Who does this describe? (For an enlightening experiment, when Rashi says "Israel," substitute "Yeshua" instead.)

> **4 Indeed, he bore our illnesses** Heb *aken* an expression of 'but' in all places. But now we see that this came to him not because of his low state, but that he was chastised with pains so that all the nations be atoned for with Israel's suffering. The illness that should rightfully have come upon us, he bore. **yet we accounted him** We thought that he was

hated by the Omnipresent, but he was not so, but he was pained because of our transgressions and crushed because of our iniquities. . . .

5 the chastisement of our welfare was upon him The chastisement due to the welfare that we enjoyed, came upon him, for he was chastised so that there be peace for the entire world.

11 . . . and their iniquities he would bear He would bear, in the manner of all the righteous, as it is said (Num. 18:1): "You and your sons shall bear the iniquity of the sanctuary."

12 . . . and with transgressors he was counted He suffered torments as if he had sinned and transgressed, and this is because of others; he bore the sin of the many. **and interceded for the transgressors** through his sufferings, for good came to the world through him.

Again I ask, Who does this describe?

4.7. The rabbis only applied Isaiah 52:13–15, not 53:1–12, to the Messiah son of David.

> Absolutely not. In fact, an Orthodox anti-missionary made this very claim—quite emphatically—in a live radio debate with me in 1991. Needless to say, he had to come back on the air and admit his error.

The question here is not whether the traditional rabbis applied this passage to Jesus (obviously, they did not, or else they would not have been traditional rabbis). Rather, the question is whether they applied it to the Messiah *son of David* (as opposed to the Messiah *son of Joseph*, the suffering Messiah of Jewish tradition; see vol. 2, 3.23)—and it is a question in which I have a special interest. As I explained in volume 2 (pp. 225–26):

> I am especially familiar with these interpretations due to an unusual event that took place when holding a live radio debate with anti-missionary Rabbi Tovia Singer in May of 1991. As we were discussing Isaiah 53, Rabbi Singer stated that not one traditional Jewish Bible commentary interpreted the passage with reference to Messiah son of David. I differed with him emphatically, stating that several traditional commentaries did, in fact, say that Isaiah 53 referred to the Messiah. To this Rabbi Singer gave me a challenge: If he could prove me wrong, would I become a traditional Jew? "Yes," I responded (since I was sure I was right in my position), asking him in return, "Would you become a Messianic Jew if I could prove you wrong?" To this he in turn responded, "Yes."

Right then and there, we shook hands on it. And he was wrong indeed! In fact, we got on the air again a few weeks later (together with the host and moderator, Messianic Jewish leader Sid Roth), and Rabbi Singer explained that what he meant to say was that no traditional Jewish commentary applied Isaiah 53 to the *death* of the Messiah son of David—a subject that had never come up once in our previous discussion.

Of course, Sid and I released Rabbi Singer from his promise (I never expected him to become a believer in Jesus just because he made a mistake in the middle of a live debate), but an unforgettable lesson was learned: Even traditional Jewish commentators referred Isaiah 53 to *the* Messiah, meaning Messiah son of David.[127]

What commentators did I have in mind? Most prominently, I pointed to Nachmanides (the Ramban), one of the greatest of all medieval Jewish thinkers, a commentator, a mystic, a philosopher, and a legal scholar. He claimed that Isaiah spoke of "the Messiah, the son of David . . . [who] will never be conquered or perish by the hands of his enemies."[128] Other commentators have interpreted this key passage with reference to the sufferings of Messiah son of David. Rabbi Moshe Kohen Ibn Crispin (or Ibn Krispin), first described the highly exalted nature of the Messiah (following a famous midrash to Isaiah 52:13; see vol. 2, 3.22) and then spoke of his sufferings in great detail, explaining that he would share Israel's "subjugation and distress and be exceedingly afflicted."[129] Rabbi Mosheh El-Sheikh (or Alshekh), claimed that "our Rabbis with one voice accept and affirm the opinion that the prophet is speaking of the King Messiah" and also referred to a midrash that stated, "of all the sufferings which entered into the world, one third was for David and the fathers, one for the generation in exile, and one for the King Messiah."[130] There is no debating this!

4.8. It is not true that the medieval rabbis were the first to apply Isaiah 53 to Israel instead of the Messiah. The Israel interpretation is actually very ancient.

You're partially correct. The earliest reference to this interpretation is found in a second-century Christian source recounting a discussion between a Gentile follower of Jesus and some Jewish teachers who did not believe in him. But aside from one passing reference in Midrash Rabbah (where part of one verse is interpreted with reference to the righ-

> teous), a specific identification of Isaiah 53 with Israel is
> not found in any Rabbinic literature until almost one thou-
> sand years after Jesus. (In other words, it is not found in
> the Talmuds, the Targums, or in the midrashim.) There-
> fore, the view that Isaiah 53 spoke of Israel can hardly be
> considered a standard (or ancient) Rabbinic interpretation,
> and for the traditional Jew, that's what really matters.

There is really nothing puzzling here at all. The evidence is well known and has been fully accessible for centuries. The Rabbinic data is as follows:

- Targum Jonathan interprets Isaiah 52:13–53:12 (which, for sim-
  plicity in this discussion, we will simply call Isaiah 53) with reference to the Messiah, despite the fact that the Targum virtually rewrites the entire passage, changing the verses that speak
  clearly of the servant's sufferings so that they speak instead of
  the suffering of the nations. This means the Messianic interpretation of the passage must have been quite prominent when
  the Targum was being formed, since it would have been much
  easier to *not* add the explicit reference to the Messiah (in 52:13)
  rather than to virtually rewrite the verses that seemed to contradict the expected role of the Messiah.[131]

- The Talmud interprets various verses in this section with reference to righteous individuals within Israel (including the Messiah) but *never once* with reference to the nation of Israel as a
  whole.[132] The Jerusalem Talmud (Shekalim 5:1) applies 53:12 to
  Rabbi Akiva, while the Babylonian Talmud applies 53:4 to the
  Messiah in Sanhedrin 98b, 53:10 to the righteous in general in
  Berakhot 5a, and 53:12 to Moses in Sotah 14a.

- Midrash Rabbah interprets 53:5 with reference to the Messiah
  (Ruth Rabbah 2:14), while interpreting 53:12 with reference to
  Israel in exile (Numbers Rabbah 13:2). This last interpretation,
  offered in a passing interpretation of Song of Solomon 5:1, is
  the one and only time in the first *thousand years* of recorded
  Rabbinic literature that any portion of any verse in Isaiah 53 is
  applied to Israel as a nation.

- Yalkut Shimoni (a thirteenth-century compilation of earlier
  midrashic writings) applies 52:13 to the Messiah, stating that
  the Messiah—called the great mountain according to the

Yalkut's interpretation of Zechariah 4:7—is "greater than the patriarchs . . . higher than Abraham . . . lifted up above Moses . . . and loftier than the ministering angels" (2:571; see also 2:621). Isaiah 53:5 is applied to the sufferings of "King Messiah" (2:620),[133] while 53:12 is applied to Moses (2:338), as in the Talmudic passage referred to above.

Reviewing the above evidence, one thing is clear: The ancient rabbis—traditional Judaism's most authoritative sources—almost always interpreted Isaiah 53 with reference to *an individual* rather than to Israel as a whole or to the righteous within Israel, and this individual was most commonly interpreted to be *the Messiah*. Once again, I cannot underscore how important this is for a traditional Jew, nor can I emphasize enough how this fact has largely been obscured by later interpreters: The Messianic interpretation was common among the ancient rabbis! As we noted above (4.6), even Rabbi Sa'adiah Gaon, the renowned leader of Babylonian Jewry in the ninth century, who did not interpret this chapter as Messianic, still follows the individual interpretation of the passage, explaining it with reference to Jeremiah. Surely, if the national interpretation had been common, he would have endorsed it, especially since it would have helped him in his polemics against the Christianity of his day.

The first authoritative recorded instance of Isaiah 53 being interpreted with reference to national Israel is found in the commentary of Rashi (eleventh century), who interpreted it, however, in terms of the *righteous remnant* of Jacob. Not surprisingly, Ibn Ezra (twelfth century), who also read Isaiah 53 as speaking of the people of Israel, began his comments with the words, "This is an extremely difficult passage." But when we read it with reference to Yeshua, it is not difficult at all. Rather, it is wonderfully clear, giving the reader the distinct feeling that the chapter was written *after* the Messiah's crucifixion and resurrection. Despite the fact that Rashi, Ibn Ezra, and Radak (twelfth to thirteenth century) as well all stated that the servant of the Lord in Isaiah 53 was national Israel (or the righteous remnant within the nation)—rather than the prophet himself or the Messiah—many other Jewish commentators, even in our day, still claim that the servant of the Lord in Isaiah 53 is the Messiah.

As stated above (4.6), the only ancient reference of any kind to the national interpretation of Isaiah 53 is actually found in a non-Jewish source, namely, a polemical work entitled *Contra Celsum*, written by the second-century Christian scholar Origen. In this work Origen refutes the arguments of an opponent of both Judaism and Christianity named Celsus, and while discussing Messianic prophecies, Origen makes reference to a disputation he once had with some learned Jews, stating that the Jews interpreted Isaiah 53 in terms of Israel's national suffering:

> Now I remember that, on one occasion, at a disputation held with certain Jews, who were reckoned wise men, I quoted these prophecies; to which my Jewish opponent replied, that these predictions bore reference to the whole people, regarded as one individual, and as being in a state of dispersion and suffering, in order that many proselytes might be gained, on account of the dispersion of the Jews among numerous heathen nations. And in this way he explained the words, "Thy form shall be of no reputation among men;" and then, "They to whom no message was sent respecting him shall see;" and the expression, "A man under suffering."

Origen had an immediate reply to this line of interpretation:

> Many arguments were employed on that occasion during the discussion to prove that these predictions regarding one particular person were not rightly applied by them to the whole nation. And I asked to what character the expression would be appropriate, "This man bears our sins, and suffers pain on our behalf;" and this, "But He was wounded for our sins, and bruised for our iniquities;" and to whom the expression properly belonged, "By His stripes were we healed." For it is manifest that it is they who had been sinners, and had been healed by the Savior's sufferings (whether belonging to the Jewish nation or converts from the Gentiles), who use such language in the writings of the prophet who foresaw these events, and who, under the influence of the Holy Spirit, applied these words to a person. But we seemed to press them hardest with the expression, "Because of the iniquities of My people was He led away unto death." For if the people, according to them, are the subject of the prophecy, how is the man said to be led away to death because of the iniquities of the people of God, unless he be a different person from that people of God? And who is this person save Jesus Christ, by whose stripes they who believe on Him are healed, when "He had spoiled the principalities and powers (that were over us), and had made a show of them openly on His cross?"[134]

Outside of this one lone reference—from an ancient Christian source, not an ancient Jewish source—there are no ancient Jewish references to this national interpretation, an interpretation that does not become prominent until the biblical commentary of Rashi, who wrote more than four hundred years after the completion of the Babylonian Talmud.

From this survey, it should be clear that your objection is completely unfounded.

4.9. Isaiah 53 contains the words of the repentant kings of the nations rather than the words of the Jewish people.

> This is not possible. The servant of the Lord in Isaiah 53 was smitten for the sins of his people, while he himself was guiltless. In complete contrast to this, the Torah promised that the people of Israel would be smitten for their own sins, not for the sins of the nations. Even more importantly, the sufferings of the servant of the Lord in Isaiah 53 bring healing to those for whom he suffered, whereas when Israel was smitten by its enemies because of its sins, God subsequently judged those nations for overdoing the punishment. Israel's suffering brought judgment rather than healing to Assyria, Babylon, Greece, and Rome—to name just a few of the nations used by God to judge his people Israel. (For more on these points, see above, 4.5–4.6.) At any rate, the text plainly says that the servant was suffering for the sins of "my people," which in context must refer to Israel, with either God speaking ("My people") or the prophet speaking ("my people").

Although this objection may seem odd at first glance, it appears to have some textual support, since Isaiah 52:15 says, "Kings will shut their mouths because of him [i.e., the servant of the Lord]. For what they were not told, they will see, and what they have not heard [from the root sh-m-'], they will understand." The very next verse, 53:1, opens with the question, "Who has believed our message [also from the root sh-m-'] and to whom has the arm of the LORD been revealed?" Doesn't this indicate that these kings are the ones raising this question, asking who has believed their report? Certainly not; the rest of the chapter simply does not support this thesis.[135]

Now, I could simply point out that it is somewhat ludicrous to put one of the loftiest theological statements in the Bible into the mouths of pagan, idol-worshiping kings. This is not only illogical; it is without precedent. Even the case of God speaking through the pagan prophet Balaam (Numbers 22–24) does not offer a true parallel to this, since (1) Isaiah 53 is presented as thoughtful reflection whereas Balaam's prophecies are divinely inspired utterances delivered contrary to his own desires, and (2) the Balaam oracles do not present deep redemptive truths, such as the theology of vicarious suffering outlined in Isaiah 53, but rather messages concerning God's choosing of Israel out of the nations.

But there are more substantial arguments that invalidate this objection. First, there is a fundamental theological flaw in the interpretation that the Gentile kings are the speakers in Isaiah 53. According to Jeremiah 30:11, God would completely destroy the nations among whom he scattered his people. While he promised to discipline his people—hence their scattering among these nations—he would eventually judge those nations for their sins against Israel. So, God's people would suffer for their own sins, often at the hands of their enemies, but then the Lord would destroy those enemies. This is the opposite of what Isaiah 53 states: The servant was guiltless, suffering for the sins of his guilty people, who are then healed by his suffering. How then can the Gentile kings—kings who are promised judgment, not blessing, for inflicting pain on the Jewish people—be pictured as the speakers in this chapter? If they were the speakers, they should have said, "We inflicted great suffering on the people of Israel, who were guilty of great sin against God, but we went too far in our punishments, and now Israel's God will utterly destroy us." There's quite a difference!

Look at Isaiah 10:5–34. God used Assyria to judge his sinning people (Israel and Judah), but Assyria was full of pride and was especially vicious. As a result, God said he would bring devastating destruction on that proud nation, which is exactly what he did. Similarly, in Habakkuk 1 the Lord said he would use the Babylonians (literally, Chaldeans) to judge Judah, but then in the next chapter the prophet is told that the Lord would judge godless Babylon for its treatment of the Jewish people. This is also a prominent theme in Jeremiah, where Nebuchadnezzar, Babylon's greatest leader, is actually called the Lord's servant (e.g., Jer. 27:6). Yet Babylon itself would be judged and utterly destroyed (see Jeremiah 50–51). It is abundantly clear, then, that the kings of these nations would hardly be declaring that they were *healed* through Israel's *innocent* suffering at their hands. Not at all! Israel's suffering was because of national sin, and the nations that inflicted that suffering were then destroyed by the Lord.[136] Therefore, from a theological, scriptural perspective, it is not possible that the Gentile kings are speaking in this passage.

Second, there is a serious contextual and grammatical flaw in this viewpoint. Look carefully at the consistent language of the entire passage. First person singular is only used by God: *my* servant (52:13), *my* righteous servant (53:11), therefore *I* will . . . (53:12). The same holds true for *my* people in 53:8.[137] God himself is speaking about his servant suffering for his people Israel, rather than the kings speaking of their people individually. This becomes even more clear when we realize that *the onlookers* in this passage (according to this objection, the Gentile kings) *always* express themselves in the first person plural: *our* message (53:1); to attract *us* . . . that *we* should desire him (53:2); *we* esteemed him not (53:3); *our* infirmities . . . *our* sorrows . . . *we* considered him (53:4); *our* transgressions . . . *our* iniquities . . . brought *us* peace . . . *we* are healed (53:5); *we* all . . . each of *us* . . . the iniquity of *us* all (53:6)—and then this language stops in verse 6. No more "we, us, our"—not once—indicating that whatever group is speaking, be it the people of Israel as a whole or the alleged kings of the nations, they are no longer speaking after verse 6. The narrator must be either the prophet or (much more likely) God, speaking in the first person singular and describing the sufferings of the servant in the third person singular. And this means that the only possible meaning of *my* people in Isaiah 53:8 is that the servant of the Lord suffered for the people of Israel, *not* that the servant was actually the people of Israel themselves.[138]

So then, even if someone tried to make the (highly unlikely) case that foreign kings were actually speaking in the first six verses of Isaiah 53, it is clear that their words stop right there, God (or possibly the prophet) stating clearly that the servant was suffering for the sins of his people Israel (and by extension, for the sins of the nations). So, even if the opening verses described the words of the astonished kings (again, an interpretation with little support), the verses describe their words of astonishment when they recognize Yeshua, the despised and rejected one, as the highly exalted servant of the Lord.[139]

In concluding the answer to this objection, I'd like you to consider something of great importance: If the subject of this chapter—the righteous, suffering servant of the Lord who was mocked, rejected, despised, and killed—is actually Jesus of Nazareth, who then are the speakers in this chapter who say, "We didn't understand that he was suffering for *our* sins. We thought God had rejected him and he was suffering for *his own* disobedience. We didn't realize he was dying *for us!*" Read these words carefully:

> He was despised and rejected by men,
> a man of sorrows, and familiar with suffering.
> Like one from whom men hide their faces
> he was despised, and we esteemed him not.
> Surely he took up our infirmities
> and carried our sorrows,
> yet we considered him stricken by God,
> smitten by him, and afflicted.
> But he was pierced for our transgressions,
> he was crushed for our iniquities;
> the punishment that brought us peace was upon him,
> and by his wounds we are healed.
> We all, like sheep, have gone astray,
> each of us has turned to his own way;
> and the LORD has laid on him
> the iniquity of us all.

Isaiah 53:3–6

Is the picture coming into focus for you now? These are not the words of the Gentile kings, the great majority of whom had no idea what was happening in Judea two thousand years ago. These are the words of our own people! These are the words of the Messiah's blood brothers: "We thought he was dying a criminal's death. We had no idea he was dying for us!" And this continues to be the attitude of most of our people to this day: "We don't know why Jesus was crucified. Apparently he was some kind of threat to the Roman government. Or maybe he was just a false prophet. Obviously, he did something wrong and paid for it." Not so! Rather, *we* did something wrong—every one of us born into this world—and *he* paid for *that*. That is good news!

But the story doesn't end there. A careful reading of the passage from Isaiah 53 quoted above tells us something else: Although our people did not initially realize why Yeshua the Messiah was dying, and although to this very day most of our people continue to misunderstand the nature and purpose of his sacrifice for our sins, eventually our people will see it clearly. Remember, according to the text, they are the ones who declare, "We all, like sheep, have gone astray, each of us has turned to his own way; and the LORD has laid on him the iniquity of us all" (Isa. 53:6). Suddenly, the light went on, the revelation came, and the incredibly rich spiritual confession was made *by our people*. So be it!

Who was it who failed to understand why Yeshua was suffering, believing that Yeshua was suffering for his own sins and not for the sins of the world? Historically, it is clear that my people Israel—including some who are even now reading this book—have done *exactly* what Isaiah prophesied. And this leads to only one conclusion: Jewish friend, your healing comes from him!

4.10. Several key words in Isaiah 53 speak of a servant in the plural.

> I'm surprised that you're still using this objection. It is simply not true, as can be seen by checking even leading Jewish translations of the Bible. Those who claim that there are references to a plural servant in Isaiah 53 failed to realize the specific Hebrew grammatical forms being used and consequently mistranslated or misinterpreted the Hebrew text. These objections were answered decisively decades ago.

Readers of English translations of Isaiah 53 might find this argument very surprising. Isn't the subject of this chapter spoken of throughout in the singular? Well, for hundreds of years now, it has been claimed that there are two words found in two separate verses that hint toward a plural subject: *lamo* in verse 8 (in the phrase *nega' lamo*, "a stroke for them/him") and *bemotayw* in verse 9 (literally, "in his deaths"). It is claimed that these words provide the clue that the singular servant is actually a nation—hence the plurals. The translation of the important part of these verses would then be: "for the transgression of my people [supposedly spoken by Gentile kings; see objection 4.9] there is a stroke *for them*" (i.e., the people of Israel); "and he [i.e., the servant of the Lord, taken to be Israel] was with the rich in his *deaths*" (as explained by Radak, the Jews have suffered all kinds of deaths at the hands of their enemies—by the sword, by burning, etc.).

What is wrong with these interpretations? Plenty! First, the phrase *nega' lamo*, as rightly understood by the NJPSV, most likely means that *the servant* receives a stroke *for them*—in other words, for those for whom he is suffering. Second, Isaiah elsewhere uses *lamo* to mean "to it," not "to them," (in 44:15: "he makes an idol and bows down *to it*"). So, even if you wanted to take *lamo* to refer to the servant (which, as stated, is unlikely), it could still mean "for him" as opposed to "for them."[140] Third, the reason *deaths* is in the plural in verse 9 is because it is an intensive plural, referring here to a violent death. Such usage of intensive plurals is extremely common in Hebrew, as recognized by even beginning students of the language. Thus, the word for compassion is an intensive plural, *rahamim,* while the word for God is *'elohim* (see vol. 2, 3.1). More specifically, in Ezekiel 28:8 the prophet declares, "And you [singular] will die the *deaths* [plural] of one slain [singular] in the depths of the sea" (translated literally). It is difficult to question the meaning here! (See also Ezek. 28:10: "the *deaths* [plural] of the uncircumcised you will die [singular].") Whenever the Hebrew Bible refers to the *deaths* of an individual, it speaks of a violent death.[141]

You might still be thinking, "I know the idea of two 'hints' to a plural-yet-singular servant in this chapter doesn't make a lot of sense, and your points on the Hebrew grammar seem clear enough. I guess even Jewish scholars and translators agree with you on this. But why don't the anti-missionaries accept your arguments?" Simple. Old arguments die hard. Still, I think this one is just about to give up the ghost.[142]

4.11. Isaiah 53 cannot refer to Jesus because it says no one was interested in the servant of the Lord or attracted to him, yet the New Testament records that large crowds followed Jesus.

> Actually, the New Testament record agrees with the picture of the servant of the Lord described in Isaiah 53, despite the fact that great crowds did follow Jesus at numerous times during his ministry. This is because he spent most of his life almost unknown, and then once he became popular, he became the center of controversy and was vehemently rejected by many religious teachers and influential leaders, ultimately dying a criminal's death on the cross. This is certainly in harmony with Isaiah 53.

At first glance, this objection might seem odd. After all, wasn't Jesus rejected by his own people, and didn't he die a horrific, humiliating death on the cross? Doesn't he clearly fulfill the image of the suffering servant of the Lord described in Isaiah 53? And don't the anti-missionaries sometimes claim that the authors of the New Testament *made up* details about the life of Jesus in order to give the impression that he was fulfilling Messianic prophecies? How then can they claim that the picture of Yeshua painted by the writers of the Gospels actually *contradicts* the words of the prophets?

Obviously, there is something self-contradictory in these two objections: arguing on the one hand that Yeshua, as described in the New Testament, did not fulfill the Messianic prophecies, while arguing on the other hand that the very same New Testament gives a false picture of Yeshua in order to make it appear that he fulfilled those very same prophecies. I address this contradiction directly in vol. 4, 5.14. For now, however, we will simply deal with the objection raised here, an objection based on the fact that the Gospels record that great crowds often followed Jesus, whereas Isaiah prophesied that he would be despised, rejected, and unpopular.

The key relevant verses in Isaiah 52:13–53:12 of the servant of the Lord are these:

> Just as there were many who were appalled at him—
>   his appearance was so disfigured beyond that of any man
>   and his form marred beyond human likeness . . .
>
> He grew up before him like a tender shoot,
>   and like a root out of dry ground.
> He had no beauty or majesty to attract us to him,
>   nothing in his appearance that we should desire him.
> He was despised and rejected by men,
>   a man of sorrows, and familiar with suffering.
> Like one from whom men hide their faces
>   he was despised, and we esteemed him not.
>
> Surely he took up our infirmities
>   and carried our sorrows,
> yet we considered him stricken by God,
>   smitten by him, and afflicted.
>
>   Isaiah 52:14; 53:2–4

Isn't this picture contradicted by New Testament passages stating that "large crowds" followed Jesus? Verses such as these are fairly common: "Large crowds from Galilee, the Decapolis, Jerusalem, Judea and the region across the Jordan followed him. . . . When he came down from the mountainside, large crowds followed him. . . . Such large crowds gathered around him that he got into a boat and sat in it, while all the people stood on the shore" (Matt. 4:25; 8:1; 13:2; see also Matt. 19:2; Luke 14:25, among other passages). How does this agree with the verses from Isaiah, just cited, that say "he had no beauty or majesty to attract us to him" and "he was despised and rejected by men"?

Let's examine these verses in greater detail, without twisting anything, rewriting anything, or taking anything out of context. What does the text actually say? It begins with the servant's humble, inauspicious origins: "He grew up before him like a tender shoot, and like a root out of dry ground. He had no beauty or majesty to attract us to him, nothing in his appearance that we should desire him" (Isa. 53:2–3). This agrees well with the humble, inauspicious origins of Jesus. He was raised by (apparently) poor parents in Nazareth,[143] his foster father, Joseph, was a carpenter, and there is only one mention of Jesus doing anything of prominence in his first thirty years of life (Luke 2:41–51; 3:23a). Truly, he grew up like a tender shoot, like a root out of dry ground, and when he began his public ministry, those who knew him were taken aback: " 'Isn't this the carpenter's son? Isn't his mother's name Miriam, and aren't his brothers Jacob, Joseph, Simon and Judah? Aren't all his sisters with us? Where then did this man get all these things?' And they took offense at him" (Matt. 13:55–57 NIV, with Hebraized names).

The fact that Jesus hailed from Nazareth in Galilee also raised some eyebrows. When Nathaniel, who became one of the Messiah's followers, was introduced to "Jesus of Nazareth," he exclaimed, "Nazareth! Can anything good come from there?" (John 1:45–46). And when the religious leaders heard talk about Jesus being the Messiah, some of them protested asking, "How can the [Messiah] come from Galilee?" and again, "Look into it, and you will find that a prophet [or the Prophet] does not come out of Galilee" (John 7:41, 52).

The prophet Isaiah stated, "he had no beauty or majesty to attract us to him, nothing in his appearance that we should desire him" (53:2b), and this too accords well with the Gospel witness, since *there is not a single reference* to Yeshua's having a stately appearance or imposing physical presence. This is in clear contrast with the descriptions of some of Israel's leaders of old, men like Saul, who was head and shoulders above his people in height (1 Sam. 10:23), or David, who was "ruddy, with a fine appearance and handsome features" (1 Sam. 16:12b). Nothing like this is said of Yeshua!

Isaiah also stated that the servant of the Lord was "despised and rejected by men," something that very accurately describes the ministry of Jesus. No sooner did he preach his inaugural message in the synagogue in Capernaum than some of the people tried to *kill* him (Luke 4:16–30). Such murderous plots against Jesus followed him wherever he went—because of both his teachings and his miracles— right up to the time of his betrayal and crucifixion (see, e.g., Mark 3:1–6; Luke 22:47–71). Religious leaders accused him of being a demon-possessed Samaritan and of healing the sick by satanic power (John 8:48; Matt. 12:22–24). This certainly qualifies as being "despised and rejected," especially when you realize that the rejection followed him more closely than the crowds did!

And there was something else about these crowds: They were fickle! For example, John 6:2 records that "a great crowd of people followed him because they saw the miraculous signs he had performed on the sick." But by the end of the chapter, after hearing him teach some hard things, it is written that "many of his disciples turned back and no longer followed him" (John 6:66). In fact, it was common for Jesus to present a hard teaching to the big crowds that followed him in order to expose their hypocrisy and the shallowness of their commitment (see Luke 14:25–34). That's why it is no surprise that one day great crowds could shout, "Crown him! Crown him!" when he entered Jerusalem and then shout "Crucify him! Crucify him!" only a few days later. As Christian leader Dan Harman pointed out, "So long as Jesus was misunderstood He was followed by the crowd. When they came to really understand Him, they crucified Him."[144]

It is the graphic portrait of a crucified Messiah that Isaiah so powerfully describes: "His appearance was so disfigured beyond that of any man and his form marred beyond human likeness" (Isa. 52:14b)— the result of the savage beating he endured before his crucifixion (Matt. 26:67; 27:26–30); "we considered him stricken by God, smitten by him, and afflicted" (Isa. 53:4b)—as he hung on the cross dying a criminal's death; he was pierced and crushed and punished and wounded (Isa. 53:5). "He was oppressed and afflicted, . . . led like a lamb to the slaughter, . . . cut off from the land of the living; . . . he poured out his life unto death, and was numbered with the transgressors" (see Isa. 53:7–8, 12). How could the picture be any clearer? Only transgressors were flogged and nailed to a cross. Jesus was numbered among them! (See 4.12, below.)

It should be perfectly clear, then, to any unbiased reader of the text that Isaiah 53 accurately describes the life, ministry, and sufferings of Jesus the Messiah. Go back and read the chapter again for yourself, or ask a Jewish friend who is unfamiliar with this chapter to read it and then ask him or her, "Who does this describe?" You might be surprised with the response.[145]

4.12. Isaiah 53 cannot refer to Jesus because it says the servant of the Lord was sickly and died of disease.

> This is the least likely interpretation of the relevant verses in the Hebrew, as confirmed by many major translations, both Jewish and Christian. The text indicates that the servant of the Lord will be a man who is intimately associated with pain, grief, and sickness, a man suffering at the hands of people and crushed by the Lord as a guilt offering on our behalf. Such an understanding of the words is found in some Rabbinic interpretations too.

There are a number of expressions in Isaiah 52:13–53:12 that clearly describe violent acts committed against the servant of the Lord rather than simply describing the servant as sickly. According to 53:5, he was pierced, crushed, and wounded; according to 53:7, he was oppressed and afflicted, led as a lamb to the slaughter; according to 53:8, he was taken away by oppression and judgment.[146] This explains what is written in 52:14: "There were many who were appalled at him—his appearance was so disfigured beyond that of any man and his form marred beyond human likeness." This is also in keeping with the New Testament description of the sufferings of Jesus, as he was beaten, flogged, abused, and mocked before his crucifixion.

Classical Rabbinic commentaries that interpreted Isaiah 53 with reference to Israel's sufferings also emphasized the violent deaths that the Jewish people have suffered at the hands of their enemies rather than speaking only of sickness and disease (see, e.g., Radak). This too agrees with a Messianic Jewish reading of the text.

What then of the passages that apparently speak of the servant's own sickness? As rendered in the Orthodox Jewish Stone edition, Isaiah 53:3 reads, "He was despised and isolated from men, a man of pains and accustomed to illness. As one from whom we would hide our faces; he was despised, and we had no regard for him." This could mean that the servant was sickly to the point of being disfigured and thus rejected. But it could plausibly mean that the servant was hated and misunderstood, totally identified with sick and hurting humanity. The NJPSV renders this passage, "He was despised, shunned by men, a man of suffering, familiar with disease," a rendering that indicates the ambiguity of the Hebrew. (The rendering in the NIV is very similar: "He was despised and rejected by men, a man of sorrows, and familiar with suffering.") This interpretation is confirmed by the following verses, which tell us clearly that (1) he actually *carried our sickness and bore our pains,* bringing healing to us through his wounds, and (2) he suffered the penalty *for our sins,* bringing us forgiveness and redemption. Thus, the servant himself was not sick, neither did he himself sin; rather, he identified with us in our sicknesses and sins, bringing us restoration in body and spirit.

What then of Isaiah 53:10a, which states, "But the LORD chose to crush him by disease" (NJPSV)? Once again, the original text is certainly not clear and unambiguous, as indicated by the footnote to this verse in the NJPSV, which states that the meaning of the Hebrew is uncertain. That's why it is no surprise that the Stone edition renders this verse, "*HASHEM* desired to oppress him and He afflicted him," even though this same translation spoke of the servant's sickness in 53:3 (as cited above). The fact is that there are other, totally valid ways to understand the Hebrew, as reflected once again in the NIV: "Yet it was the LORD's will to crush him and *cause him to suffer.*" The reason there are such differences in translation is simply that the Hebrew root *hlh* can mean "to be sick" or it can mean "to be debilitated," both definitions coming from a root meaning "to be weak."[147]

An excellent example of the root *hlh* being used to mean "weak" is found in Judges 16:7, where Samson tells Delilah, "If anyone ties me with seven fresh thongs that have not been dried, I'll become as weak as any other man" (see also 16:11, 17). The meaning "sick" stems from this root meaning of "weak." In a similar way, someone who was severely wounded or hurt could say, "I have become *hlh*"—and it is obvious that the meaning here is not "sick." Thus, after King Ahab was mortally wounded when he was struck by an archer's arrow, he said to his chariot driver, "I am severely wounded!" (1 Kings 22:34 and 2 Chron. 18:33 NASB). The Hebrew says *hohaleti* (literally, "I have been made *hlh*"), which is identical in form to 2 Chronicles 35:23, where King Josiah, also struck by a fatal arrow, says to his attendants, "I am badly wounded"—the Hebrew word *me'od,* "very," being added here. It makes perfect sense, then, to understand this same verb in Isaiah 53:10 as stating that the Lord severely *afflicted* his righteous servant, allowing him to suffer in the most terrible and inhumane ways at the hands of wicked men, since the Hebrew verb *heheli* does not only mean "made sick" but can also mean "made to suffer, made weak, afflicted" (see further the lengthy discussion of the fifteenth-century Jewish commentator Don Isaac Abravanel).

Would even an anti-missionary object to such a reading of the passage if it were interpreted with reference to the people of Israel rather than Yeshua? Would the text refer only to those Jews who were smitten with sickness and disease, while it would not refer to those Jews who were expelled from their countries, or imprisoned and tortured, or starved to death in ghettos, or executed in gas chambers? Would not all of these varied sufferings fit under the heading of "being afflicted"? The simple fact is that the Hebrew root does not have exclusive reference to sickness and disease, and even when it does refer to sickness, it can have a metaphorical meaning, as in Deuteronomy 29:22[21], where the text speaks of God's judgments on the *land* of Israel as *diseases*.

How then do we explain Isaiah 53:3, which states that the servant of the Lord was "a man of suffering and acquainted with infirmity" (NRSV)? There is actually some ambiguity in the Hebrew text, since: (1) The nouns *mak'ob* and *holi* can refer to either physical or metaphorical pain and sickness (see, e.g., Exod. 3:7 for *mak'ob* and Eccles. 6:2 for *holi*). (2) The Hebrew does not say that the servant of the Lord was sick and in pain but rather that he was "a man of pains" and "intimate with sickness/suffering."[148] This describes Jesus quite accurately: He was often in anguish and pain because of the depth of human suffering (and human sinfulness), sometimes sighing or groaning under the burden of it all, at other times being moved to tears (see, e.g., Mark 7:31–34; John 11:32–36). Truly, he was a man of sorrows and pains, intimately involved with sick and afflicted people.[149] (3) The Stone edition renders Isaiah 53:4b as, "but we had regarded him diseased *[nagu'a]*, stricken by God, and afflicted!" It is this verse—in particular the word *nagu'a* (rendered here as "diseased")—from which the Talmud drew the concept of the "leper Messiah" (see b. Sanhedrin 98b).[150] *Nagu'a*, however, can simply mean "smitten," with no reference to leprosy or sickness, as can be seen from the use of the word in Psalm 73:14, where it speaks of the psalmist's spiritual chastisements.[151]

Jesus spent a tremendous amount of his time pouring himself out for those who were severely ill, crippled, lame, blind, and even demonized—a ministry not nearly as glamorous as it sounds. These were often the outcasts, the untouchables, the beggars, the wretched; people with terrible wounds and sores and disfiguring skin conditions; screaming lunatics and wild men; epileptics tormented with seizures, foaming at the mouth. At times the stench of sickness and death must have been unbearable. At other times the horrific sights of twisted bodies and sightless eyes must have been overwhelming. And the crowds never stopped coming to him with their sick and dying family members and friends, even removing the roof of a house to get a paralytic to Jesus when there was no other way to reach him because of the throngs (Mark 2:1–12). And the text records that Yeshua healed them all! (See, e.g., Matt. 4:24; 8:16–17; 9:35; 12:15; 14:14, 35–36; 15:30–31; 21:14; Mark 6:53–56; Luke 4:40; 6:17–19; 17:12–19.)

This helps us to understand Isaiah 53:4, which states, "He has borne our infirmities and carried our diseases" (NRSV). He did not bear our sicknesses by becoming sick, nor did he carry our diseases by becoming diseased; rather, he bore our sicknesses by healing them and carried our diseases by removing them. And in the agonies of crucifixion, suffering in body and spirit, he became our ideal substitute. As his disciple Peter taught, "He himself bore our sins in his body on the tree, so that we might die to sins and live for righteousness; by his wounds you have been healed. For you were like sheep going astray, but now you have returned to the Shepherd and Overseer of your souls" (1 Peter 2:24–25).

4.13. Isaiah 53 does not actually say the servant would die.

This objection actually contradicts two of the previous objections (specifically, 4.10 and 4.12), both of which understand that according to Isaiah 53, the servant of the Lord would die. Many standard Rabbinic interpretations recognize this, either interpreting the text with reference to Israel's suffering and death at the hands of their enemies or with reference to the suffering and death of the Messiah (either Messiah ben Joseph or Messiah ben David).

Some years ago, I was invited by Christian students at Yale University to speak at an open forum titled "Will the Real Messiah Please Rise?" The object of the forum was to have me compare the Messianic qualifications of Yeshua with those of the Lubavitcher Rebbe, Menachem Schneerson. (The forum took place in 1993, when many of Rabbi Schneerson's followers were expecting him to miraculously rise up from his paralysis, caused by a stroke he suffered in 1992. At such time, they believed he would declare himself to be the Messiah.) When I finished my presentation, I opened the floor for questions and arguments. Leading the way in this discussion and debate were representatives of the Lubavitch community, including the campus Lubavitch rabbi, who was quite aggressive in his presentation.

At some point in the evening, the discussion turned to Isaiah 53, and the Lubavitch leader and I engaged in a lively debate, going back and forth on the interpretation of the text until something fascinating became apparent to the listening audience: When I argued that Isaiah 53 spoke of the death of Jesus the Messiah, the Lubavitch leader adamantly denied that the text spoke of the death of the servant of the Lord. Then he turned around and argued that the text should be applied to the many deaths suffered by the Jewish people at the hands of their adversaries. How revealing! (Of course, I immediately pointed out this contradiction, and no defense was offered.)

This incident reminds us of the obvious: The text of Isaiah 53 explicitly speaks of the death of the servant of the Lord, using numerous expressions to make this perfectly clear, and there is no valid reason to deny this unless one is trying to evade the obvious sense of the chapter. In addition to the clear expressions describing the servant's suffering (see above, 4.10 and 4.12), note the following: 53:7 says he was brought as a lamb to the slaughter; 53:8 says he was cut off from the land of the living; 53:9 speaks of his grave and death(!); 53:10 says he will be offered up as a guilt offering; 53:12 says he poured out his life unto death. What could be clearer?

Not surprisingly, when reading the text in terms of Israel, the three most respected Rabbinic commentators, Rashi, Ibn Ezra, and Radak, saw numerous references to the servant's death(s). Radak, for example, claimed that 53:8 spoke of the fact that the people of Israel "used to be put to death in many ways: Some were burnt, some were slain, and others were stoned—they gave themselves over to any form of death for the sake of the unity of the Godhead."[152] This again reminds us that the text points explicitly to the death of the servant of the Lord, not only to his suffering and pain.

It's also interesting to note that after the Lubavitcher Rebbe's death, his followers pointed to Isaiah 53, claiming that it spoke of *his* death, which is not surprising, given the clear sense of the original Hebrew. Thus, they rightly interpreted it as a prophecy of the *death of the Messiah* but wrongly interpreted *the identity of the Messiah*.[153]

4.14. Isaiah 53 does not say the servant will rise from the dead.

> If, as we have demonstrated, Isaiah 53 speaks of the servant's death, then it must be accepted that the text speaks just as clearly of his continued activities after his death. Thus, there is only one possible explanation: The servant rises from the dead!

According to Hebrew University Professor David Flusser,

Although no Jewish interpretation of this passage, which would explain that the Servant will be the prophet or the Messiah who will be killed, is preserved, such an interpretation could have existed. If an interpretation of Isa. LIII in this vein ever existed in Judaism, this would have been important for the concept that the prophet will again come to life. Though the Servant "was pierced for our transgressions, tortured for our iniquities" (v. 5), he "shall enjoy long life and see his children's children" (v. 10). So Isa. LIII could be understood not only as speaking about the death of the Servant (see also v. 8 and 9), but implicitly also about his resurrection.[154]

Professor Flusser has raised an important point: The text clearly speaks of the continued ministry of the servant of the Lord, and since his death is also clearly foretold, his resurrection is also implied.

As we observed previously (see above, 4.13), Isaiah 53 uses almost every possible description to communicate to us that the servant would die, saying explicitly that he would be cut off from the land of the living (v. 8) and making reference to his grave and his violent death (v. 9). Yet in verse 10 we read, "he will see his offspring and prolong his days." How does someone *die* and yet *prolong his days?* There is only one way: resurrection! It is written that the servant of the Lord would be offered up as a guilt offering (v. 10) and pour out his life unto death (v. 12), yet the Lord says of him, "I will give him a portion among the great, and he will divide the spoils with the strong" (v. 12). This can only happen if he is raised from the dead.

Such an interpretation is self-evident, providing the most natural and obvious reading of the text. The wonderful truth is that Yeshua *did* indeed die and rise from the dead, paying for our sins, bearing our transgressions, and carrying our pains. By his wounds we can be healed (Isa. 53:5). And because he is risen, death can no longer touch him. "Therefore he is able to save completely those who come to God through him, because he always lives to intercede for them" (Heb. 7:25).

4.15. Isaiah 53 cannot refer to Jesus because it says the servant of the Lord did no violence, yet Jesus drove out the Temple money changers with a whip.

Jesus, who was known for his meekness and gentleness—all the way to the cross—did not engage in "violence" in the Temple courts. There is no record of anyone being hurt or injured, and in contrast to some of the ancient Israelite prophets like Moses, Joshua, or Samuel, Jesus did not put anyone to death in the name of the Lord. Obviously, he used a whip—not a sword—because his design was to clear the area, not to hurt anyone. This is hardly "violence" according to the standards of the Hebrew Scriptures. In fact, it's unlikely he used a whip to drive people out; rather, the whip was used to drive out the animals.

It is interesting to note that Mahatma Gandhi and Dr. Martin Luther King Jr.—the two twentieth-century leaders best known for putting the principle of nonviolent resistance into practice—both learned this principle from Jesus. He was the ultimate example of a totally nonviolent man involved in radical action and change. The witness of the New Testament is very clear on this, even pointing out that Jesus fulfilled the words of Isaiah 42:1–4:

> Here is my servant whom I have chosen,
> 　the one I love, in whom I delight;
> I will put my Spirit on him,
> 　and he will proclaim justice to the nations.
> He will not quarrel or cry out;
> 　no one will hear his voice in the streets.

> A bruised reed he will not break,
>> and a smoldering wick he will not snuff out,
> till he leads justice to victory.
>> In his name the nations will put their hope.

Matthew 12:18–21

This is hardly the picture of a violent individual!

The specific question being raised here, however, does not have to do with the whole of Yeshua's life but rather with his driving out the money changers from the Temple. Was not *this* an act of violence?

Let's first consider what the Tanakh means by "violence" (Hebrew, *hamas*), since Isaiah 53:9b specifically states that the servant did no *hamas*. What exactly does this mean? The Hebrew noun *hamas*, "violence," occurs sixty times in the Hebrew Bible, along with eight occurrences of the verb *h-m-s*, "to act violently, do violence." What kind of actions are called "violent"? Actions such as murder, bloodshed, and robbery are, quite clearly, acts of violence, and the subject of Isaiah 53, as stated explicitly in verse 9, could *not* have committed any such acts. In keeping with this and true to his character, Jesus did not murder or shed blood, neither did he strike, hurt, rob, or assault anyone at any time, nor did he allow his followers to do so. In fact, when the Temple guards came to take him away by force in the middle of the night, his overzealous disciple Peter struck one of those guards, cutting off his ear. But Jesus rebuked him for his violence, telling him to put his sword away—before healing the man's ear (John 18:10–11; see also Matt. 26:52b, where the Messiah taught that "all who draw the sword will die by the sword").

As for Yeshua's controversial actions in the Temple, the text is clear: He made a whip of cords, drove out *the sheep and cattle* with that whip, overturned the money tables, scattered the coins, and ordered the money changers to get out, exclaiming, "Get these out of here! How dare you turn my Father's house into a market! . . . It is written . . . 'My house will be called a house of prayer,' but you are making it a 'den of robbers'" (John 2:16; Matt. 21:13). This is hardly "violence"!

It is understandable that some have failed to read the varied accounts in the four Gospels carefully and therefore have failed to put together the fact that John 2 mentions Jesus making a whip of cords (with which he drove out the sheep and cattle) while Matthew 21, Mark 11, and Luke 19 mention that he drove out the people selling. But the whip was for the animals; sharp words of rebuke were for the people. It is interesting that all four Gospels speak of this event (some believe it was actually two separate events), which indicates the great importance attached to the Messiah's prophetic actions in the Temple.[155] He was cleaning out his Father's house, and it was a praiseworthy deed motivated by zeal for God and the work of God (see John 2:17). We should also point out that none of the Gospels record a single word of criticism from the Jewish leadership for Jesus' actions here, even when false witnesses were being brought to slander and attack him (Matt. 26:59–61). Not a word about this incident was spoken by any of his accusers—obviously because there was nothing worth mentioning. (None of the Rabbinic literature mentions this incident either, despite the fact that there are some ugly attacks on Yeshua in that literature. See vol. 1, pp. 136–39, for more on these anti-Jesus hostilities.)

Returning again to the specific nature of *hamas*, "violence," in the Tanakh, we must remember that Moses, Joshua, David, Samuel, and other great leaders put people to death at God's command, yet they were not called "violent" because of their deeds. That is because *hamas* speaks of illegal violent acts, as opposed to simply carrying out God's righteous judgments against sinners. Thus, when Moses called on the Levites to put their fellow Israelites to death for their idolatry, they were not committing violence (Exod. 32:25–28); when Joshua killed the five Canaanite kings, he was not committing violence (Josh. 10:16–27), nor was Samuel when he chopped up the Amalekite king, Agag (1 Sam. 15:32–33). How then could anyone say Jesus acted violently when he drove out animals with a whip and overturned the tables of money changers? This is certainly not violence!

What I find most ironic is that anti-missionaries say Isaiah 53 cannot possibly apply to Yeshua because of his alleged violence in cleansing the Temple, yet they freely apply Isaiah 53 to the nation of Israel (or the righteous remnant within Israel; see above, 4.6). Yet our people have been at their most heroic historically when they have used *armed, forceful resistance* against their adversaries—be it the warring Maccabees in the second century c.e., the courageous fighters of the Warsaw Ghetto uprising during the Holocaust, or the Israeli Defense Forces (IDF) who recaptured the Golan in 1973. We commend our people for heroic acts of war! How then can we apply Isaiah 53 to Israel—as a nonviolent people—while disqualifying Yeshua, the greatest example of nonviolence the world has ever known? Obviously, we cannot.

4.16. Isaiah 53 cannot refer to Jesus because it says the servant of the Lord would not lift up his voice or cry out, yet Jesus cried out several times on the cross, once in near blasphemy (Psalm 22:1).

> One of the most striking aspects of the suffering and death of Jesus was that he went as a lamb to the slaughter, not resisting those who arrested him, not defending himself before his accusers, and even forgiving those who crucified him. In this, he has become the worldwide symbol of a man who truly "turned the other cheek." As for his quoting Psalm 22:1 on the cross—a beloved passage of Scripture—how is this "near blasphemy"?

Isaiah 53:7 says of the servant of the Lord: "He was oppressed and afflicted, yet he did not open his mouth; he was led like a lamb to the slaughter, and as a sheep before her shearers is silent, so he did not open his mouth." This quite accurately describes the actions and attitudes of Yeshua the Messiah when he "was oppressed and afflicted." In fact, his followers pointed to this very text to indicate that he, quite clearly, was the one of whom the prophet Isaiah spoke (see Acts 8:26–39). That's why Peter, an eyewitness of the Messiah's suffering and death, could write of him, "When they hurled their insults at him, he did not retaliate; when he suffered, he made no threats. Instead, he entrusted himself to him who judges justly" (1 Peter 2:23).

Let's look for a moment at the specific details of Jesus' arrest, trials, beatings, mockings, flogging, and crucifixion:

- When Jesus was arrested in the Garden of Gethsemane, he did not allow his disciples to fight on his behalf, saying to Peter, "Put your sword back in its place, for all who draw the sword will die by the sword" (see Matt. 26:52). Thus, he went as a lamb to the slaughter.
- When all kinds of false charges were brought against him at his bogus trial before the high priest, the Scriptures record, "The high priest stood up and said to Jesus, 'Are you not going to answer? What is this testimony that these men are bringing against you?' But Jesus remained silent" (Matt. 26:62–63a). Here is a man being falsely accused, with the death penalty hanging

over his head, and he refuses to defend himself! It is only when the high priest orders him to state whether he is the Messiah, the Son of God, that he says, "Yes, it is as you say. . . . But I say to all of you: In the future you will see the Son of Man sitting at the right hand of the Mighty One and coming on the clouds of heaven" (Matt. 26:64, pointing his accusers to the prophetic picture of the Son of man in Daniel 7:13–14). When some of those at the trial then began to spit on him and punch him, he did not say a word (Matt. 26:67). His trial before Pontius Pilate, the Roman governor, was conducted along similar lines:

> Early in the morning, all the chief priests and the elders of the people came to the decision to put Jesus to death. They bound him, led him away and handed him over to Pilate, the governor.
>
> Matthew 27:1–2

> Meanwhile Jesus stood before the governor, and the governor asked him, "Are you the king of the Jews?"
>   "Yes, it is as you say," Jesus replied.
>   When he was accused by the chief priests and the elders, he gave no answer. Then Pilate asked him, "Don't you hear the testimony they are bringing against you?" But Jesus made no reply, not even to a single charge—to the great amazement of the governor.
>
> Matthew 27:11–14

Once again, we see Yeshua going as a lamb to the slaughter—without resistance of any kind—and his refusal to defend himself amazes the governor.[156]

• After Pilate sentenced him to be crucified, Jesus was flogged and then abused by the Roman soldiers. The Gospels record the picture quite graphically. But note carefully: At no point does Jesus resist; at no point does he respond to his captors; at no point does he raise his voice and revile those attacking him. He suffers silently like a lamb.

> Then the governor's soldiers took Jesus into the Praetorium and gathered the whole company of soldiers around him. They stripped him and put a scarlet robe on him, and then twisted together a crown of thorns and set it on his head. They put a staff in his right hand and knelt in front of him and mocked him. "Hail, king of the Jews!" they said. They spit on him, and

> took the staff and struck him on the head again and again. After they had mocked him, they took off the robe and put his own clothes on him. Then they led him away to crucify him.
>
> Matthew 27:28–31

- Comparing the verses just cited with some of the other related accounts penned by Yeshua's followers, we see that in each stage of his suffering, it is stated that he was *led away,* just as a lamb being led to slaughter: First, he was seized and *led away* to his trial at the home of the high priest (Luke 22:54); second, he was bound and *led away* to his trial before Pilate (Matt. 27:2; Mark 15:1); third, he was *led away* to be crucified after being flogged and abused (Matt. 27:31; Luke 23:26). This is exactly what Isaiah prophesied: "He was oppressed and afflicted, yet he did not open his mouth; he was *led like a lamb* to the slaughter, and as a sheep before her shearers is silent, so he did not open his mouth" (Isa. 53:7).

And what does our blessed Messiah say when he is being crucified? He prays that his Father would *forgive* those nailing him to the cross! (See Luke 23:34.) And when the soldiers and religious leaders mock him as he hangs there naked and humiliated, challenging him to demonstrate that he is the Messiah, the Son of God, he says nothing in defense. He doesn't utter a word! Nor does he reply to the two criminals crucified on either side of him, both of whom initially mock him as well (see Matt. 27:38, 44). It is only when one of these men comes to his senses and recognizes that there is something different about Jesus, that he is in fact God's chosen one, that Jesus says, "I tell you the truth, today you will be with me in paradise" (Luke 23:43). So, he only speaks to show mercy, not to retaliate. This goes *beyond* the noncombative qualities of a lamb!

His only other utterances on the cross are (1) his recitation of Psalm 22:1, pointing those listening to the words of the righteous sufferer who would be delivered from death by God (Matt. 27:46; see also below, 4.24); (2) his committing his mother's care into the hands of his disciple John (John 19:26–27); (3) the words, "I am thirsty" (John 19:28);[157] and (4) his last words, namely, "It is finished" and "Father, into your hands I commit my spirit" (John 19:30; Luke 23:46; see also Matt. 27:50). None of these utterances, in spirit or in letter, violate the words of Isaiah 53. Rather, like a lamb, he did not resist his oppressors nor did he seek to defend himself. Like a sheep silent before his shearers, he did not raise his voice when mocked, ridiculed, beaten, flogged, and crucified. And when he did speak, it was to commune with his Father, to pronounce mercy and forgiveness for the guilty, and to commit his mother to the care of one of his trusted followers. Truly, this was the Lamb of God! (See John 1:29.)

4.17. Isaiah 53 cannot refer to Jesus because it says the servant of the Lord would see seed, an expression always meaning physical descendants when used in the Hebrew Bible.

> Actually, the passage you refer to is the only occurrence of the Hebrew expression "see seed" in the Tanakh, so it is not wise to be so dogmatic about the meaning of the expression, especially since "seed" is sometimes used metaphorically in the Scriptures and since it can sometimes refer simply to a future generation. This much is certain: Through his continued life after his resurrection, we can honestly and fairly say that Jesus the Messiah fulfills the description of "seeing seed."

It was while debating Rabbi Professor J. Immanuel Schochet on March 30, 1995, that I first heard the argument that the Hebrew expression "see seed" *(yireh zera')* always referred to literal offspring in the Hebrew Bible. With all due respect to Rabbi Schochet's scholarship, I must confess I was surprised to hear this, since this idiom is found only one time in the Tanakh, namely, in Isaiah 53. How then can it be argued that this expression *always* refers to literal offspring in the Tanakh when it occurs only once? Of course, one could simply argue that the Hebrew word *zera'* always refers to literal seed (= physical offspring), never to metaphorical seed (such as disciples or spiritual offspring), and therefore the verse would mean that the servant of the Lord had children. If this were true, it would rule out Jesus as a candidate. This argument, however, is not compelling for a number of reasons.

First, *zera'*, "seed," is sometimes used metaphorically in the Hebrew Scriptures, including the Book of Isaiah. Thus, Isaiah called Israel "a seed of evildoers," "a seed of an adulterer," and "a seed of falsehood" (Isa. 1:4; 14:20; 57:3–4). While some of these phrases could be intended in a literal sense (that is, the Israelites were literally children of evil, adulterous, lying people), more likely they are intended metaphorically (that is, they were wicked, adulterous, dishonest people to the very core of their beings). According to the standard Hebrew lexicon of Brown, Driver, and Briggs, in cases such as these, seed means "as marked by moral quality = persons (or community) of such a quality,"[158] thus, "a seed of evildoers" would really mean "a community of evildoers" or "evildoers to the core." In the context of Isaiah 53:10, this would mean that the servant of the Lord would see godly, spiritual posterity, true disciples transformed by means of his labors on their behalf. As Isaiah 53:10 explains, this is tied in with his "prolong[ing] his days," referring to his resurrection (see above, 4.13).

Second, *zera'* is sometimes used with reference to "a future generation" without referring to the specific descendants of one individual in particular. Thus, Psalm 22 declares that as a result of the mighty deliverance experienced by the righteous sufferer (see below, 4.24), "posterity *[zera']* will serve him; future generations will be told about the Lord. They will proclaim his righteousness to a people yet unborn—for he has done it" (Ps. 22:30–31[31–32]).[159] As rendered in the NJPSV: "Offspring shall serve Him; the Lord's fame shall be proclaimed to the generation to come; they shall tell of His beneficence to people yet to be born, for He has acted." In the context of Isaiah 53:10, this would mean that the servant of the Lord would see future generations of his people serving the Lord. Cannot this be rightly applied to the hundreds of thousands of Jews who have followed Yeshua, the servant of the Lord, through the centuries? Certainly, this would be true to the context, especially since the text does not say that he would literally father a seed (= offspring), but rather that he would *see* offspring.

Third, the weakness of this argument is seen when we realize that no less a traditional Jewish authority than Sa'adiah Gaon applied Isaiah 53 to Jeremiah the prophet, yet God commanded Jeremiah never to marry or have children (Jer. 16:1; see above, 4.6). More recently, Isaiah 53 was applied to the late Lubavitcher Rebbe, yet he and his wife were unable to have children. How then could this be applied to either of these two candidates? Obviously, the text does not explicitly state that the servant of the Lord had to bear children of his own, hence the passage could be applied to these other Jewish leaders, albeit incorrectly. (In other words, many of the other specifics of the text cannot possibly apply to either Jeremiah or the Rebbe, while they apply perfectly to Yeshua.) We can see, then, that this argument has very little, if any, force.

Having concluded our discussion of Isaiah 53, let me once again encourage you to read the entire passage for yourself (beginning in Isaiah 52:13) while asking yourself honestly before the Lord, Of whom does the prophet speak? I trust you will see an amazing prophetic portrait of our Messiah, the righteous Lamb of God, who died that we could live. In fact, the description is so clear that you will understand why the charge has been raised that this section of the Bible was removed from the weekly Scripture portions read in the synagogue. It sounds too much like Yeshua! But is this charge really true?

Oxford professor Geza Vermes has argued that the Ten Commandments were once read every week in the synagogues and then were removed because of Hellenizing Jews who claimed that God gave Israel only the Ten Commandments.[160] If true, this would mean there might have been polemical factors that dictated which portions of the Bible would be read aloud in the synagogue—at least in some extreme cases. Similarly, it has been argued that Isaiah 52:13–53:12 was also removed from its place because Christians often pointed to the text as a clear prophecy of Jesus, and it sounded too much like him to be read in the synagogues. More specifically, we see that Isaiah 51:12–52:12 (the section immediately preceding Isaiah 52:13–53:12) was read in conjunction with Deuteronomy 15:18–21:9 (called Parashat Shoftim) from the Torah, while Isaiah 54:1–10 (the section immediately following Isaiah 52:13–53:12) was read in conjunction with the next Torah passage, Deuteronomy 21:10–25:19 (called Parashat Ki Tetzei). What happened to Isaiah 53?

It is possible the text was simply skipped because it did not fit properly with the Torah portion in question, since the reading from the Prophets coincided in some way with the reading from the Torah. In keeping with this, the Jewish scholar Raphael Loewe has pointed to ancient synagogal traditions from Palestine that seem to indicate that Isaiah 53 was *never* read as part of the weekly portion. On the other hand, Loewe pointed to equally ancient synagogal traditions from Egypt that seem to indicate the opposite, namely, that Isaiah 53 *was* originally read one week out of every year, but it was subsequently removed, apparently for polemical reasons.[161] How interesting! Of course, we may never know which tradition is accurate (or if both traditions are accurate, reflecting different customs in different parts of the world). Yet we do know this: Isaiah 53 has not been read aloud in the synagogues for many centuries, but there is nothing stopping you from carefully and prayerfully reading the text for yourself. I urge you to follow the truth wherever it may lead.

Having examined all the major objections that have been raised against the Messianic Jewish/Christian interpretation of Isaiah 53, it is clear that none of them have any substance. It is equally clear that the passage describes Jesus the Messiah with striking accuracy. What do you say?

4.18. Daniel 9:24–27 has nothing to do with *the* Messiah.

> There is no question that Christian versions translating the Hebrew word mashiach as "the Messiah" in this passage are reading something into the text. However, what they are reading into the text is correct, since the prophecy is clearly about the work of the Messiah.

Two things are immediately apparent in this short section of the Book of Daniel: First, these four verses are of great importance, serving as the climax to the angelic revelation concerning God's plan for Jerusalem and the Jewish people;[162] second, they are fraught with interpretive difficulties, as noted by Abraham Ibn Ezra, who pointed to the chronological questions (since the text describes events that will take place over a period of seventy sevens of years) as well as to questions concerning the meaning of individual words (since several key verbs can be interpreted in very different ways and there are textual variations in the Masoretic manuscripts that affect the overall meaning of the passage). It is clear, then, that special attention should be given to the interpretation of these verses, and it is not surprising that both Jewish and Christian translations and commentaries have offered many different solutions to the problems presented in Daniel 9:24–27. It is also not surprising that anti-missionaries have strongly rejected traditional Christian translations of these verses, since believers in Jesus have often pointed to them as containing one of the most important Messianic prophetic announcements in the Tanakh.

Anti-missionary author Gerald Sigal attacks the Christian interpretation of this passage, claiming that the King James Version here "contains the grossest errors, which are, in whole or in part, duplicated by other Christian versions of the Bible." He observes that "the King James Version puts a definite article before 'Messiah the Prince' (9:25)," whereas "the original Hebrew text does not read 'the Messiah the Prince,' but, having no article, it is to be rendered 'a *mashiach* ['anointed one,' 'messiah'], a prince,' i.e., Cyrus (Isaiah 45:1, 13; Ezra 1:1–2)." He also claims that "the word *mashiach* is nowhere used in the Jewish Scriptures as a proper name, but as a title of authority of a king or a high priest. Therefore, a correct rendering of the original Hebrew should be: 'an anointed one, a prince.'" (see <http://www.jewsforjudaism.org/j4j-2000/index.html>.)

What then does the text mean, and how should it be translated? And are the Christian translations guilty of "the grossest errors"? Let's look at the larger context of this passage in order to see just how important this prophetic revelation really is. We can then answer the specific questions that have been raised.

Daniel 9 begins with these words:

> In the first year of Darius son of Xerxes (a Mede by descent), who was made ruler over the Babylonian kingdom—in the first year of his reign, I, Daniel, understood from the Scriptures, according to the word of the LORD given to Jeremiah the prophet, that the desolation of Jerusalem would last seventy years. So I turned to the Lord God and pleaded with him in prayer and petition, in fasting, and in sackcloth and ashes.
>
> Daniel 9:1–3

This is the background: Daniel, one of the godliest men spoken of in the Scriptures, was as a young man among the first exiles brought to Babylon, almost twenty years before the Temple was destroyed in 586 B.C.E. He was now an old man, having spent almost all of his life in exile, and he had read in the Book of Jeremiah that Judah's exile was to last for seventy years (Jeremiah 29). The seventy years were almost completed, at least beginning with the time of Daniel's own exile in 604 B.C.E. So he gave himself to brokenhearted prayer and fasting, pleading with God to have mercy on his scattered people and to restore them to their homeland.

The verses that follow in Daniel 9 (vv. 4–19) contain one of the deepest penitential prayers in the entire Bible. I would encourage you to stop for a moment and read Daniel's prayer and confession aloud, and as you read, take note of the *larger* picture: Israel had sinned so grievously against God that he had judged his people with such severity that the Temple was destroyed and the people were exiled from their land. This was a public tragedy that far exceeds anything we in our contemporary society can relate to on a national level, a horrific series of events that brought extraordinary shame and guilt.[163] That's why Daniel cried out with such contrition and pain: He was praying for the very destiny of his people. He was praying that God would bring full restoration—both to the Temple and to the people—with everything in his prayer focused on Jerusalem. (Note that he describes his confession in 9:20 as "confessing my sin and the sin of my people Israel and making my request to the LORD my God *for his holy hill*"— meaning the Temple mount in Jerusalem.)

It was during this time of prayer and fasting that the angel Gabriel appeared to him—this was serious business, to say the least—and said:

> Daniel, I have now come to give you insight and understanding. As soon as you began to pray, an answer was given, which I have come to tell you, for you are highly esteemed. Therefore, consider the message and understand the vision:
>
> Seventy 'sevens' are decreed for your people and your holy city to finish transgression, to put an end to sin, to atone for wickedness, to bring in everlasting righteousness, to seal up vision and prophecy and to anoint the most holy.

Daniel 9:22b–24[164]

It is important that we grasp the full significance of this event. Daniel was so esteemed by heaven that God sent the mighty angel Gabriel (see Dan. 8:15–27) on a personal visit to Daniel, giving him one of the most significant revelations in the Scriptures. We can paraphrase this critically important message as follows: "Daniel, you are praying about a period of seventy years and are yearning to see the return of your people to the land and the restoration of the Temple. But I will go far beyond your request and speak to you about a period of *seventy sevens of years* (490 years), a period in which final atonement will be made, a period of even greater importance for the Temple and the people. I will speak to you about the Messianic era!"[165]

To give us a traditional Jewish perspective on the passage as a whole, let's listen now to Rashi's opening comments on this passage. As rendered by A. J. Rosenberg, the preeminent translator of Rashi today, Rashi explains as follows:

> **Seventy weeks [of years] have been decreed** on Jerusalem from the day of the first destruction in the days of Zedekiah until it will be [destroyed] the second time. **to terminate the transgression and to end sin** so that Israel should receive their complete retribution in the exile of Titus and his subjugation, in order that their transgressions should terminate, their sins should end, and their iniquities should be expiated, in order to bring upon them eternal righteousness and to

anoint upon them (sic) the Holy of Holies: the Ark, the altars, and the holy vessels, which they will bring to them through the king Messiah. The number of seven weeks is four hundred and ninety years. The Babylonian exile was seventy [years] and the Second Temple stood four hundred and twenty [years].[166]

Note carefully Rashi's comments that this prophecy involves a time of restoration brought about "through the king Messiah," indicating that it is not only Christians who see clear Messianic overtones in this prophecy. The difference, however, is that Christians have a clear basis for their Messianic interpretation of Daniel 9:24–27, namely, that the Messiah died for the sins of the world during the very times specified by Daniel, whereas Rashi simply appends a reference to the Messiah to the end of the passage, without explanation.[167] This becomes more clear when we focus on Rashi's comments to Daniel 9:26:

> **26 And after** those weeks. **the anointed one will be cut off** Agrippa, the king of Judea, who was ruling at the time of the destruction, will be slain. **and he will be no more** Heb. *we'en lo* and he will not have. The meaning is that he will not be. **the anointed one** Heb. *mashiah* This is purely an expression of a prince and a dignitary. **and the city and the Sanctuary** lit. and the city and the Holy. **and the people of the coming monarch will destroy** [The monarch who will come] upon them. That is Titus and his armies. **and his end will come about by inundation** And his end will be damnation and destruction, for He will inundate the power of his kingdom through the Messiah, and until the end of the wars of Gog the city will exist. **cut off into desolation** a destruction of desolation.

Let's look carefully at some of Rashi's comments here. First, he identifies "the anointed one" as the Judean King Agrippa, "who was ruling at the time of the destruction" of the Second Temple in 70 C.E., which was approximately forty years after Yeshua's death. Second, he interprets the destruction of the city and the sanctuary as pointing to that same event under Titus the Roman general. As translated by Jewish historian Heinrich W. Guggenheimer, "the power of his reign [i.e., Titus] will be blown away by the Messiah."[168] Third, he makes reference again to God's kingdom coming in power through the Messiah, but once more, it is merely appended without explanation. In other words, Rashi's references to the Messiah have nothing to do with the immediate context, which speaks of events that culminate in the first century of this era. Yet that is when Jesus, the real Messiah, *did* come and visit our people, dying and rising from the dead, providing final atonement for mankind. Strangely, Rashi recognized the Messianic implications of the prophecy yet failed to see the Messianic prophecies contained therein.

In the Stone edition, the footnote to the words "the anointed one" in Daniel 9:26 summarizes Rashi's views as follows: "I.e., Agrippa, the last Jewish king, at the end of the Second Temple Era. After his death, the prince of this verse, the Roman Titus, would command the destruction of the Temple, which will not be rebuilt until after the War of Gog and Magog, in Messianic times." So, Rashi taught that the prophecy pinpointed the death of Agrippa and the destruction of the Temple—major events in the last generation of the Second Temple era—but then simply drifted off to the distant future in terms of the final fulfillment of the prophecy. Despite Rashi's brilliance as a biblical and Talmudic interpreter, we have to admit that his interpretation is lacking cohesion and clarity, to say the least.[169]

All this is underscored by Rashi's comments on the end of Daniel 9:27: "**and until destruction and extermination befall the dumb one** and the ruling of the abomination will endure until the day that the destruction and extermination decreed upon it [will] befall it, in the days of the king Messiah." Once again, Rashi sees Daniel's prophecy as ultimately pointing to the Messiah and his reign, but in a way that is completely unrelated to the passage. It is almost like counting down for the launch of a rocket, with everyone gathered around the launchpad in great expectation, then the countdown is completed, liftoff is announced . . . but the rocket doesn't take off for two thousand years. Something is wrong with this picture. Yet that is exactly what happens with Rashi's interpretation of the passage: He explains how all the prophesied events culminate and unfold in a time period one generation after Jesus and then says, "And the real end of the story will take place in the days of the Messiah"—which, according to traditional Judaism, still have not arrived, now two thousand years later.

I find it interesting that Rachmiel Frydland, a well-known Messianic Jewish scholar, became a believer in Yeshua with the help of Rashi's commentary on Daniel 9:24–27. Raised as an ultra-Orthodox Jew in Poland, Frydland narrowly escaped death in the Holocaust, enduring terrible suffering and deprivation in his flight from his homeland.[170] During an intensive time of seeking the truth about the Scriptures as a teenager, he read Rashi's commentary and thought to himself—to paraphrase—"He has the time frame right, but he got the wrong anointed one!" Soon he realized, "It is not Agrippa who was cut off; it was Yeshua." His reasoning makes perfect sense. After all, the death of Agrippa was of no great significance in terms of God's eternal purposes for his people Israel, neither was it of great consequence in terms of the future of the Jewish people, the city of Jerusalem, or even the Temple itself. But the death of Jesus affected the entire world! And it was because our people did not recognize him when he came that the Temple was destroyed, just as Daniel prophesied. Viewed in this light, Gabriel's revelation to Daniel is very clear, as we will see in responding to the next three objections.

You might say, "Even if your interpretation has some merit, there is still no justification for translating the Hebrew word *mashiach* as 'the Messiah.' There is no definite article here, so the translation should say 'a' rather than 'the'; and *mashiach* should simply be translated as 'anointed one,' just as it is throughout the Tanakh."

Actually, I agree with your basic position. I simply believe you have overstated it and, in so doing, have thrown out the baby with the bathwater. First, traditional Christian translations are not the only ones that add the word "the" before "anointed one" in Daniel 9:26. In fact, the oldest Jewish translation, the Septuagint, translates *mashiach* as *tou christou* ("the anointed one"), while the most recent traditional Jewish translation, the Stone edition, renders it "the anointed one" rather than "an anointed one."[171] This is because the Hebrew language can sometimes specify a particular person or event without using the definite article, as recognized in the standard grammars and, in certain phrases, in virtually all translations. Thus, it is not just any anointed one that the prophecy describes, but one particular anointed one. Some translators, both Christian and Jewish, feel that this concept is best expressed by using the word "the" to identify that particular subject. Second, later Jewish usage made the word *mashiach* into a proper name, as in the Jewish bumper sticker that says, "We want Moshiach now!" For many centuries, in the Jewish mind the word *mashiach* has not simply meant "an anointed one" but rather "*the* anointed one, King Messiah." Some Christian translations simply interpreted Daniel 9:26 in the light of their own Messianic traditions and views, finding in this verse the most overt reference to *the Messiah*—identified as such—in the Hebrew Scriptures.

Now, I agree it is reading too much into the text to justify the *translation* "the Messiah" (still reflected in the NASB). But that does not mean the *interpretation* is wrong. Quite the contrary. The verse does speak of the death of the Messiah, and Christian interpreters are fully justified in explaining Daniel 9:24–27 in Messianic terms (see below, 4.19–4.21, for more on this). A simple translation, however, should either speak of "an anointed one" (as does the NRSV), "the anointed one" (as in the Stone edition), or possibly, but with much less likelihood, "Messiah" (without the definite article, as in the NKJV).[172] The bottom line is that this prophecy foretells the Messiah's atoning death, and Christian translators can be forgiven if they sought to bring this meaning out even more clearly than the original author intended, since the anointed one of whom Daniel spoke in 9:26 is none other than King Messiah.[173]

4.19. Daniel 9:24 was clearly *not* fulfilled by Jesus.

> Since Daniel 9:24–27 speaks of events that must be fulfilled before the destruction of the Second Temple (which took place in 70 c.e.), the question that must be asked is this: If Jesus did not fulfill Daniel 9:24, who did? Who was it that ushered in everlasting righteousness and made atonement for iniquity before 70 c.e. if not Jesus the Messiah? In reality, if Jesus did not fulfill Daniel 9:24, then no one fulfilled it and the prophecies of Daniel cannot be trusted.

Daniel 9:24 sums up the main events to be accomplished during the period of the seventy weeks of years (see above, 4.18): "Seventy 'sevens' are decreed for your people and your holy city to finish transgression, to put an end to sin, to atone for wickedness, to bring in everlasting righteousness, to seal up vision and prophecy and to anoint the most holy" (NIV). The Stone edition reads, "Seventy septets have been decreed upon your people and upon your holy city to terminate transgression, to end sin, to wipe away iniquity, to bring everlasting righteousness, to confirm the visions and prophets, and to anoint the Holy of Holies." It can be seen, then, there is not much difference between these two translations, the former reflecting traditional Christian scholarship, the latter reflecting traditional Jewish scholarship.[174] The question is one of interpretation and application: What does this verse mean and did it come to pass?

Professor Walter Kaiser presents the traditional Christian understanding of verse 24:

> God uses six infinitives to describe his divine purposes for Israel during these 490 future years for the nation. . . . All the transgressions

against God must be completed. The final sacrifice that will put an end to sin has to be offered so that atonement can be made. God will need to bring in everlasting righteousness during this period, and the visions and prophecies about the future will remain enigmatic to the Jewish people. Finally, the most holy person, the Messiah himself (or does it refer to the temple as the Most Holy *Place*?) will need to be anointed somewhere during this same 490 years.[175]

More detailed is the interpretation of conservative Christian scholar James E. Smith. He explains the sixfold promise of Daniel 9:24 as follows:

1. *To fill up* [or restrain] *the transgression.* Within the 490 year period the people of Israel would commit their final transgression against God. Jesus indicated that the leaders of his generation were about to fill up the measure of the sin of their forefathers (Matt. 23:32). . . .[176]
2. *To seal up the sin.* The perfect sacrifice for sin offered by Jesus Christ provided the means by which the sin problem of mankind could be dealt with decisively (Heb. 10:12). . . .
3. *To make atonement for iniquity.* The necessary sacrifice would be offered and would become the basis upon which iniquity could be forgiven. In Christ there is redemption, the forgiveness of sins (Col. 1:14). His once-for-all sacrifice is able to make perfect those who accept it as their own (Heb. 10:12–14).
4. *To bring in everlasting righteousness.* It is obviously God who brings in this righteousness, and he does that through the Messiah. This righteousness by its very perpetuity must belong to the age of the Messiah. . . .
5. *To seal up vision and prophecy* [lit., vision and prophet]. . . . On two occasions Jesus cited the prophecy in Isaiah 6:9–10 regarding the obtuseness of [his fellow] Jews.[177] . . . The sealing of vision and prophecy in their midst—the failure to understand that the long awaited Messiah was ministering in their midst—was one of the penalties suffered by the Jewish nation because of their hardness of heart. [Smith further notes that some scholars think "the sealing refers to the fulfillment of prophecies in Christ."]
6. *To anoint the most holy.* The expression could refer to the anointing of the most holy person,[178] the anointed one *par excellence.* . . .

In summary, it is clear that all six objectives stated in Daniel 24 were accomplished by the time Jesus of Nazareth ascended to heaven in A.D. 30, or shortly thereafter.[179]

Very different is the translation and commentary of Professor John J. Collins, reflecting a critical historical interpretation of the verse (bracketed quotations are also from Collins and convey his understanding of the text):

> Seventy weeks are determined for your people and for your holy city, to finish the transgression ["the idea is that evil must run its course until the appointed time"], to bring sins to completion [as in Daniel 8:23, where the meaning is that the sins will reach their full measure] and to expiate iniquity ["*kpr*, with God as subject, means to 'cancel' or 'absolve'"], to bring in everlasting righteousness, to seal vision [as authentic], and to anoint a most holy place ["The reference is to the rededication of the Jerusalem Temple, which was actually accomplished by Judas Maccabee late in 164 B.C.E. (1 Macc. 4:36–39)"].[180]

Which view is right? In favor of the traditional Christian interpretation are the following points: (1) It recognizes the magnitude and scope of Daniel 9:24–27, understanding the lasting significance of the events described there; (2) it does not downplay concepts such as bringing in "everlasting righteousness"; and (3) it recognizes the accuracy of the prophecies in terms of a 490-year window of fulfillment. Against this interpretation the following objections could be raised: (1) It struggles with the meaning of anointing a most holy, applying this to Jesus instead of to the Temple, and (2) it seems to fall short of the mark in terms of total fulfillment, since the world is still filled with sin and unrighteousness (this, of course, is the core of the overall objection we are presently discussing).

In favor of the historical-critical interpretation of these verses are the following: (1) It points to a definite series of well-documented historical events; (2) it agrees with the critical dating of the Book of Daniel, placing the book within the time frame of the events described; and (3) it has a simple explanation for the phrase "to anoint a most holy place," as explained above by Collins. There are, however, some fatal flaws to this interpretation. (1) It actually makes Daniel mistaken in his dates, since the specific period of years that he predicts simply does not pan out. The interpretation is actually off by fifty to one hundred years![181] As summarized by Old Testament scholar John Goldingay, "The critical view has usually been that the seventy sevens extend as one sequence from some point in the sixth century to the period of Antiochus Epiphanes. Daniel 9 is then an overestimate and Daniel is faulted for its 'wrongheaded arithmetical calculations.'"[182] (2) It places Daniel in the second century B.C.E. rather than in the sixth century B.C.E. (where the Hebrew Bible explicitly places him), claiming that all the prophecies of the book are not prophecies at all, but rather history passing itself off as prophecy. That is to say, it claims that the author of Daniel was not really Daniel at all but a second-century B.C.E. Jew who *looked back* at the history of the previous four centuries and then created a mythical figure named Daniel, claiming that this man Daniel lived four hundred years earlier and *predicted* the historical events described in the book.[183] (3) It does not recognize the significance of Daniel 9:24–27 and fails to do justice to some of the specific promises, such as bringing in "everlasting righteousness." For these reasons alone, this interpretation must be rejected.

What then of the problems with the Christian view? The answer to this question is really quite simple. Since the prophesied events had to take place before the destruction of the Temple in 70 C.E., and since the most natural interpretation of these events points to Yeshua's atoning death, it is only logical to begin with him and ask to what extent he fulfilled each of the six divine promises in Daniel 9:24. Having done this, we can easily resolve any remaining difficulties. Let's consider the six phrases one by one, asking if, in fact, they point to Jesus the Messiah and the events of his day.

1. *"To finish transgression."* This probably means bringing sin to its ugly, final climax, as opposed to bringing it to an end. According to one Christian view, as represented by Old Testament and Semitic scholar Gleason Archer, "The culmination of the appointed years will witness the conclusion of man's 'transgression' or 'rebellion' *(peša')* against God—a development most naturally entered into with the establishment of an entirely new order on earth. This seems to require nothing less than the inauguration of the kingdom of God on earth. Certainly the crucifixion of Christ in A.D. 30 did not put an end to man's iniquity or rebellion on earth, as the millennial kingdom of Christ promises to do."[184] Archer, then, would posit the fulfillment of this event during the last of Daniel's seventy weeks of years, which Archer believes has yet to take place. A more plausible view, however—and one that does not call for such an extended gap between the sixty-ninth and seventieth weeks—is to take seriously Yeshua's words spoken in Matthew 23:32, when he sarcastically exhorted the hostile Jewish leaders of his day, "Fill up, then, the measure of the sin of your forefathers!" Thus, the generation that rejected the Messiah would suffer the culmination of the sins of all the previous gen-

erations: "Upon you will come all the righteous blood that has been shed on earth. . . . I tell you the truth, all this will come upon this generation" (Matt. 23:35a, 37).[185] This is similar to God's word to Abram in Genesis 15:12–16, explaining that Abram's descendants would have to wait four hundred years to inherit the Promised Land because "the sin of the Amorites [who then inhabited the land] has not yet reached its full measure."

2. *"To put an end to sin."* This phrase also could be interpreted in one of two ways, as speaking of a still-future event that will be ushered in with Messiah's return (this is the position of Archer and others) or as referring to Messiah's atoning death on the cross, an event of cosmic proportions that did, in fact, deal a deathblow to the power of sin. As other New Testament writers explain, everything necessary for forgiveness and redemption was accomplished by the death and resurrection of Jesus. It need only be applied and appropriated (cf. 2 Cor. 5:14–21).

3. *"To atone for wickedness."* This statement sums up the very heart of the Messiah's mission on the earth. Archer is correct in stating that this "certainly points to the Crucifixion, an event that ushered in the final stage of human history before the establishment of the fifth kingdom (cf. [Dan.] 2:35, 44)."[186] It is only fair to ask, If one of the central redemptive events described in Daniel's prophecy was "to atone for wickedness," and if this event was to take place before the Temple's destruction in 70 C.E., and if this was the whole focus of Yeshua's ministry, why then seek a different explanation and overlook the most important atoning event in human history?

4. *"To bring in everlasting righteousness."* As with the first two phrases, this could point either to the culmination of the Messiah's work when he returns and establishes God's righteous kingdom on the earth (again, Archer's position) or to Messiah's work on the cross, which brought about "the gift of righteousness" spoken of by Paul in Romans 5:17: "For if, by the trespass of the one man [Adam], death reigned through that one man, how much more will those who receive God's abundant provision of grace and of the gift of righteousness reign in life through the one man, Jesus [the Messiah]." As explained by Peter, "He himself bore our sins in his body on the tree, so that we might die to sins and live for righteousness; by his wounds you have been healed" (1 Peter 2:24). Thus, "if anyone is in [the Messiah], he is a new creation; the old has gone, the new has come!" This is because, "God made him who had no sin [the Messiah!] to be sin [or, a sin offering] for us, so that in him we might become the righteousness

of God" (2 Cor. 5:21). From citations such as these you can see that Paul and Peter, two devoted Jewish followers of Jesus the Messiah, had no problem explaining how "everlasting righteousness" was inaugurated by Jesus' atoning work.[187]

5. *"To seal up vision and prophecy."* This could mean "to authenticate" or "to hide." Either one would be applicable to Jesus, since (1) his coming fully validated the prophetic witness of the Hebrew Scriptures (if he did *not* come at the appointed time, this would have *invalidated* both vision and prophecy), and (2) God judged those who rejected him with hardness of heart, thus hiding the truth of the prophetic Scriptures from them.[188]

6. *"To anoint the most holy."* This is perhaps the most difficult phrase to explain with reference to Jesus. However, since the first five phrases can so readily be explained with reference to him, it seems only logical to see if this phrase too could apply to him. What then does it mean? According to Archer, "This is not likely a reference to the anointing of Christ (as some writers have suggested) because *qodeš qad^{a}šîm* nowhere else in Scripture refers to a person. Here the anointing of the 'most holy' most likely refers to the consecration of the temple of the Lord, quite conceivably the millennial temple, to which so much attention is given in Ezekiel 40–44."[189] Once again, this pushes the fulfillment of this event to the final seven-year "week," which according to Archer culminates with Yeshua's return. As I have stated throughout this section, I find this poisition unnecessary, although it still points to fulfillment in Jesus. Archer's point, however, is well taken in terms of the meaning of the Hebrew phrase "most holy" (lit., "holy of holies") never referring to a person—with one possible exception, namely, 1 Chronicles 23:13, as observed by Smith (see n. 178). It is true that most translations understand this verse to state that Aaron was set apart "to consecrate the most holy *things*" (NIV; cf., e.g., KJV, NKJV, RSV, NRSV, NLT). Yet there are other translations, both Christian and Jewish (e.g., NASB and *Stone*), that interpret the Hebrew with reference to Aaron himself: "Aaron was set apart to sanctify *him* as most holy" (NASB; for the *Stone* rendering, see n. 178).[190] If this is an accurate understanding of the Hebrew, then there would be biblical precedent for taking "the most holy" to refer to a person, not just to a place in the Temple or to items in the Temple. And to what person could the anointing of the most holy better refer than to our righteous Messiah, our priestly King?[191] As far back as the eighteenth century, C. Schöttgen cited no less an authority than Nachmanides as having stated that "the Holy of holies is naught else than the Messiah,

the sanctified one of the sons of David."[192] This view may also be supported by the Septuagint, and it is certainly supported by the Syriac Peshitta, composed in the first centuries of this era.[193] If "the most holy" refers to a place (or to sacred things) rather than to a person, then it could refer to the *spiritual Temple*—i.e., the redeemed people of God, who, according to the New Testament authors, have become a holy dwelling place for the Spirit. This Temple was, in fact, inaugurated by Jesus the Messiah, and the community of believers who make up this Temple are, in fact, anointed by the Spirit of God. On the other hand, the reference could be to a still-future Temple, the Messiah's millennial Temple in Jerusalem.[194]

Where then does this leave us? As I see it, only two choices are viable, and both point to fulfillment through Yeshua. (1) We have seen that all six divine declarations found in Daniel 9:24 could apply to the work accomplished through the death and resurrection of the Messiah, the anointed one cut off in the very time period prophesied by Daniel. Thus, everything Daniel recorded in 9:24–27 reached its fulfillment by 70 C.E. (2) It is also possible that *on the basis of our Messiah's atoning work*, the ultimate fulfillment of Gabriel's revelation to Daniel in this key section of Scripture will take place at the end of this age, when Jesus returns. But this is not a cheap cop out, as frequently charged by anti-missionaries, who claim that the whole concept of the Messiah's second coming is a simple way of escaping the fact that Jesus, in their opinion, failed to fulfill the real Messianic prophecies (see further 4.33 and vol. 4, 5.15). Hardly! To the contrary, this interpretation is realistic and honest, remaining true to the text and true to history, since Daniel 9:24–27 points to major redemptive events that had to take place before the destruction of the Second Temple. And if it is true—as the Jewish commentator Rashi and the Christian commentator Gleason Archer both claim—that these verses speak of events that took place more than nineteen hundred years ago as well as events that culminate in the end of the age, then it is only the Christian interpretation that makes sense. This is because it is the only interpretation that explains *why* the events that took place in the first century of this era will have an impact at the end of this age, when the Messiah's kingdom will be established on the earth.

In other words, it was during his first coming that Yeshua died for the sins of the world, making atonement for iniquity and bringing in everlasting righteousness, in accordance with Daniel 9:24. Since that time our righteous Messiah has extended his spiritual kingdom through his followers on the earth, to the point that more than one billion people now worship the God of Israel through him. When the good news of his death and resurrection has been shared around the world, the end will come—apparently on the heels of great worldwide wars—Messiah will return, and his kingdom will be established on the earth.

I reiterate, then, my premise: If all the events spoken of in Daniel 9:24–27 had to be fulfilled before 70 C.E., then Jesus must be the central, anointed figure involved in their fulfillment, bringing redemption and forgiveness to his people. If the events spoken of in the text were partially fulfilled before 70 C.E. and will only reach their total fulfillment at the end of this age, then this too can only be interpreted with reference to Jesus, since it is only through what he accomplished *before* 70 C.E. that the culminating events of this age will take place.

There is one last important piece of corroborating evidence in the book of Daniel, namely, his prophecy of the kingdom of God destroying and displacing the greatest of the kingdoms of man. I refer here to Daniel 2, in which the prophet interpreted king Nebuchadnezzar's symbolic dream with reference to four ancient kingdoms: first, the Babylonian empire, represented by gold; second the Medo-Persian empire, represented by silver; third, the Greek empire, represented by bronze; and fourth, the Roman empire, represented by iron mixed with clay. But those kingdoms would not endure. Rather, the Scripture declares, "In the time of those kings, the God of heaven will set up a kingdom that will never be destroyed, nor will it be left to another people. It will crush all those kingdoms and bring them to an end, but it will itself endure forever. This is the meaning of the vision of the rock cut out of a mountain, but not by human hands—a rock that broke the iron, the bronze, the clay, the silver and the gold to pieces" (Dan. 2:44–45a).

Notice the opening words of this passage, "In the time of those kings, the God of heaven will set up a kingdom that will never be destroyed" (2:44a). What does this mean? According to Rashi, "**And in the days of these kings** in the days of these kings, when the kingdom of Rome is still in existence. **the God of heaven will set up a kingdom** The kingdom of the Holy One, blessed be He, which will never be destroyed, is the kingdom of the Messiah. **it will crumble and destroy** It will crumble and destroy all these kingdoms."[195] Exactly! The Messianic kingdom *was* established in the Roman era— just as the New Testament writings declare—and it has been growing and increasing around the world ever since. As Daniel explained to the astonished Babylonian king, Nebuchadnezzar,

While you were watching, a rock was cut out, but not by human hands. It struck the statue on its feet of iron and clay and smashed them. Then the iron, the clay, the bronze, the silver and the gold were broken to pieces at the same time and became like chaff on a threshing floor in the summer. The wind swept them away without leaving a trace. But the rock that struck the statue became a huge mountain and filled the whole earth.

Daniel 2:34–35

Yes, this "rock" *is* becoming a huge mountain that is filling the whole earth. But its origins were in the days of Rome, when Jesus the Messiah inaugurated the kingdom of God on earth. This is also the key to understanding Daniel 9:24–27: Everything written there is fulfilled through Messiah Yeshua, beginning with his atoning death on the cross and culminating with his return to earth, when the kingdom of God will be fully established on the earth. Do you see it?

With Yeshua in the middle of the picture, Daniel 9:24–27 makes perfect sense. Take Yeshua out, and these verses become completely obscure and unintelligible. I trust the picture will be clear for you! As the psalmist wrote, "Whoever is wise, let him heed these things and consider the great love of the LORD" (Ps. 107:43). Or in the words of the prophet Hosea, "Who is wise? He will realize these things. Who is discerning? He will understand them" (Hosea 14:9a). I pray you will be counted among the wise.

4.20. Christian translations of Daniel 9:24–27 divide the seventy weeks incorrectly, and the dates have no relation to the times of Jesus.

> There are two different ways to understand the division of the seventy weeks, but both of them are legitimate and in keeping with the rules of Hebrew grammar. More important, both equally support the Messianic interpretation of the text, and the dates involved clearly point to the times of Jesus. That's one of the reasons why many Christians point to this text as an important Messianic prophecy.

We noted previously (above, 4.18) that Rashi understood the anointed one mentioned in Daniel 9:26 to refer to Agrippa and that he interpreted Daniel 9:27 with reference to the destruction of the Second Temple in 70 C.E.[196] In other words, without stating it—or perhaps without even being conscious of it—Rashi dated some of the key events described in this prophecy to the generation after Yeshua. Like most Jewish commentators and translators, however, he understood the text in harmony with the Masoretic accents and divided the weeks into three periods of time: seven weeks, sixty-two weeks, and one week. This is reflected in the New Revised Standard Version, a liberal Christian translation:

> Seventy weeks are decreed for your people and your holy city: to finish the transgression, to put an end to sin, and to atone for iniquity, to bring in everlasting righteousness, to seal both vision and prophet, and to anoint a most holy place. Know therefore and understand: from the time that the word went out to restore and rebuild Jerusalem until the time of an anointed prince, there shall be seven weeks; and for sixty-two weeks it shall be built again with streets and moat, but in a troubled time. After the sixty-two weeks, an anointed one shall be cut off and shall have nothing, and the troops of the prince who is to come shall destroy the city and the sanctuary. Its end shall come with a flood, and to the end there shall be war. Desolations are decreed. He shall make a strong covenant with many for one week, and for half of the week he shall make sacrifice and offering cease; and in their place shall be an abomination that desolates, until the decreed end is poured out upon the desolator.

> Daniel 9:24–27

Other Christian translations, however, following the pattern of the King James Version, divide the weeks into two main periods: (1) seven weeks + sixty-two weeks, and (2) one week. As rendered in the KJV:

> Seventy weeks are determined upon thy people and upon thy holy city, to finish the transgression, and to make an end of sins, and to make reconciliation for iniquity, and to bring in everlasting righteousness, and to seal up the vision and prophecy, and to anoint the most Holy.

> Know therefore and understand, that from the going forth of the commandment to restore and to build Jerusalem unto the Messiah the Prince shall be seven weeks, and threescore and two weeks: the street shall be built again, and the wall, even in troublous times.

> And after threescore and two weeks shall Messiah be cut off, but not for himself: and the people of the prince that shall come shall destroy the city and the sanctuary; and the end thereof shall be with a flood, and unto the end of the war desolations are determined.

> And he shall confirm the covenant with many for one week: and in the midst of the week he shall cause the sacrifice and the oblation to

cease, and for the overspreading of abominations he shall make it desolate, even until the consummation, and that determined shall be poured upon the desolate.

Daniel 9:24–27

Translating the text in this way makes quite a difference. According to traditional Jewish thought (reflected also in the rendering of the NRSV, cited earlier), verse 25 should be translated as follows: "From the time that the word went out to restore and rebuild Jerusalem until the time of an anointed prince, there shall be seven weeks"—meaning that forty-nine years would elapse from the time of the initial decree (somewhere in the sixth or fifth century B.C.E.; we will return to this subject later) until the time of this anointed prince. Obviously, this could not refer to Jesus, who was born more than four hundred years later. The KJV, however, rendered this verse, "Know therefore and understand, that from the going forth of the commandment to restore and to build Jerusalem unto the Messiah the Prince shall be seven weeks, and threescore and two weeks: the street shall be built again, and the wall, even in troublous times." Using the date of 457 B.C.E. as our starting point, as suggested by some scholars, and putting the two sets of weeks together ($7 \times 7 + 7 \times 62$), we would arrive at a total of 483 years, ending in 27 C.E.—the very year that Jesus began his public ministry.[197] What an incredibly accurate prophecy this would be!

It is understandable why anti-missionaries would oppose this view so strongly, arguing that a proper understanding of the Hebrew text would *exclude* fulfillment in the time of Yeshua. In reality, however, the original text presents no such problems for at least two reasons: First, if we follow the traditional Jewish division of the weeks, then we would also follow the traditional Jewish understanding that there are two anointed figures mentioned in the text (see below, 4.21). This understanding is quite natural, since there would be at least 434 years (7×62) between the two *mashiachs*. Second, the Hebrew text was originally written without vowel signs or accents (also called cantillation marks), both of which were added to the written biblical text centuries after its completion, and both of which sometimes reflect erroneous and/or variant readings.[198] Thus, to argue for an interpretation *based primarily on the accents* is to give them a weight of authority they do not deserve (since they simply reflect the tradition of the Tiberian Masoretes) and to admit that the original, consonantal text is subject to varied interpretation. If this is not the case, why not simply argue that the text can only be read one way *without* pointing to the accents for proof?

Basically, however, the difficulty in joining the two groups of weeks together—seven weeks of years and sixty-two weeks of years—is not grammatical. It is logical and contextual. If the purpose of the prophecy was to state that there would be 483 years until the coming of the Messiah—as indicated in many Christian versions—why not simply state, "Know therefore and understand, that from the going forth of the commandment to restore and to build Jerusalem unto the Messiah the Prince shall be sixty-nine weeks" rather than "seven weeks, and threescore and two weeks"? For those maintaining the Messianic position, only one answer makes sense: There was a prophetic significance to these two specific sets of weeks, the first set covering 49 years, being the time during which Jerusalem was restored and rebuilt, and the second set covering 434 years, being the time between the completion of Jerusalem's physical restoration and the coming of the Messiah.

As Gleason Archer explained,

> If, then, the terminus a quo for the decree in v. 25 be reckoned as 457 B.C. (the date of Ezra's return to Jerusalem), then we may compute the first seven heptads as running from 457 to 408, within which time the rebuilding of the walls, streets, and moats was completed. Then from 408 we count off the sixty-two heptads also mentioned in v. 25 and come out to A.D. 26 (408 is 26 less than 434). But actually we come out to A.D. 27, since a year is gained in our reckoning as we pass directly from 1 B.C. to A.D. 1 (without any year zero in between). If Christ was crucified on 14 Abib A.D. 30, as is generally believed (cf. L. A. Foster, "The Chronology of the New Testament," *EBC*, 1:598–99, 607), this would come out to a remarkably exact fulfillment of the terms of v. 25. Christ's public ministry, from the time of his baptism in the Jordan till his death and resurrection at Jerusalem, must have taken up about three years. The 483 years from the issuing of the decree of Artaxerxes came to an end in A.D. 27, the year of the "coming" of Messiah as Ruler *(nasi)*. It was indeed "after the sixty-two 'sevens'"—three years after—that "the Anointed One" was "cut off."[199]

Could this interpretation be true? We will return to it in a moment, examining some of its premises in more detail. For now, let's follow the traditional Jewish division of the sixty-nine weeks into two distinct periods, with each period centering in on a *mashiach* (anointed one). This does not necessarily mean I believe the traditional Christian translations are in error in their division of the sixty-nine weeks, since it is certainly grammatically and contextually possible to follow the KJV rendering of verse 25. I do believe, however, that the traditional Jewish rendering is more natural and that there is no problem with seeing two anointed ones in the prophecy. And with both interpretations, we still come out to the same general time frame for the activity—and death!—of the second *mashiach*. Thus, following Archer's view, "we may compute the first seven heptads as running from 457 to 408, within which time the rebuilding of the walls, streets, and moats was completed." This would then lead to the one referred to as *mashiach nagid*. "Then," continuing to cite Archer, "from 408 we count off the sixty-two heptads also mentioned in v. 25 . . . and come out to A.D. 27."[200]

To simplify all this, let me restate both positions: Traditional Jewish interpreters believe there will be a period of forty-nine years beginning with the word to restore and build Jerusalem, at the end of which (or during which) an anointed leader will do something of significance; this will be followed by a period of 434 years, at the end of which an anointed one will be cut off. Then there will be a final period of seven years, during which another leader will destroy the Temple. So, the sequence is as follows: (1) The decree to restore and build Jerusalem is given; (2) after forty-nine years an anointed leader appears on the scene; (3) the restoration of Jerusalem is complete and the city remains intact, even in troublous times, for a period of 434 years, after which an anointed one is killed; (4) over the final seven years, Jerusalem will be destroyed.

As we have stated, traditional Christian interpreters believe there will be a period of 483 years, beginning with the word to restore and build Jerusalem, at the end of which an anointed leader (the Messiah) will be cut off.[201] During the first forty-nine years of this 483-year period, the city will be rebuilt; at the end of the 483-year period, there will be a final seven-year period, during which another leader will destroy the Temple. Note also that some Christian commentators understand the text to state that it is in the middle of the last seven-year period that the Messiah is killed. As explained by Christian commentator Albert Barnes,

the whole time of the seventy weeks is broken up into three smaller portions of seven, sixty-two, and one—designating evidently some important epochs or periods, Dan. 9:25, and the last one week is again subdivided in such a way, that, while it is said that the whole work of the Messiah in confirming the covenant would occupy the entire week, yet that he would be cut off in the middle of the week, Dan. 9:27.[202]

This would be in keeping with Daniel 9:27, which divides the events of the seventieth week of years into two parts. It would mean, however, that the first half of that week ended with Messiah's death in 30 C.E. (as it is written, "he will put an end to sacrifice and offering," meaning by his once-and-for-all atoning death on the cross) but the second half of that week did not unfold for almost forty more years (specifically, from 67–70 C.E.), as the text states, "And on a wing ⌐of the temple⌐ he [meaning the Roman general Titus] will set up an abomination that causes desolation, until the end that is decreed is poured out on him" (Dan. 9:27b). It would also mean that the "he" of Daniel 9:27a is different than the "he" of Daniel 9:27b, if we follow the rendering of the NIV. For these reasons, even from a Messianic Jewish perspective, I believe it is best to understand all the events of the seventieth week as referring to the destruction of the Temple under Titus.[203]

You might say, "This is so confusing, and you've hardly scratched the surface! How in the world can we be sure of anything?"

That's an excellent question, since there are literally hundreds of different interpretations that have been presented by both Jewish and Christian scholars, offering all kinds of solutions to the difficulties in the text, including those that slavishly follow the Masoretic accents and those that categorically reject some of these accents. We have barely touched on all the interpretative difficulties involved, both chronological and exegetical. Having said this, however, I am quite sure that (1) there are some extremely clear truths taught in this very important scriptural passage, (2) God gave this Scripture to us to bring clarity and not confusion, and (3) the key events described in this passage point decisively to the death of Yeshua the Messiah. When we major on the majors, the minors become less important.

What then are the majors? First, Daniel's seventy weeks begin with the rebuilding of Jerusalem and end with the destruction of Jerusalem. These are the chronological "bookends" within which these major redemptive events will take place, also identifying the general time periods involved: from the sixth to fifth centuries B.C.E. to the first century C.E. Second, several key players are specified, including one or two anointed ones *(mashiachs)*. Concerning the anointed one mentioned in 9:26, it is explicitly stated that he will be killed ("cut off"). Third, there are six spiritual acts of great significance that must be accomplished within this 490-year period (for details on this last point, see above, 4.19).

All the other questions and issues are somewhat secondary, almost like disputed calls made by a referee in the course of a game that ultimately have no impact on the outcome of that game. The final score is not disputed, nor is it disputed that the better team won. The only thing disputed is whether the referee made some of the minor calls correctly, not the outcome of the game. It's the same with Daniel 9:24–27. The final outcome is clear: The Messiah came and brought final atonement before the Second Temple was destroyed, regardless of the interpretation of some of the disputed details of textual interpretation.

Various dates have been suggested as the starting point of the seventy weeks (called by scholars the *terminus a quo*), identified in Daniel 9:25 as "the issuing of the decree [lit., "word"] to restore and rebuild Jerusalem." The following dates, suggested by both Jewish and Christian commentators, are among the most common:[204]

- Jeremiah's receiving of the word of Jerusalem's future restoration after seventy years in exile (Jer. 25:11–12), dating to 605 B.C.E. (Also suggested is Jeremiah 29:10, dating to 597 B.C.E.) This view, however, has very few proponents, since it is clearly *not* the issuing of a word to restore and rebuild Jerusalem—the city had not yet been destroyed!—and because it does not make sense of the 490-year period, finding no significance in the divisions of 49 years, 434 years, and 7 years.
- The decree of Cyrus in 538 B.C.E. (see 2 Chron. 36:22–23; Ezra 1:1–4. Note that this also correlates to within one year of the very revelation of the seventy weeks of years to Daniel, dating to 539–538 B.C.E.). One major problem with this interpretation is that this decree, despite its great importance, applied only to the rebuilding of the Temple, not the city.
- The decree of Darius in 521 B.C.E. (see Ezra 6:1–12), although this too focuses on the Temple rather than on the city and simply renews the earlier decree of Cyrus from 538 B.C.E.
- The decree of Artaxerxes I in 457 B.C.E. (see Ezra 7:12–26). While this royal edict focused on the funding of the rebuilding of the Temple, Ezra was given permission by the king to use the designated funds as needed, and other relevant texts suggest that both Ezra and Nehemiah may have associated this decree with

the wider issue of the restoration of Jerusalem itself (see Ezra 9:9; Neh. 1:4).

- The commission of Artaxerxes I in 446 B.C.E. (see Neh. 2:5–8). The biggest problem with this view is that it is hard to imagine that this commission—hardly even a royal edict—would have been recognized as the *terminus a quo* of the prophecy. It would have been all too easy to overlook this commission. Moreover, 483 years after 446 B.C.E. brings us to 38 C.E., more than seven years after the Messiah's crucifixion, leaving no plausible explanation as to the identity of the anointed one who would be killed at that time.[205]

Which of these dates is most accurate? In all candor, Daniel 9:25 simply does not give us enough details to be entirely sure; therefore it is wise not to be dogmatic. The suggestion of James Smith, however, is worthy of consideration, namely, that the "word" spoken of in the text does not necessarily refer to a specific royal decree or published prophetic message. It could simply refer to the divine proclamation that Jerusalem's rebuilding begin, in which case evidence in Ezra and Nehemiah points us to a time period very close to the decree of Artaxerxes in 457 B.C.E., since that is when the actual rebuilding of the city's walls began. This line of reasoning, then, brings us to the approximate date of the decree by deductive reasoning that asks the basic question, When did the work begin? The answer to that question provides us with the *terminus a quo* of Daniel's seventy weeks.

In reviewing the overall chronology, we should consider the possibility that there are some minor gaps between the specific periods mentioned, meaning that the 490-year period might not be totally consecutive. (Rashi is one of many interpreters who posits such gaps.) These gaps, however, could only be justified under three conditions: (1) The grouping of the weeks would still have to make sense. In other words, there would have to be something distinct and identifiable about the three periods of 49, 434, and 7 years; otherwise, they cease to have meaning and significance. (2) The gaps could not be so large as to disrupt the overall chronological flow that makes this 490-year period so important. (3) The gaps could not cause the 490-year period to end later than the time specified in the text.

Despite these words of caution, however, we can safely identify the boundaries of the fulfillment of this prophecy—beginning somewhere after 538 B.C.E. and ending in 70 C.E.—with the major events taking place over the course of 490 years. If there are no major gaps between the first 483 years (49 + 434), then only the last two dates suggested above are plausible (457 B.C.E. or 446 B.C.E.), since they alone end up close to 70 C.E. And since Daniel 9:26 indicates that the anointed one will be killed *after* the 483-year period, the starting date of 457 B.C.E. is extremely attractive, leaving the final seven-year period to unfold barely one generation later. This interpretation works well even with traditional Jewish translations, such as the Stone edition:

> Then, after the sixty-two septets, the anointed one will be cut off and will exist no longer; the people of the prince [who] will come will destroy the city and the Sanctuary; but his end will be [to be swept away as] in a flood. Then, until the end of the war, desolation is decreed. He will forge a strong covenant with the great ones for one septet; but for half of that septet he will abolish sacrifice and meal-offering, and the mute abominations will be upon soaring heights, until extermination as decreed will pour down upon the mute [abomination].

Daniel 9:26–27[206]

It appears, then, that some time could elapse between the end of the sixty-ninth septet (i.e., seven-year period) and the beginning of the seventieth septet. The sequence would be as follows: The period of 483 years ends; after this the anointed one is cut off; there are wars and conflicts, terminating with a final seven-year period that sees the destruction of the city and the Temple.[207]

We can also reverse our approach and count backwards, asking ourselves, What is the *terminus ad quem* (the ending point) of the seventy weeks? Clearly, as recognized by the Talmud and key Jewish interpreters, the key final event prophesied in Daniel 9:24–27 is the destruction of the city of Jerusalem and the sanctuary. Therefore, the seventieth and last seven-year period must culminate in 70 C.E. Before this last week of years, we come to the end of the previous two periods, totaling 483 years (7 weeks of years + 62 weeks of years), after which the anointed one described will be cut off. So, this anointed one will be killed at some point before 63 C.E. If we subtract 483 from 63 C.E. (remembering that there is no "zero year"), we arrive at a date of 421 B.C.E., which is later than any of the dates suggested by scholars and commentators, as we have seen. This means we can safely say there must be some gaps in the 490-year period. Based on the evidence reviewed here, the best interpretation would be this: The seventy weeks of years began somewhere in the 450s B.C.E., the first forty-nine of which focused on the rebuilding of Jerusalem, and the next

434 of which led up to the death of the Messiah. His death was followed by a gap of approximately thirty-three years, after which the final week of years unfolded.

The conclusion of Walter Kaiser is sound: "It is enough to know that there are some 483 years between the time that God began to fulfill this word mentioned to Daniel and the time of the first advent of Messiah, without trying to nail down the precise day and month."[208] Has anyone come up with a better interpretation?[209]

4.21. Daniel 9:24–27 speaks of *two* anointed ones.

> It is possible that the text does speak of two anointed ones, the first in 9:25 and the second in 9:26. This depends on how the seventy weeks of years are divided (see above, 4.20). This does not present a problem, however, since it is clear that (1) if there are two anointed ones, the second anointed one is the Messiah, and (2) the Messianic era had to be inaugurated before the Second Temple was destroyed, thus pointing decisively to Jesus as the key figure of whom the text speaks.

I can understand why this could seem like a significant objection to some readers, since a number of Christian translations see only *one* anointed one in the text, namely, Jesus. And according to these translations (as noted above, 4.19–4.20), this anointed one will appear at the end of a period of 483 years (49 + 434), culminating around the time of Jesus. But if the text speaks of an anointed one who is active after a period of 49 years, it could not possibly be Jesus, since this anointed one would have to live for *more than 434 additional years* if it is one and the same person. This is, quite obviously, totally preposterous, and it would necessitate the appearance of *two* anointed ones, not just one. It would also mean that *mashiach* should not be rendered in either case as "Messiah"—unless someone believed that Daniel spoke of two Messiahs! In light of these arguments, I do recognize the force of this objection.

In reality, however, there is no problem with this objection at all. If Daniel 9:24–27 speaks of only one anointed one who lived and died in the first century C.E. (see above, 4.21), that anointed one is Yeshua. If Daniel 9:24–27 speaks of two anointed ones, one living in the fifth century B.C.E. and the other living and dying in the first century C.E., the second one is Yeshua. It's that simple. As for the question of the proper translation of *mashiach* in this passage, we have agreed that it is going too far to render this as "the Messiah." At the same time, however, we have pointed out that the specific anointed one who will be cut off and have nothing (Dan. 9:26) is, in fact, the Anointed One par excellence, the Messiah.

It's also worth noting that Daniel 9:24–27 makes reference to a *mashiach nagid* ("an anointed ruler" or "the anointed ruler"; 9:25); a *mashiach* ("anointed one"; 9:26); and a *nagid* ("ruler"; 9:26). It is possible, then, that the text is speaking of *three* different people, two of whom are called rulers (the first and the last), and two of whom are called anointed ones (the first and the second). There are several different players involved in this divine drama! The one who fulfills what is promised in Daniel 9:24 (see above, 4.19), however, is the most important individual in this drama, the one who alone is recognized around the world as *the mashiach*. A careful review of the previous three objections should make this abundantly clear.

Still, it is only fair to ask, If there are two anointed ones spoken of in the text, who is the first one? And for the sake of argument, if the second one is not Yeshua, then who is it? Candidates for the first anointed one include the Medo-Persian king Cyrus among non-Israelites and either Joshua the high priest or Zerubbabel the governor (spoken of throughout Ezra and Nehemiah, as well as in the Book of Zechariah) among Israelites. None of these figures, however, can be decisively identified as the anointed leader of whom the text speaks, nor is there a rock-solid interpretation that explains how the forty-nine-year period beginning with Daniel 9:25 ends with any of them. Some of them are certainly potential candidates, but there are either chronological problems (as in the case of Cyrus)[210] or problems in determining exactly why the text singled them out or how someone would identify them as the anointed one in question. Why them?

The point of this is simple: While it is certainly possible that Daniel 9:24–27 speaks of two anointed ones rather than one Anointed One (= Messiah), it is difficult to see why the first one was mentioned at all, especially in the context described (i.e., coming after a period of forty-nine years). This suggests that it is fair to revisit the traditional Christian division of the weeks suggested above (4.18 and 4.20), since that interpretation puts the emphasis on the proper division of the years (49 years for the rebuilding of Jerusalem, followed by 434 years until the Messiah's death) and explains why such emphasis was placed on this *mashiach*.

As to the question of the identity of some of the non-Messianic candidates for the second anointed one—whose death is described in Daniel 9:26—reference is often made to the high priest Onias III, who was displaced by his brother Jason in 172 B.C.E. and then killed by Menelaus in 171 B.C.E. A later candidate would be King Agrippa I, who died in 44 C.E. However, the association with Onias III is based on the assumption that Daniel got his chronology entirely wrong (see above, 4.19), while the association with Agrippa I, which is the most common view among traditional Jewish interpreters, fails to explain why he would be singled out as a special anointed one whose death was of such significance. More important, it would mean that *the* Anointed One whose atoning death changed the course of world history, the candidate who fits the chronological data to a tee, was bypassed entirely in favor of a man whose death about fifteen years later was of no lasting significance at all.[211] Similar questions could be raised about the other potential candidates who allegedly answer to the description of the anointed one mentioned in Daniel 9:26, a man whose death occurred shortly before the destruction of the Second Temple.

To repeat our premise, then, we can safely state that (1) if the text speaks of two anointed ones, the second of these two is Jesus the Messiah, and (2) if the text speaks of one anointed one, all the more can we be sure that it refers to our Messiah and King. Honestly, now, can anyone claim that there is one candidate who even remotely displaces Yeshua as the obvious, central subject of the text? I think not.

4.22. Psalm 2:12 should not be translated as "kiss the Son." Only the King James Version and modern Christian fundamentalist translations still maintain this incorrect rendering.

The words "kiss the son" in Psalm 2:12 are actually not quoted in the New Testament, but one of the greatest of the medieval Rabbinic commentators, along with some noted modern Hebrew scholars argued for the "kiss the son" rendering. A good case can be made for this translation. In any case, regardless of the translation of this verse, the psalm is filled with important Messianic imagery.

Psalm 2 is a coronation psalm, celebrating the enthronement of the Davidic king, called God's son. As I pointed out in vol. 2, 3.3, the psalm reaches its ultimate fulfillment in the Messiah, the greatest Davidic king of all. The connection between psalms of David and Messianic psalms is reflected in the comments of Rashi on verse 1 of this psalm, "Our Sages [in the Talmud, b. Berakhoth 7b] expounded the passage as referring to the King Messiah, but according to its apparent meaning, it is proper to interpret it as referring to David himself, as the matter is stated (II Sam. 5:17)." Similarly, Ibn Ezra states, "The correct [interpretation] in my opinion is that one of the [court] poets composed this psalm concerning David when he was anointed, thus it is written, Today I have begotten you. Or, it concerns the Messiah."[212] As I understand Messianic prophecy, *both interpretations are true:* Psalm 2 was originally written concerning David (or one of his descendants) at the time of coronation, and this psalm reaches its fulfillment in the life of the Messiah (see the principles articulated in the appendix).

There is also a Talmudic reference to Psalm 2:7–8 in b. Sukkah 52a, the famous section dealing with Messiah ben Joseph, which is applied to Messiah son of David. It is written there:

> Our Rabbis taught: The Holy One, blessed be He, will say to the Messiah, son of David (may he reveal himself speedily in our days!), "Ask of Me anything, and I will give it to you," as it is said, "I will tell of the decree, etc., this day have I begotten you. Ask of me and I will give the nations for your inheritance" (Ps. 2:7–8). But when he will see that Messiah son of Joseph is slain, he will say to him, "Lord of the universe, I ask of You only the gift of life." "As to life," He would answer him, "Your father David has already prophesied this concerning you," as it is said, "He asked life of You, and You gave it to him [even length of days for ever and ever]" (Ps. 21:4[5]).

This text reminds us that the language of sonship is prominent in this psalm, as proclaimed by the king himself—the Messiah according to the Talmudic passage just cited—in verse 7b: "I am obliged to proclaim that HASHEM said to me, 'You are my son, I have begotten you this day'" *(Stone).*[213] And throughout the psalm, there are two key subjects: the Lord and his anointed one (Hebrew, *mashiach*), as stated in the opening verses: "Why do the nations conspire and the peoples plot in vain? The kings of the earth take their stand and the rulers gather together against the LORD and against his Anointed One. 'Let us break their chains,' they say, 'and throw off their fetters'" (Ps. 2:1–3). How preposterous—the nations of the earth want to overthrow the Lord and his anointed king! No chance, says the Lord. "I have installed my King on Zion, my holy hill" (v. 6a). And this king, as stated in verse 7b, was God's son.

Why then should it be considered odd that the psalm would close with a twofold admonition, namely, to "serve the LORD with fear" (v. 11a) and "kiss the son" (v. 12a)? The primary issue is not the translation of the verb "kiss" *(nashaq)*, nor is it the meaning of the word, since "kiss" can be used in the sense of paying homage, either to an idol (1 Kings 19:18; Hosea 13:2; cf. m. Sanhedrin 7:6) or to an earthly ruler (1 Sam. 10:1). The bigger issue is the word "son," since it is not the normal Hebrew noun *ben* (as in v. 7) but rather the Aramaic word for son, *bar,* which is rarely found in the Hebrew Bible (see Prov. 31:2). Thus, the oldest versions are divided on the phrase's meaning,[214] while traditional Hebrew commentators have suggested widely varied renderings, including reading *bor* ("purity") rather than *bar,* and understanding the text to say something like, "worship [the Lord] in purity." But this is far from certain, as can be seen by comparing recent Jewish translations: "pay homage in good faith" (NJPSV, with a note that the meaning of the Hebrew is uncertain); "yearn for purity" (*Stone,* understanding the verb *nashaq* to mean "yearn," as suggested by Rashi); "arm yourselves with purity" (Rosenberg, following another interpretation suggested by Rashi).

Aside from the confusion as to the text's actual meaning, there is a contextual problem as well, since the psalm centers around the figure of the Davidic king, installed by the Lord, and it is against the Lord *and* his anointed king that the nations rage. But, if any of these Jewish translations are followed, the closing verses of the psalm, which contain a stern word of warning *addressed to these very nations,* contain no mention of the Messianic King at all! In traditional Christian translations, however, there is no such problem, since the foreign kings are admonished to serve the Lord and reverence the son, lest God's wrath come upon them.[215]

"But that's the whole problem," you say. "It's only the Christian translations that understand *bar* to mean 'son.'"

Not so. Abraham Ibn Ezra, possibly the most exacting of the medieval Jewish commentators and a man with no sympathy for Christian interpretations of the Tanakh, understood *bar* to mean "son," with reference to Proverbs 31:2. Other Jewish scholars—some traditional and some not—have also interpreted the text in similar terms, including A. B. Ehrlich, A. Sh. Hartom (in his fairly traditional Psalms commentary, where "son" is mentioned as a possibility),[216] and Samuel Loewenstamm and Joshua Blau, leading Israeli scholars, in their *Thesaurus*.[217] (Note that David Kimchi also understands *bar* to refer to the king, although reading the text in terms of *bar lebab* ["purity of heart"], hence "the pure one" or, with another interpretation, "the elect one."[218]) Thus, Ibn Ezra states, "'Serve the Lord refers to the Lord, while 'Kiss the son' refers to his anointed one, and the meaning of *bar* is like [the meaning of *bar* in the phrase] 'What my son *[beri]* and what, son of my womb *[bar bitni; Prov. 31:2].' And thus it is written, 'You are my son' [Ps. 2:7]. And it is a custom of the nations in the world to put their hands under the hand of the king, as the brothers of Solomon did [see 1 Chr. 29:24 in the Hebrew], or for the servant [to put his hand] under the thigh of his master [see Gen. 24:2], or to kiss the king. And this is the custom until today in the land of India."[219]

There is also an interesting mystical interpretation provided in the Zohar that equates *bar* with the son of God: "You are the good shepherd; of you it is said, 'Kiss the son.' You are great here below, the teacher of Israel, the Lord of the serving angels, the son of the Most High, the son of the Holy One, may His name be praised and His Holy Spirit [Shekhinah]."[220]

As to the question of why an Aramaic word would occur in a Hebrew psalm, some scholars have suggested that just as in Jeremiah 10:11, where the *foreign nations* are addressed *in Aramaic* (the most widely used Semitic language of the day, similar to Arabic today in the Muslim world) in an otherwise totally Hebrew context, so also the final warning to the *foreign kings* reminds them in the most common Semitic term (Aramaic *bar* for "son") that the king in Jerusalem is God's son.

We can safely say, then, that there are excellent reasons to accept the translation of "kiss the son" and no compelling reasons to reject it. In context, it reminds us of the central role played by the Messianic King in Jerusalem, the son/Son of God.

4.23. Psalm 16 does not speak of the resurrection of the Messiah.

> According to the biblical record, Psalm 16 is a psalm of David, in which he expresses his confidence that he will be delivered from death and will not rot in the grave. But since David did, in fact, ultimately die and see physical corruption, the New Testament learns from this that he was speak-

ing prophetically about his greatest descendant, the Messiah, who would actually be resurrected from the grave.

As rendered in the NJPSV, the key verses from Psalm 16 state:

> I am ever mindful of the LORD's presence;
>   He is at my right hand; I will never be shaken.
> So my heart rejoices,
>   my whole being exults,
>   and my body rests secure.
> For You will not abandon me to Sheol,
>   or let Your faithful one see the Pit.
> You will teach me the path of life.
> In Your presence is perfect joy;
>   delights are ever in Your right hand.
>
> Psalm 16:8–11

What exactly does this mean? Does David simply express the hope that he will not die before his time? Or is it something more? Is he actually saying that God will not *let his body stay in the grave?* As the nineteenth-century biblical scholar J. A. Alexander observed, the text does not say that God will not leave him *in* the place of the dead (Sheol) but rather that God will not leave him *to* that place, meaning "abandon to, give up to the dominion or possession of another."[221] And this is reinforced by the next phrase, namely, that God will not let his "faithful one see the Pit," meaning, see the corruption and decay of death.[222] This seems to indicate more than "You will keep me from dying prematurely."[223] In fact, some of the traditional Jewish commentators, including Rabbi David Kimchi, interpreted David's words in verse 9 ("my body rests secure," my translation) to mean that "when the Psalmist dies his body will not decompose."[224]

As Rozenberg and Zlotowitz explain:

> The Talmud points out that seven biblical heroes were preserved whole in the earth: Abraham, Isaac, Jacob, Moses, Aaron, Miriam, and Benjamin. Regarding David this is a difference of opinion as to whether the expression, "my body" includes David among the others, which would make it eight or that David's prayer was wishful thinking (B.B. 17A).[225]

How interesting! Even the Talmud takes up the question of exactly what David meant in some of these important phrases, while other traditional sources interpret some of the expressions "to allude to immortality."[226] This emphasis on the future life seems to be confirmed by the closing verse of the psalm, speaking of the path of life, God's presence, perfect joy, and unending delights. As Rashi explains, "Endless joy. That is the joy of the future."[227]

In light of all this, Peter's comments on this psalm—as he preached to a Jewish audience from around the world, gathered at the Temple in celebration of Shavuot (the Feast of Weeks, or Pentecost)—make perfect sense:

> Brothers, I can tell you confidently that the patriarch David died and was buried, and his tomb is here to this day. But he was a prophet and knew that God had promised him on oath that he would place one of his descendants on his throne. Seeing what was ahead, he spoke of the resurrection of the [Messiah], that he was not abandoned to the grave, nor did his body see decay. God has raised this Jesus to life, and we are all witnesses of the fact.
>
> Acts 2:29–32; cf. also 13:35–37

"There's only one problem," you say. "David spoke this about himself, not about some future descendant of his. So how can it refer to the Messiah?"

Actually, it is possible that he looked ahead into the future and saw himself supernaturally preserved from death and decay (as suggested by some of the rabbis, as we have read), but what he was actually seeing was not his own deliverance from death (in reality, resurrection) but rather that of his progeny, the Messiah.[228] And this would really not be surprising at all, since in the biblical mentality, one's future hope and ongoing life were intimately tied in with one's descendants, and to die childless would be to die without a future.[229] That's why King Hezekiah pleaded with God to deliver him from death: At the time of his sickness, he had no son. How then could his line be preserved? How then could his destiny be fulfilled? When he was healed, he proclaimed, "The living, the living—they praise you, as I am doing today; *fathers tell their children about your faithfulness*" (Isa. 38:19). The chain of life is kept intact from father to son.

This mentality is also reflected in names such as Simon Bar Jonah (Simon son of Jonah, in the New Testament) or Abraham Ibn Ezra (Abraham son of Ezra, in the middle ages): You do not stand alone; rather, you are your father's son. Even more interesting is the Arabic custom reflected in such names as Abu Walid (meaning father of

Walid). How can a *father* be named after his *son*? The reverse is what we expect! The answer is fascinating: In some Arabic cultures, when the firstborn son is named, *the father changes his name*. And so, to give an example, when a man named Salim has his first son and names him Muhammad, Salim now becomes known as Abu Muhammad, father of Muhammad. His future is bound up with his son, and his offspring carries out his destiny in an unbroken chain. This is similar to the biblical mentality and shows why it was considered such a curse to die childless.

It is therefore totally logical from a biblical standpoint that David, a prophet of God inspired by the Spirit, actually foresaw the resurrection of the Messiah as he pondered his own future hope. The New Testament application of this verse to Yeshua's resurrection is fitting and appropriate, not twisting the force of the original but rather gleaning an important insight from the text. We do well to take this interpretation seriously, especially since David's prophetic hope was *not* fulfilled in his life but rather in the life of his greater son, the Messiah.

4.24. Psalm 22 is the story of David's past suffering. There is nothing prophetic about it.

Actually, Psalm 22 is the prayer of a righteous sufferer, brought down to the jaws of death and then rescued and raised up by God in answer to prayer, a glorious testimony to be recounted through the ages. As such, it applies powerfully to Jesus the Messiah, the ideal righteous sufferer, surrounded by hostile crowds, beaten, mocked, crucified, and seemingly abandoned by man and God, but delivered from death itself and raised from the dead by the power of God, a story now celebrated around the globe. That's why he quoted words from this psalm with reference to himself when he hung on the cross. How strikingly they apply to him! What is also interesting is that some of the great Rabbinic commentators—including Rashi—interpreted the psalm as a prophecy of Israel's future suffering and exile, not as the story of David's past suffering. Not only so, but a famous Rabbinic midrash composed about twelve hundred years ago said that David spoke of the Messiah's sufferings in Psalm 22. We can therefore say with confidence that the application of this psalm to the death and resurrection of the Messiah is in keeping with the clear meaning of the text.

According to anti-missionary rabbi Tovia Singer,

> missionaries are confronted with another remarkable problem as they seek to project the words of this Psalm into a first century crucifixion story. In the simplest terms, this text that Christians eagerly quote is not a prophecy, nor does it speak of any future event. This entire Psalm, as well as the celebrated Psalm that follows it, contains a dramatic monologue in which King David cried out to God from the depths of his personal pain, anguish, and longing as he remained a fugitive from his enemies. Accordingly, the stirring monologue in this chapter is all in the first person. The author himself is crying out to God, and there is no doubt who the faithful speaker is in this Psalm; the very first verse in this chapter explicitly identifies this person as King David.[230]

Unfortunately, Rabbi Singer's interpretation flies in the face of many traditional Jewish commentators who plainly say that Psalm 22 *is* prophetic. For example, at the outset of his comments on this psalm, Rashi says, "They [meaning the people of Israel] are destined to go into exile and *David recited this prayer for the future.*"[231] Commenting on the words "I am a worm" in 22:6[7], Rashi notes that David "refers to all Israel as one man," and he interprets specific verses with reference to later historical figures such as Nebuchadnezzar (22:14[15]). How then can Rabbi Singer claim that the psalm does not "speak of any future event"? Jewish tradition says that it does![232] In fact, Rashi explains verse 26[27] with reference to "the time of our redemption in the days of our Messiah," then interprets verses 27–29[28–30] with reference to the Gentile nations turning to the Lord, the end of the age, and the final judgment. These certainly are future events, also underscoring the worldwide redemptive implications of this psalm.[233]

There is no need, however, even to press this argument about the futuristic interpretation of Psalm 22, since it does not have to be prophetic to be applied to the Messiah, for two primary reasons: (1) Many events in the life of David were repeated in the life of the Messiah, since David, in many ways, was the prototype of the Messiah (see further, below, 4.26 and 4.29); and (2) as part of the canon of Scripture, Psalm 22 was the psalm of the righteous sufferer miraculously delivered from death, and without doubt, many righteous sufferers have recited the words of this psalm to the Lord in their times of distress. But none could recite it with as much meaning and application as could Jesus the Messiah, the ideal and ultimate righteous sufferer, resurrected from death itself, resulting in worldwide praise to God. Really, the psalm applies to him in many unique ways, and whereas the author of the psalm (according to tradition, David) may have spoken of his own situation with some poetic hyperbole, there was no hyperbole when applying the words to Yeshua. Just look at how aptly his death and resurrection are described in this psalm.

First is the picture of a public, agonizing, humiliating death—extraordinarily applicable to death by crucifixion:[234]

> Many bulls surround me,
>> mighty ones of Bashan encircle me.
> They open their mouths at me,
>> like tearing, roaring lions.
> My life ebbs away:
>> all my bones are disjointed;
>> my heart is like wax,
>> melting within me;
>> my vigor dries up like a shard;
>> my tongue cleaves to my palate;
>> You commit me to the dust of death.[235]
> Dogs surround me;
>> a pack of evil ones closes in on me,
>> like lions [they maul] my hands and feet.
> I take the count of all my bones
>> while they look on and gloat.
> They divide my clothes among themselves,
>> casting lots for my garments.
>
> Psalm 22:12–19[13–20] NJPSV[236]

Surrounded, hemmed in, with his life ebbing away, brought down to the dust of death, the psalmist then prays for a mighty deliverance:

> But you, O LORD, be not far off;
>> O my Strength, come quickly to help me.
> Deliver my life from the sword,
>> my precious life from the power of the dogs.
> Rescue me from the mouth of the lions;
>> save me from the horns of the wild oxen.
>
> Psalm 22:19–21[20–22]

And God heard his cry, answering the anguished sufferer with a deliverance so extraordinary that it resulted in: (1) worldwide praise and adoration, (2) a lasting testimony of God's saving power to be recounted through the generations of Israel, and (3) *the turning of the Gentile nations to God*, as Rashi himself noted, even associating this final event with the Messianic era (as we observed, above). As the text declares:

> You who fear the Lord, praise him!
>> All you descendants of Jacob, honor him!
>> Revere him, all you descendants of Israel!
> For he has not despised or disdained
>> the suffering of the afflicted one;
> he has not hidden his face from him
>> but has listened to his cry for help.
>
> From you comes the theme of my praise in the great assembly;
>> before those who fear you will I fulfill my vows.
> The poor will eat and be satisfied;
>> they who seek the Lord will praise him—
>> may your hearts live forever!
> All the ends of the earth
>> will remember and turn to the Lord,
> and all the families of the nations
>> will bow down before him,
> for dominion belongs to the Lord
>> and he rules over the nations.
>
> All the rich of the earth will feast and worship;
>> all who go down to the dust will kneel before him—
>> those who cannot keep themselves alive.
> Posterity will serve him;
>> future generations will be told about the Lord.
> They will proclaim his righteousness
>> to a people yet unborn—
>> for he has done it.

Psalm 22:23–31[24–31]

Little wonder, then, that this was understood to be a Messianic psalm by the writers of the New Testament. What other individual's deliverance from extreme suffering and death was worthy of being recounted again and again in the assembly of Israel? What other individual's deliverance from extreme suffering and death was worthy of worldwide attention to the point that the nations actually *turned to the God of Israel* because of it? Only the death and resurrection of the Messiah, the perfectly righteous one, the ultimate fulfillment of Psalm 22.[237]

As expressed by James E. Smith,

> No Old Testament person could have imagined that his personal deliverance from death could be the occasion for the world's conversion. Such a hope must be restricted to the future Redeemer. Under inspiration of the Holy Spirit, David in Psalm 22 saw his descendants resembling, but far surpassing, himself in suffering. Furthermore, the deliverance of this descendant would have meaning for all mankind.[238]

In light of all this, it is very interesting to see how Pesikta Rabbati, the famous eighth-century midrash, put some of the words of this psalm on the lips of the suffering Messiah (called Ephraim, but associated with the son of David), citing Psalm 22:8, 13–14, and 16 in the context of Messiah's sufferings. In fact, the midrash explicitly states that "it was because of the ordeal of the son of David that David wept, saying *My strength is dried up like a potsherd* (Ps. 22:16)." Did you catch that? According to this respected Rabbinic homily, David described the Messiah's sufferings in Psalm 22!

Let's look at the key texts more fully:

> During the seven-year period preceding the coming of the son of David, iron beams will be brought low and loaded upon his neck until the Messiah's body is bent low. Then he will cry and weep, and his voice will rise to the very height of heaven, and he will say to God: Master of the universe, how much can my strength endure? How much can my spirit endure? How much my breath before it ceases? How much can my limbs suffer? Am I not flesh and blood?

> It was because of the ordeal of the son of David that David wept, saying *My strength is dried up like a potsherd* (Ps. 22:16). During the ordeal of the son of David, the Holy One, blessed be He, will say to him: Ephraim, My true Messiah, long ago, ever since the six days of creation, thou didst take this ordeal upon thyself. At this moment, thy pain is like my pain.

At these words, the Messiah will reply: "Now I am reconciled. The servant is content to be like his Master" (Pesikta Rabbati 36:2).[239]

It is taught, moreover, that in the month of Nisan the Patriarchs will arise and say to the Messiah: Ephraim, our true Messiah, even though we are thy forbears, thou art greater than we because thou didst suffer for the iniquities of our children, and terrible ordeals befell thee. . . . For the sake of Israel thou didst become a laughingstock and a derision among the nations of the earth; and didst sit in darkness, in thick darkness, and thine eyes saw no light, and thy skin cleaved to thy bones, and thy body was as dry as a piece of wood; and thine eyes grew dim from fasting, and thy strength was dried up like a potsherd—all these afflictions on account of the iniquities of our children.

Pesikta Rabbati 37:1[240]

Ephraim is a darling son to Me . . . My heart yearneth for him, in mercy I will have mercy upon him, saith the Lord (Jer. 31:20). Why does the verse speak twice of mercy: In mercy I will have mercy upon him? One mercy refers to the time when he will be shut up in prison, a time when the nations of the world will gnash their teeth at him every day, wink their eyes at one another in derision of him, nod their heads at him in contempt, open wide their lips to guffaw, as is said *All they that see me laugh me to scorn; they shoot out the lip, they shake the head* (Ps. 22:8); *My strength is dried up like a potsherd; and my tongue cleaveth to my throat; and thou layest me in the dust of death* (Ps. 22:16). Moreover, they will roar over him like lions, as is said *They open wide their mouth against me, as a ravening and roaring lion. I am poured out like water, and all my bones are out of joint; my heart is become like wax; it is melted in mine inmost parts* (Ps. 22:14–15).

Pesikta Rabbati 37:1[241]

How striking all this is, especially in light of the objection raised here, namely, that Psalm 22 has nothing to do with the Messiah. To the contrary, when Psalm 22 is rightly understood, and when the true Messiah is recognized—our suffering, dying, and rising Savior—the application of this psalm to him is totally appropriate, to say the least.

4.25. Psalm 22 does not speak of death by crucifixion. In fact, the King James translators changed the words of verse 16[17] to speak of "piercing" the sufferer's hands and feet, whereas the

Hebrew text actually says, "Like a lion they are at my hands and feet."

It is interesting to note that verse 16[17] is not quoted in the New Testament even though other verses from Psalm 22 are cited in the Gospels. This means that verse 16[17] was not the primary verse on which the New Testament authors focused. As to the allegation that the King James translators intentionally changed the meaning of the Hebrew text, their translation ("they pierced my hands and feet" versus "like a lion [they are at] my hands and feet") actually reflects an ancient Jewish interpretation along with some important variations in the medieval Masoretic manuscripts. In other words, it's as much of a Jewish issue as it is a Christian one! In any case, there really is no problem. With either rendering, the imagery is one of extreme bodily violence done to the sufferer's hands and feet, corresponding to the realities of crucifixion.

Psalm 22 is the great psalm of the righteous sufferer, publicly mocked and shamed, brought down to the jaws of death in the midst of terrible suffering and humiliation, and miraculously delivered by God, to the praise of his name (see above, 4.24). It was quoted in the Gospels with reference to the Messiah's crucifixion (see Matt. 27:35 KJV; John 19:24). In fact, Jesus himself drew our attention to Psalm 22 while hanging on the cross, using the familiar words of verse 1[2] in his prayer to his heavenly Father, "My God, my God, why have you forsaken me?" (Matt. 27:46 and parallels).

Interestingly, the very verse that is the subject of so much controversy (namely, verse 16[17]) is a verse that the New Testament never quotes. Not once! Still, the charge is made that *later Christian translators*—specifically, the translators of the King James Version, the most influential and widely used English version in history—intentionally altered the meaning of the Hebrew text of this verse, introducing the word "pierced" in place of the Hebrew "like a lion." To quote anti-missionary rabbi Tovia Singer once again:

Needless to say, the phrase "they pierced my hands and my feet" is a Christian contrivance that appears nowhere in the Jewish scriptures.

Bear in mind, this stunning mistranslation in the 22nd Psalm did not occur because Christian translators were unaware of the correct meaning of this Hebrew word. Clearly, this was not the case.[242]

Rabbi Singer does, however, note that this alleged "Christian contrivance," this so-called stunning mistranslation, does not go back to the New Testament itself. He asserts,

> It must be noted that the authors of the New Testament were not responsible for inserting the word "pierced" into the text of Psalm 22:17. This verse was undoubtedly tampered with years after the Christian canon was completed.
> . . . The insertion of the word "pierced" into the last clause of this verse is a not-too-ingenious Christian interpolation that was created by deliberately mistranslating the Hebrew word *kaari* [the word found in Psalm 22:16(17) in most Masoretic manuscripts] . . . as "pierced."[243]

Once again, Rabbi Singer is typical of the anti-missionaries, who not only take issue with quotations of Hebrew Scriptures in the New Testament and with later Christian translations of the Bible but also claim that there has been willful mistranslation and premeditated, purposeful duplicity—accusations that are quite serious indeed.[244] How should we respond to such charges? It is best to answer these charges in a dispassionate and calm spirit, simply weighing the evidence and asking the question, What is the verdict of honest, non-biased scholarship? Following this method, it will quickly be seen that there is *no* substance to the anti-missionary polemic here.

We must also bear in mind that there is actually no need to try to defend or vindicate the translators of the King James Version or other Christian versions. The truth of the New Testament surely doesn't rise or fall on the accuracy of translations completed more than fifteen hundred years later! That would be like questioning the reliability of the Hebrew Bible based on an alleged mistranslation of a particular passage made by a panel of rabbis centuries later. How does a mistranslation by later translators affect the accuracy or reliability of the original? Obviously, it does not.

"But that's where I differ," you say. "This type of falsification is common in Christianity. It's the only way the New Testament authors can support their case, and it's the only way later translators can support the whole argument."

Hardly! The reason so many scholars, intellectuals, educated Jews, and thinking people of all faiths have put their faith in Jesus the Messiah is because the truth about Yeshua can withstand every kind of scholastic or emotional attack. In keeping with this, we will clearly demonstrate (see vol. 4, 5.1–5.5) that the New Testament authors showed great understanding and sensitivity in their use of the Tanakh. As for the honesty and integrity of later translators, I have no question that Christian translators display a Christian bias, while Jewish translators display a Jewish bias. It's easy to document this practice on numerous occasions, and it has nothing to do with dishonesty or lack of integrity. Rather, it has to do with human beings trying to grapple honestly with textual and translation difficulties. Thus, if manuscript evidence for a certain reading is equally divided between two possible variants, and one reading is in harmony with "Christian" interpretation and the other reading is in harmony with "Jewish" interpretation, it is quite natural for the decision of the translators to reflect their particular religious background.

As for Psalm 22:16[17], almost all of the standard medieval Hebrew manuscripts (known as Masoretic) read *ka'ari,* followed by the words "my hands and my feet." According to Rashi, the meaning is "as though they are crushed in a lion's mouth," while the commentary of Metsudat David states, "They crush my hands and my feet as the lion which crushes the bones of the prey in its mouth." Thus, the imagery is clear: These lions are not licking the psalmist's feet! They are tearing and ripping at them.[245] Given the metaphorical language of the surrounding verses (cf. vv. 12–21[13–22]), this vivid image of mauling lions graphically conveys the great physical agony of the sufferer. Would this in any way contradict the picture of a crucified victim, his bones out of joint, mockers surrounding him and jeering at him, his garments stripped off of him and divided among his enemies, his feet and hands torn with nails, and his body hung on pieces of wood?[246]

"But you're avoiding something here," you argue. "Where did the King James translators come up with this idea of 'piercing' the hands and feet? That's not what the Hebrew says."

Actually, the Septuagint, the oldest existing Jewish translation of the Tanakh, was the first to translate the Hebrew as "they pierced my hands and feet" (using the verb *oruxan* in Greek), followed by the Syriac Peshitta version two or three centuries later (rendering with *baz'u*). Not only so, but the oldest Hebrew copy of the Psalms we possess (from the Dead Sea Scrolls, dating to the century before Yeshua) reads the verb in this verse as *ka'aru* (not *ka'ari,* "like a lion"),[247] a reading also found in about a dozen medieval Masoretic manuscripts—recognized as *the* authoritative texts in traditional Jewish thought—where instead of *ka'ari* (found in almost all other Masoretic manuscripts) the texts say either *ka'aru* or *karu.*[248] (Hebrew scholars believe this comes from a root meaning "to dig out" or "to bore through.")

So, the *oldest Jewish translation* (the Septuagint) translates "they pierced"; the *oldest Jewish manuscript* (from the Dead Sea Scrolls) reads *ka'aru*, not *ka'ari*; and *several Masoretic manuscripts* read *ka'aru* or *karu* rather than *ka'ari*. This is *not* a Christian fabrication. I have copies of the manuscript evidence in front of my eyes as I write these words.[249]

There is also an interesting notation made by the Masoretic scholars in the margin to Isaiah 38:13, where the Hebrew word *ka'ari*, "like a lion," also occurs—the only other time in the Tanakh that *ka'ari* is found with the preposition *k-*, "like," joined to this form of the word.[250] In this instance, however, *ka'ari* occurs with a verb explaining the lion's activity ("break"), whereas in Psalm 22:16[17] the meaning is ambiguous. As noted by Franz Delitzsch, "Perceiving this, the Masora [i.e., the marginal system of notation of the Masoretic scholars to the Hebrew biblical text] on Isaiah xxxviii. 13 observes, that *k'ry* in the two passages in which it occurs (Ps. xxii. 17, Isa. xxxviii. 13), occurs in two different meanings [Aramaic *lyshny btry*], just as the Midrash then also understands *k'ry* in the Psalm as a verb used of marking with conjuring, magic characters."[251] So, the Masoretes indicated that *k'ry* in Psalm 22 was to be understood differently than *k'ry* in Isaiah 38, where it certainly meant "like a lion."

In light of this, Singer's charges of deliberate and deceitful alteration of the text by Christians become all the more outrageous. Listen again to his words:

> Notice that when the original words of the Psalmist are read, any allusion to a crucifixion disappears. The insertion of the word "pierced" into the last clause of this verse is a *not-too-ingenious Christian interpolation* that was created by *deliberately mistranslating the Hebrew* word *kaari* . . . as "pierced." The word *kaari*, however, does not mean "pierced," it means "like a lion." The end of Psalm 22:17, therefore, properly reads "like a lion they are at my hands and my feet." Had King David wished to write the word "pierced," he would never use the Hebrew word *kaari*. Instead, he would have written either *daqar* or *ratza*, which are common Hebrew words in the Jewish scriptures. Needless to say, the phrase "they pierced my hands and my feet" is a *Christian contrivance* that appears nowhere in the Jewish scriptures.
>
> Bear in mind, this *stunning mistranslation* in the 22nd Psalm did not occur because Christian translators were unaware of the correct meaning of this Hebrew word. Clearly, this was not the case.[252]

In reality, there is no stunning mistranslation, no Christian inter-polation, no Christian contrivance to be found. Rather, the Christian translations vilified by the anti-missionaries simply reflect an ex-tremely honest and valid attempt to accurately translate the Hebrew text based on ancient Jewish manuscripts and translations. Those are the facts.

4.26. Some of the so-called Messianic prophecies in the Psalms actually speak of the psalmist's *sin* and *folly*. How can you apply *this* to Jesus?

> No one tries to apply every verse in each "prophetic" psalm to the Messiah. Rather, there is a simple principle behind the Messianic interpretation of these important psalms: As it was with David, so it is with the Messiah. In other words, there are striking parallels between the life of King David and the life of King Messiah, and it is these parallels that are highlighted in the New Testament's quotation of cer-tain psalms. For example, just as David was betrayed by one of his closest friends, so also the Messiah was betrayed by one of his closest friends, as noted by Jesus himself (see Psalm 41 and John 13:18). But it is obvious that the details of the betrayal don't have to be the same (e.g., David was betrayed by Ahithopel, Jesus was betrayed by Judas; David's betrayal led to his temporary exile, Yeshua's betrayal led to his death).

If you are familiar at all with the Talmud and the Midrash, you will know that the rabbis applied all kinds of obscure verses to the Mes-siah and to the Messianic era, often taking them totally out of con-text (for a representative sampling, see below, 4.34). For the most part, these Jewish sages clearly were *not* looking at an entire portion of Scripture—a whole psalm or chapter—when they cited the verses in question. Rather, what got their attention was a word association, or an association of ideas, or an even more distant link connecting the given verse or phrase with the Messiah. This was quite common in Rabbinic interpretation during the first thousand years of this era, but it was not limited to the Rabbinic writings, especially two thou-sand years ago. At that time it was common in other, non-Rabbinic Jewish circles to cite verses atomistically (i.e., without relation to the larger context). This is especially common in the Talmudic and midrashic writings, and while the New Testament authors sometimes engage in this practice, for the most part their method was more sober and systematic than this. It should not surprise us, then, if the New Testament sometimes applies just one relevant verse from a larger context that is not relevant. This was normal *Jewish* interpretation for the day.[253]

At other times, there were specific principles that fueled the New Testament citations of passages from the Tanakh: As it was with David (or, more broadly, with the righteous psalmist), so it was with the Messiah. That explains why the New Testament can cite Psalm 41:9[10] with reference to Jesus ("Even my close friend, whom I trusted, he who shared my bread, has lifted up his heel against me"), when several verses earlier the psalmist had exclaimed, "O Lord, have mercy on me; heal me, for I have sinned against you" (v. 4[5]).

Anti-missionaries will point to this and say, "Either the New Testament quoted a psalm that cannot apply to Jesus or else Jesus must have sinned!" Not at all. Instead, we must remember that there were certain events in the life of David that stood out above the others, such as his betrayal by a close friend or his being hunted and treated like a criminal. When these striking events occurred again in the life of Yeshua, he was quick to point out these parallels (see, e.g., Matt. 21:33–42, quoting Ps. 118:22–33). In this very tangible sense, "the scripture was fulfilled" (e.g., John 19:36–37).

When you consider that David was the prototype of the Messiah, and the Tanakh was both the record of the past and the witness of the future, it is quite fitting that such an interpretative method was used, making us remember how wonderfully the Messiah's life was laid out in advance in the Scriptures. Once he came to earth and died and then rose from the dead, opening the eyes of his followers to the truth of the biblical prophecies (Luke 24:44–45), it became very clear that (1) the Tanakh laid out the details of the Messiah's coming, both in history and in prophecy, and (2) Jesus was the promised Messiah.

Let me close this discussion with a personal anecdote. In the early 1990s, I was teaching a course on Messianic prophecy in Maryland and an Orthodox rabbi from Israel, who had come to faith in Yeshua a few years earlier, sat in on the class one day. It was amazing to hear him explain how passage after passage in the Tanakh applied to Yeshua—including verses that I would never have thought of applying to him. I can still remember him sitting there, with his Hebrew Bible in hand, raising his hand enthusiastically and saying in Hebrew,

"In my opinion, this is Yeshua." Yes, it seemed he found Jesus *everywhere* in the Tanakh. This was because his Rabbinic upbringing led him to find references to Torah everywhere in the Tanakh—I literally mean everywhere—and now that he understood that Jesus was the Messiah, he began to find references to him everywhere in the text.[254]

In comparison with this rabbi's passionate but unscientific approach to the Scriptures, the interpretation of the New Testament writers makes a lot of sense.

4.27. Psalm 40 is absolutely not Messianic in any way.

> Did you know that the Talmudic rabbis interpreted all kinds of obscure verses to be Messianic? They saw hints and allusions to the Messiah in hundreds of unusual biblical texts, in passages that are totally unrelated to anything Messianic. In contrast with this, Psalm 40 has some very important Messianic themes.

As we noted in the previous answer, the Talmudic rabbis applied all kinds of scriptural passages to the Messiah, many of which seem quite far-fetched. Can the same be said of the use of Psalm 40 in the Letter to the Hebrews in the New Testament? Let's consider the evidence.

Several verses from Psalm 40 are quoted with reference to Jesus the Messiah in Hebrews 10 (see Heb. 10:1–10). The author's point in that chapter is that "the law is only a shadow of the good things that are coming—not the realities themselves. For this reason it can never, by the same sacrifices repeated endlessly year after year, make perfect those who draw near to worship" (Heb. 10:1). He finds support for his view in Psalm 40 where the psalmist (who is David, according to tradition) states:

> Sacrifice and offering you did not desire,
>   but my ears you have pierced;
> burnt offerings and sin offerings
>   you did not require.
> Then I said, "Here I am, I have come—
>   it is written about me in the scroll."
>
> Psalm 40:6–7

What then is the problem? For many, it is that these words are attributed to Jesus in Hebrews: "Therefore, when [Messiah] came into the world, he said: 'Sacrifice and offering you did not desire, but a body you prepared for me;[255] with burnt offerings and sin offerings you were not pleased. Then I said, 'Here I am—it is written about me in the scroll—I have come to do your will, O God'" (Heb. 10:5–7). How can these statements be attributed to Jesus? And did the writer of Hebrews actually believe that Jesus spoke the words of Psalm 40? Let me explain the background and meaning of the psalm. Then you will be able to understand why Hebrews 10 quotes it in a Messianic context.

After experiencing a great deliverance, the psalmist caught a glimpse of something new (Ps. 40:3) and crucial: "God isn't looking for sacrifices and offerings, he wants me—my total, unreserved obedience." In other words, "God doesn't want me endlessly offering sacrifices for my sins and disobedience. He wants me to obey!" And as the psalmist—David?—considered the words of the Torah, repeatedly calling for sacrifices to be offered up on the altar of the Lord, he said to himself, "Sacrifice and offering you did not desire, but my ears you have pierced; burnt offerings and sin offerings you did not require. Then I said, 'Here I am, I have come—it is written about me in the scroll'" (vv. 6–7).[256]

What does he mean? There are many different interpretations given by the commentators, both Jewish and Christian, but I personally believe he was saying, "When I read about the offerings in the scroll of the Law, I came to realize that it really speaks of your desire for me—my life given wholly over to you." Unfortunately, just a few verses later, the psalmist goes on to lament his own sins and failures: "For troubles without number surround me; my sins have overtaken me, and I cannot see. They are more than the hairs of my head, and my heart fails within me" (v. 12). What a confession! He is saying, "I see that God wants my life wholly yielded to him. *That* is the sacrifice he seeks. But I'm a sinner, overwhelmed by my iniquity." He saw the lofty ideal of the Torah; he failed miserably to live it out.

Once this psalm became part of the Hebrew Bible, it took on a life of its own, as Israelite worshipers would sing and pray these words for themselves—and every one of them would fall short of the ideal, just as the psalmist did. And this continued until the one perfect Israelite came into the world, the Messiah, the only one who was completely obedient, the one who could truly say, "In the scroll of the book it is written about *me*," since he was the ultimate sacrifice, the perfect offering, the one who fulfills the image of the sacrifices of atonement and cleansing. His life satisfied the real meaning of the sacrificial system. He was not just the one who was totally yielded to the will of the Father; he was the one who actually offered himself up as a sin offering (see above, 4.1).

So, according to Hebrews 10, when Jesus the Messiah came into the world (not meaning the moment he was born, but typically and prophetically), he said, "God, you don't want more sacrifices and offerings. You have already received hundreds of thousands of lambs and goats and rams and bulls. You want me! I'm the one you spoke of in your Law"—and for the first time, the Scripture was fulfilled and the goal was realized. It makes perfect sense!

4.28. Psalm 45:6[7] does not say the Messiah is God.

> Try this simple test: Write out this verse in Hebrew by itself, give it to anyone who is fluent in biblical Hebrew, and ask him or her to translate the verse. They will say that the meaning of the Hebrew is "Your throne, O God, is forever and ever." The Hebrew is quite clear. The problem is that the verse refers in context to Israel's king, who was human. So, the real question is, How can an earthly king be called 'elohim? The answer is simple: This passage ultimately points to the Messiah, the divine King!

We addressed this issue at some length in vol. 2 (3.3; see also above, 4.4), and the interested reader will find much relevant information there. It will be sufficient here to summarize what we learned in our previous discussions: Psalm 45 is a royal psalm, hailing the Davidic king in highly exalted terms, even referring to him as "God" (or "divine one"). While it is stretching the limits of the Hebrew language to refer to any human king in such lofty terms, it is altogether fitting to speak of Yeshua in such terms, since he is the Word made flesh, the Son of God clothed in earthly, human garments. Thus, this psalm can only be rightly understood when it is interpreted in terms of the Messiah.

As we have explained elsewhere (vol. 2, 3.3; principle 2 in the appendix), Psalm 45 is a royal psalm, written in honor of Israel's king, which means that we should not be surprised to see it filled with Messianic imagery.[257] In keeping with this, Risto Santala, a Finnish Christian scholar of Hebrew and Rabbinic literature, points out that the rabbis commonly interpret royal psalms with reference to the Messiah, noting, "The Jews see the Messiah in the Psalms *in more or less the same contexts as do the Christians*. But since they communicate in the Psalms' own language they find there secret references which they can then apply to their own conception of the Messiah."[258] As a typical example he points to Psalm 21, observing, "In Christian circles Psalm 21 is not usually considered Messianic. The Midrash, on the other hand, see the Messiah-King in its first and fourth verses. Rashi attaches the same interpretation to verse 7, and the Targum to verse 8."[259] All this is justified by the fact that the Davidic king is the subject of the psalm (see also the related comments of Rashi and Ibn Ezra to Psalm 2, 4.22). With reference to Psalm 45, Santala writes, "The most celebrated Jewish exegetes agree that *this psalm speaks of the 'Messiah-King.'*"[260]

How then is verse 6[7] interpreted in the classic Rabbinic commentaries? Commenting on the opening clause, Rashi's explanation is translated by A. J. Rosenberg as follows: "**Your throne O judge** Your throne O prince and judge shall exist forever and ever as the matter that is stated (Exod. 7:1): 'I have made you a judge . . . over Pharaoh.' And why? Because 'a scepter of equity is the scepter of your kingdom' that your judgments are true and you are fit to govern." This is highly significant, since Rashi understands *'elohim* to be the description of the king, following the most natural sense of the Hebrew. According to this understanding, the phrase would be rendered, "Your throne, O *'elohim*, is forever and ever." The question, then, is the meaning of *'elohim*, which Rashi interprets in light of Exodus 7:1, where Moses is appointed by the Lord to be *'elohim* to Pharaoh. This leads to two important observations: (1) Even though we can assume Rashi knew that Christians used this text to point to the divine nature of the Messiah, he still interpreted it along the same grammatical lines as did the Christians; (2) Rashi's interpretation, although highly unlikely and generally not widely followed by later Jewish interpreters and translators, reminds us that *'elohim* can have varied nuances of meaning.[261] This is in keeping with Christian scholars who have rendered the clause as "Your throne, O divine one," so as to emphasize the Messiah's divinity without suggesting that his divinity caused God in heaven to cease to be God.[262]

The Targum renders this passage as, "Your throne of honor, Yahweh [abbreviated in the Targum], is forever and ever," reminding us that the meaning of the original text is clear and straightforward. Other classical Rabbinic commentaries, such as Ibn Ezra and Metsudat David, argue that the text means, "Your throne is the throne of

God," or, "Your throne is given by God" (cf. also the rendering in the Stone edition; see further vol. 2, 3.3). In their recent Psalms commentary, Rozenberg and Zlotowitz translate this clause as "Your throne from God is everlasting," explaining, "The sense is that the king's throne has God's approval because he renders justice from it in accordance with God's will. Ibn Ezra translates 'your throne is the throne of God,' adding another 'throne.'"[263] More interesting, however, is their next comment: "The Hebrew could also be rendered 'Your throne, O God, is everlasting.' This would not fit the context, which requires the king to be the subject."[264] So, if not for the contextual difficulty, the translation would be fairly straightforward. And what is the primary difficulty? It is impossible for these commentators to conceive that the human king could be called 'elohim. But if that human king is the Messiah, and if the Messiah is divine, then there is no valid reason to reject the obvious, clear rendering.

We can therefore repeat without hesitation what we stated at the outset: Psalm 45 proclaims the divine nature of the Messianic King, and we do best to take the Scriptures in their most obvious, basic sense, allowing the Bible to dictate our theology, rather than imposing our theology on the Word of God.

4.29. Psalm 110 does not say the Messiah is LORD. Also, the psalm is not written by David about the Messiah. Our traditions indicate it may have been written by Eliezer about his master, Abraham, and then added to the collection of the Psalms by David many years later. Or David wrote it for the Levites to recite about him (or a court poet wrote it about David). This much is sure: It does not teach that the Messiah is God!

Psalm 110 is an important Messianic psalm pointing to the highly exalted status of the Messiah (to the right hand of God!) and to his priestly and royal nature. For these reasons, it is quoted frequently in the New Testament with reference to Yeshua. Yeshua even quotes it himself, pointing out how the Messiah was greater than David, since David called him "my lord." However, you are mistaken in thinking that the New Testament (or Christian translations

> of the Hebrew Bible) makes the claim that the opening
> verse of this psalm means that Jesus is Lord (Yahweh).

According to anti-missionary rabbi Tovia Singer,

> Psalm 110 represents one of the New Testament's most stunning, yet
> clever mistranslations of the Jewish scriptures. Moreover, the confu-
> sion created by the Christianization of this verse was further perpetu-
> ated and promulgated by numerous Christian translators of the Bible
> as well. . . .
> The story of the church's tampering with Psalm 110 is so old that it
> begins in the Christian canon itself.[265]

These are startling claims indeed. On what basis does Singer make
such serious charges? On the basis of Yeshua's use of this psalm to
point to his own exalted status, and on the basis of subsequent Christian translations that allegedly perpetuate this misunderstanding of
the text. What is startling is not the wrongness of the "Christian" interpretation but the wrongness of Singer's arguments, in particular his
claim that the New Testament's usage of this psalm represents one
of its "most stunning, yet clever mistranslations of the Jewish scriptures."[266] This claim is absolutely without foundation.

Let's take a look at the words of Jesus himself as recorded by one
of his disciples:

> While the Pharisees were gathered together, Jesus asked them, "What
> do you think about the [Messiah]? Whose son is he?"
> "The son of David," they replied.
> He said to them, "How is it then that David, speaking by the Spirit,
> calls him 'Lord'? For he says,
> " 'The Lord said to my Lord:
> "Sit at my right hand
> until I put your enemies
> under your feet." '
> If then David calls him 'Lord,' how can he be his son?" No one could
> say a word in reply, and from that day on no one dared to ask him any
> more questions.
>
> Matthew 22:41–46

Rabbi Singer is confident that this event not only reflects a wrong
interpretation of the text but that it never even took place:

Although the above conversation could never have occurred, I am certain this narrative has been replayed over and over again in the imagination of countless Christians for nearly 1,900 years.

It's an inspiring story to the Christian believer. Jesus really showed those Pharisees how little they knew! Yet, this is precisely why this story could never have transpired. No Jew who had even a superficial knowledge of the Jewish scriptures would have ever found Jesus' argument compelling, let alone a conversation stopper. The depth of knowledge that the Pharisees possessed of *Tanach* was astounding.[267]

Notice carefully Singer's words: "No Jew who had even a superficial knowledge of the Jewish scriptures would have ever found Jesus' argument compelling, let alone a conversation stopper." To the contrary, it is *because* Jesus knew that his hearers were so familiar with the Scriptures that he raised this compelling argument. Of course, they had no answer. You see, some of the earliest Rabbinic interpretation of Psalm 110 understood the psalm to be speaking of the Messiah, and if David in fact wrote the psalm, then Yeshua's question is well taken: If the Messiah is merely David's son—and it was universally agreed that the Messiah *was* the son of David—how can David call him his lord?

"But that's the whole problem," you object. "The Christian translations claim that the Messiah is Lord—meaning God himself—whereas the Hebrew Bible says no such thing." This, in fact, is another of Rabbi Singer's points, and he argues that the second "Lord" in the text "never refers to God anywhere in the Bible. It is only used for the profane, never the sacred."[268]

But where did Jesus say "Lord" was referring to God? He simply stated that the text indicated David called the Messiah his lord—which is exactly what Singer claims that *la'doni* means: "The correct translation . . . is 'to my master' or 'to my lord.'"[269] Precisely. That was Yeshua's whole point.

Unfortunately, Singer has gotten his information completely wrong, failing to read correctly the Christian translation he cites and completely ignoring well-known Jewish translation customs. Simply stated, a tradition developed among the Jewish people that the Hebrew name for God, *yhwh*, was too sacred to pronounce.[270] Thus, whenever a Jew would read this name in the Bible, he would not say *Yahweh* (which is the most likely original pronunciation; the more common Jehovah is not correct). Rather, he would say, *'adonai*, meaning "Lord."[271] Thus, the opening verse of Psalm 110 would have been recited out loud as "'*adonay* (or '*adonai*) said to '*adoni*" ('*adoni* meaning "my lord" or "my Lord").[272]

When Jesus quoted this verse to the Pharisees, this would have been the way he said it, referring to Yahweh as '*adonai*. There were no tricks here, no sleight of hand, no cover-up, no deception, no mistranslation. Just a straightforward recitation of the Hebrew text. No one would have thought that Jesus was claiming to be Yahweh, since his hearers certainly knew the text by heart as well, and since they distinctly heard two different words for Lord and lord: '*adonai*, meaning *Yahweh*, and '*adoni*, meaning "my Lord" or "my lord."[273] And that was Jesus' whole point: How can the Messiah be merely a son of David if David calls him his lord?[274] He must not only be David's son; he must also be greater than David.

How then does Singer claim that the New Testament and later Christian translations of Psalm 110 are guilty of intentional mistranslation? It is simply because (1) he has not handled the Christian translations fairly, and (2) he has not realized how the very first Jewish translation of the Tanakh into Greek rendered Psalm 110:1.

Using the King James Version as an example, we see that Psalm 110:1 was rendered: "The Lord said unto my Lord, Sit thou at my right hand, until I make thine enemies thy footstool." Virtually all modern Christian translations follow a similar translation pattern, rendering the opening Hebrew word *yhwh* as "Lord" and then rendering the second Hebrew word '*adoni* as "my Lord" or "my lord." As we have seen, the custom of translating the Hebrew *yhwh* as "Lord" goes back to Jewish practice, not Christian practice. And just as Jewish readers distinguished between '*adonai* and '*adon* (meaning Yahweh, as opposed to any lord or the Lord), so also Christian translations into English distinguished between Lord (Hebrew, yhwh) and Lord (Hebrew, '*adon*). This is also the custom most commonly followed by *Jewish* translations of the Bible into English: Whenever *yhwh* occurs in the original text, it is written as Lord (all uppercase).

In keeping with this practice, Christian translations (and many Jewish translations as well) distinguish between *yhwh* and '*adoni* in Psalm 110:1 by rendering these words as Lord and my Lord (or my lord). Amazingly, Singer claims that the NASB (a twentieth-century Christian translation that also renders Psalm 110:1 with Lord and Lord) fails to distinguish between the two words, inviting the readers to "look at the first word 'Lord' in the verse. Now look at the second word 'Lord' (they are only three words apart). Did you notice any difference between them? You didn't because the Christian translator carefully masked what it actually says in the text of the original Hebrew." Thus, he claims, "the two English words in the NASB translation are carefully made to appear identical, in the original Hebrew text they are entirely different."[275] Absolutely not! These two words are *not* the same, as you would immediately see even at first glance: The first is all uppercase letters (you'll find this in just about any Christian translation); the second is lowercase after the initial capital *L*.

Rabbi Singer, however, takes serious issue with the fact that many Christian versions translate the second *'adon* (*'adoni*, representing the noun followed by the first-person pronominal suffix) as "my Lord" instead of "my lord," arguing that every single time *'adoni* is found in the Tanakh, it is speaking of a human being, not God (who would always be referred to as *'adonai* rather than *'adoni*). He states:

> The Hebrew word *adonee* [a phonetic spelling of *adoni*] never refers to God anywhere in the Bible. It is only used for the profane, never the sacred. That is to say, God, the Creator of the universe, is never called *adonee* in the Bible. There are many words reserved for God in the Bible; *adonee*, however, is not one of them.[276]

There are at least three problems with his argument: First, he is incorrect in stating that "my lord" is reserved "for the profane, never the sacred." Just look in Joshua 5:14, where Joshua addresses the angel of the Lord as "my lord" *('adoni)*. Yet this divine messenger is so holy that Joshua is commanded to remove the shoes from his feet because he is standing on holy ground, just as Moses was commanded when the angel of the Lord—representing Yahweh himself—appeared to him (Exod. 3:1–6). This is hardly a "profane" rather than "sacred" usage! Similar examples can be found in Judges 6:13 and Zechariah 1:9, among other places. In each of these, angels are addressed as "my lord," and in some of these cases, the angels bear the divine presence. Second, Singer's whole argument hinges on the Masoretic vocalization, which did not reach its final form until the Middle Ages. As every student of Hebrew knows, biblical Hebrew was written with consonants and "vowel letters" only; the *vowel signs* were added hundreds of years later. Yet both *'adonai* (used only for Yahweh) and *'adoni* (used for men and angels, as we just noted) are spelled identically in Hebrew, consisting of the four consonants *'-d-n-y*. How then can Rabbi Singer make such a dogmatic statement about the differences between these two forms in the Bible? His argument stands only if we accept the absolute authority of the Masoretic vocalization, which in some cases follows the original writing by almost two thousand years.[277] Third, it is not really important whether we translate with "my Lord" or "my lord," since Yeshua's whole argument was simply that David called the Messiah "lord," meaning that the Messiah had to be more than David's son. While many Christian translations do render 'adoni as "my Lord" in Psalm 110:1, they are careful to distinguish between the first Lord (i.e., LORD) and the second.

"But," you say, "I understand that the New Testament is written in Greek. Are you telling me that the writers of the New Testament followed Jewish practice and spelled the two words differently? That was not the custom in Greek, and therefore readers of the Gospels would be misled into thinking that the two 'Lords' were the same person, both referring to God."

That's a good observation. But once again, this is not a "Christian" problem but rather a "Jewish" problem dating back to the Septuagint, which was completed more than two hundred years before the writing of the New Testament. The New Testament only follows the practice of the Jewish Septuagint. It is the Greek Septuagint that first rendered *yhwh* with the Greek word *kyrios*, "Lord" or "lord." Thus, Psalm 110:1 is rendered by the Septuagint as, "The *kyrios* said to my *kyrios*,"[278] and the writers of the New Testament—themselves almost all Jews—merely quoted the Jewish translation of their day into Greek. It's that simple![279]

To review: (1) When Jesus quoted this verse in Hebrew, he would have said, *ne'um 'adonai la'adoni*. He would not have spoken the name Yahweh, but he would have distinguished between the Lord God and David's Lord/lord. (The same would apply to Aramaic if Yeshua quoted the verse in a Targumic form.) (2) Christian translations of Psalm 110:1 into English also distinguish between Yahweh and David's Lord/lord, representing the former with LORD and the latter with Lord/lord. (3) The Septuagint, not the New Testament, was the first example of a translation in which *yhwh* and *'adon* were both translated with *kyrios*. From this we can see that Singer's charges are totally erroneous and without any support in the text. We need not trouble ourselves with this for another moment.

The real questions that deserve attention are, Is this really a Messianic psalm, and, Was Yeshua correct in referring it to himself? Let's look at the whole psalm as rendered in the NIV:

> Of David. A psalm.
>
> The LORD says to my Lord:
>   "Sit at my right hand

until I make your enemies
a footstool for your feet."

The LORD will extend your mighty scepter from Zion;
you will rule in the midst of your enemies.
Your troops will be willing
on your day of battle.
Arrayed in holy majesty,
from the womb of the dawn
you will receive the dew of your youth.

The LORD has sworn
and will not change his mind:
"You are a priest forever,
in the order of Melchizedek."

The Lord is at your right hand;
he will crush kings on the day of his wrath.
He will judge the nations, heaping up the dead
and crushing the rulers of the whole earth.
He will drink from a brook beside the way;
therefore he will lift up his head.

Psalm 110

It is clear that this is a royal psalm, spoken to a Judean king about his promised worldwide reign. But what is meant by "Of David. A psalm."? We know that these opening words (called the superscription) are not necessarily part of the original text. But we also know that Jewish readers in Yeshua's day accepted this as a psalm of David. What then does this mean? Was the psalm written *by* David or *for* David (or for the Davidic king)?

An ancient Jewish interpretation, as fascinating as it is far-fetched, claims that this psalm was originally written by Eliezer, the servant of Abraham, and that David added this psalm to his collection centuries later. According to this view, the psalm was written after Abraham returned from his victorious battle with the four kings of the plain (see Genesis 14) and Melchizedek, king of Salem (Jerusalem) came out to meet him. As written in Genesis 14:19–20, Melchizedek, the priest-king of Jerusalem, greeted Abraham (still called Abram at that time) with the words: "Blessed be Abram by God Most High, Creator of heaven and earth. And blessed be God Most High, who delivered your enemies into your hand." Abraham then gave a tithe of the spoils to Melchizedek, a definite sign of honor and respect (Gen. 14:20a).

Surprisingly, some of the ancient rabbis had a problem with Melchizedek's greeting, saying that God was displeased with Melchizedek since he blessed Abram before he blessed the Lord, as a result of which the priesthood was taken from Melchizedek and given to Abram (meaning to his descendants; see b. Nedarim 32b). This is how Psalm 110:4 is explained: "The LORD has sworn and will not change his mind: 'You are a priest forever, in the order of Melchizedek.'" There is little, however, to commend this interpretation and several serious objections that can be raised against it: (1) As Ibn Ezra notes, after giving due regard to the ancient midrash just cited, it is quite difficult to explain the reference to Zion in verse 2 ("The LORD will extend your mighty scepter from Zion") with reference to Abraham. Zion is the city of David![280] (2) Abraham himself was *not* called a priest by the Lord, even if the priesthood ultimately came through the tribe of his great-grandson Levi. (3) Abraham was not a royal figure in the Torah, nor was he primarily a triumphant ruler; yet that is what Psalm 110 explicitly describes and promises. (4) There is not a shred of evidence to support the midrashic interpretation. It is simply a creative reading of the text, apparently inspired by the reference to Melchizedek in Genesis 14 and Psalm 110, the only two times his name appears in the Hebrew Bible. (5) Even some midrashic evidence is against this interpretation, since elsewhere it is said that Abraham sits at the *left hand* of God, while it is *the Messiah* who sits at the Lord's right hand.[281]

Some scholars have even argued that the interpretation of this psalm with reference to Abraham is a direct reaction to Christian interpretations that pointed to the Messiah.[282] This is certainly possible, although it is far from certain. But the extreme unlikelihood of the Abrahamic interpretation is beyond dispute.

A much more likely view is that a court poet wrote this psalm for David, perhaps when he moved his throne to Jerusalem (2 Sam. 5–6).[283] Thus, speaking prophetically, this poet declared that Yahweh said to his lord (David), "Sit at my right hand. . . ." And, as we learned previously (vol. 1, 2.1), David served as a prototype of the priestly king, a Messianic figure who himself was both priest and king. The fact that David ruled out of Jerusalem would associate him with Melchizedek, the priest-king of Salem (= Jerusalem) spoken of in Genesis 14.

There are, however, serious problems with this view as well: (1) Was David actually called a priest by the Lord? It is one thing to say that David was a priestly king; it is another thing to say that he was called "a priest forever" by God himself. Clearly, David was not.[284] (2) When was David told to sit at God's right hand until his enemies were made a footstool for his feet? It is true that the Lord granted David victory over his enemies *while he was alive.* But this psalm presents a call from God to sit at his right hand (i.e., by his heavenly throne) until all of David's enemies were defeated. When did this happen? (3) The closing verses of this psalm seem to indicate that the king spoken of here would have a worldwide reign. This cannot apply to David.[285]

Not surprisingly, a number of the ancient rabbis applied this psalm to the Messiah,[286] and it is this Messianic interpretation that is actually *presupposed* by Jesus in the New Testament. As Franz Delitzsch rightly observed:

> . . . if those who were interrogated [meaning the Pharisees and other Jewish teachers] had been able to reply that David does not there speak of the future Messiah, but puts into the mouth of the people words concerning himself, or . . . concerning the Davidic king in a general way, then the question would lack the background of cogency as an argument. Since, however, the prophetico-Messianic character of the Psalm was acknowledged at that time (even as the later synagogue, in spite of the dilemma into which this Psalm brought it in opposition to the church, has never been able entirely to avoid this confession), the conclusion to be drawn from this Psalm must have been felt by the Pharisees themselves, that the Messiah, because the Son of David and Lord at the same time, was of human and at the same time of superhuman nature; that it was therefore in accordance with Scripture if this Jesus, who represented Himself to be the predicted Christ [Messiah], should as such profess to be the Son of God and of divine nature.[287]

Simply stated, if the most common interpretation of the day did not understand this psalm to speak of the Messiah, then any of the Jewish leaders with whom Yeshua spoke could have simply said, "But this doesn't speak of the Messiah! It speaks of David." The fact that no such reply was given indicates just how widely the psalm was understood to be Messianic.

"But you're not being fair," you say. "You're basing everything on the New Testament account. How do we know that it is true?"

First, the very nature of Jesus' question points to the widespread Messianic understanding of the psalm. After all, Matthew (whom we cited above) wrote his book of good news (= Gospel) to his own Jewish people, many of whom were thoroughly versed in the Scriptures, and if Jesus' point had no relevance at all—if, indeed, it was as ludicrous and impossible as Rabbi Singer claims—then Matthew (not to mention Mark and Luke) would not have put the wool over anyone's eyes. Rather, the question posed by Yeshua would be like someone asking, "Do you believe that President Kennedy's assassination was the work of one man or part of a larger conspiracy?" The *fact* of his assassination is not in dispute, only the details. In the same way, the *fact* of the Messianic interpretation of the psalm was not in dispute, only the specific meaning of the verses. Second, despite the fact that the New Testament refers to Psalm 110 more than any other portion of Scripture in the Hebrew Bible, Talmudic rabbis still interpreted the psalm messianically. In other words (as noted above by Delitzsch), since followers of Jesus were so quick to point to Psalm 110 with reference to him as Messiah, it would only be natural to think that the later rabbis would *not* interpret this psalm as Messianic. And yet they did, with frequency. There can be no doubt, then, that this Messianic interpretation was not only ancient; it was also natural. Third, as far as we can tell, for a first-century Jewish reader "A psalm of David" would most naturally be taken to mean "A psalm written by David" unless there were good reasons to interpret it as a psalm written for David. This would mean that David wrote this psalm *about* the Messianic King rather than about himself.[288] Fourth, even if the psalm was originally written by a court poet for *his* lord, King David, it would still point to David's priestly calling (as a prototype of the Messiah) as well as to his worldwide reign, fulfilled only through David's greater descendant, King Messiah. This would mean, then, that Jesus was pointing to Jewish interpretation of the day, interpretation that attributed the authorship of this psalm to David, thereby proving that Messiah had to be greater than David, but without making a definitive statement about the authorship of the psalm.

These observations, coupled with the reasons listed above, argue for the Messianic interpretation of Psalm 110. At the least, such an interpretation makes very good sense, and therefore the New Testament writers were not out of line in frequently citing this psalm with reference to Jesus.[289]

In support of this Messianic interpretation we can also point to the comments on Daniel 7:13 attributed to the influential medieval

Jewish leader, Rabbi Sa'adiah Gaon. Explaining the words "And behold, [coming] with the clouds of heaven, one like a son of man," he stated, "This is Messiah our righteousness," contrasting this description with the Messianic prophecy found in Zechariah 9:9, where it is written that the Messiah will come meek and lowly, riding on a donkey.[290] He interpreted the clouds of heaven to mean the host of heavenly angels, noting that this is the glorious splendor that the Creator will grant to the Messiah. And how does Gaon explain the end of verse 13, where it is stated that they will bring the Messiah to the Ancient of Days (a title for the Lord)? He simply quotes the opening line of Psalm 110, "The utterance of the LORD to my lord, 'Sit at My right hand'" (translated literally). He got that exactly right!

There is one final point to be made, and it is extremely significant. We noted in vol. 1, 2.1, that two thousand years ago, many Jews were looking for *two* Messiahs, one priestly and one royal. This is reflected in the Dead Sea Scrolls in the references to the Messiahs of Aaron and David. It is also reflected in what is called the Testament of the Twelve Patriarchs, a writing of great importance in the ancient Jewish world. Reference is made there to a Messiah from the tribe of Judah and a Messiah from the tribe of Levi. The concept of a priestly and royal Messiah came directly from the Hebrew Scriptures, but it was misunderstood by the Jewish teachers in Yeshua's day. Some of these teachers were expecting *two* Messianic figures, one priestly and one royal, whereas the Tanakh only spoke of *one* Messianic figure, descended from David, who was *both* priestly (in function) and royal (in function and lineage).

After Yeshua's death and resurrection, his first followers, all of them Jews, began to understand his priestly role, and an important letter to these Jewish believers (called the Letter to the Hebrews in the New Testament) speaks of his priestly work at length (see above, 4.1). They understood that the divine son of David was, like David, a royal priest. Perhaps it was in reaction to this that Rabbinic literature, which postdates the writing of the New Testament, makes virtually no reference to the Messiah's priestly role. That's right: In literally *millions* of words of teaching and instruction, thousands of which discuss the Messiah, there is not a single reference to the priestly Messiah. Yet the scriptural hints—really, they are more than hints—were totally clear. In the person of the Messiah, identified as "the Branch" in the Tanakh, priest and king would be combined as one.

Along with Psalm 110, Zechariah 3–6 provides the clearest references to this, and some of the Rabbinic comments to these passages are striking, especially when you consider that the obvious deduction was not made, namely, if *these* passages are Messianic in content, then the Messiah should be both a priest and king. Let's focus in on Zechariah 3:8, "Listen, O high priest Joshua and your associates seated before you, who are men symbolic of things to come: I am going to bring my servant, the Branch." The Targum renders this closing phrase as, "Behold I bring my servant the Messiah." The Branch—understood to be the Branch of David—is the Messiah.

Abraham Ibn Ezra provides an interesting interpretation on the identity of the Branch:

> He is Zerubbabel, as it is said, "His name is branch" [Zech. 6:12], and the end of the passage proves it, [stating] "before Zerubbabel" [Zech. 4:7]. And many interpreters say that this branch is the Messiah, and he is called Zerubbabel because he is from his seed, as in, "and David my servant will be their prince forever" [Ezek. 37:25]. And I too can interpret this homiletically *[derek derash]*, for *tsemach* [branch] by Gematria [i.e., numerically interpreted] equals Menachem, that is, Ben Ammiel [in the Talmud, Menachem Ben Ammiel is a name for the Messiah; see b. Sanhedrin 99b, and notes of Ibn Ezra that the numeric values for the Hebrew words *branch* and *Menachem* are identical, both equal to 138].[291]

One question, however, was not adequately addressed in this interpretation: Why was Joshua the high priest, along with his companions, singled out immediately before reference was made to the Branch? Why not single out Zerubbabel, the Davidic governor, rather than single out the high priest? Many interpreters believe that Zechariah 4:14 points to Zerubbabel and Joshua as the *two anointed ones* who will serve in this world, but no reference is made to the Branch in this passage. Zechariah 6:9–15, however, is explicit: Joshua the high priest is to be *crowned*—remember that only kings were crowned—and it is he who symbolizes the Branch: "Take the silver and gold and make a crown, and set it on the head of the high priest, Joshua son of Jehozadak. Tell him this is what the LORD Almighty says: 'Here is the man whose name is the Branch [once again, the Targum calls him the Messiah], and he will branch out from his place and build the temple of the LORD'" (Zech. 6:11–12).[292] So, it is Joshua, not Zerubbabel, who is called the Branch, a high priest, wearing the crown, representing the Davidic Messiah.[293]

Why then did both Rashi and Ibn Ezra state that the Branch here was actually Zerubbabel? It was because they missed the priestly role of the Messiah.[294] Otherwise, the passage is perfectly clear: Joshua the high priest, not Zerubbabel the governor, is identified with the Branch. In fact, the text is so clear that some liberal interpreters actually believe that the text was changed and that it originally referred to Zerubbabel being crowned, not Joshua.[295] This, however, is similar to the claim of the PLO in 2002 when the Israeli forces discovered documents directly linking Yasser Arafat to terrorist activities: PLO officials claimed that the documents were forged! There is no forgery here, nor has the text been altered: It is the high priest Joshua, crowned and sitting on a throne, who is symbolic of the Branch, thus emphasizing the priestly role of the Messiah—making atonement for Israel and the nations—who is elsewhere known in the Scriptures as the royal son of David.

What makes this all the more interesting is that this man Joshua is normally known by a shortened name in the Tanakh, just as someone named Michael could be called Mike. And what is that shortened name? Yeshua! And so, the one and only man directly singled out in the Bible as a symbol of the Messiah was called *Yeshua*. The Lord knew exactly what he was doing when he laid this all out in advance, giving enough clues along the way that, once discovered, the evidence would be indisputable. Is the picture becoming clearer to you?[296]

4.30. You claim that Haggai 2 points to the fact that the Messiah had to come before the Second Temple was destroyed, since it says in verse 9 that the glory of the Second Temple would be greater than the glory of Solomon's Temple. Actually, Haggai is speaking about only the *physical splendor* of the Second Temple, which surpassed Solomon's Temple in the days of Herod.

Although there are some clear references in Haggai 2 to an abundance of gold and silver that would be used in rebuilding the Temple, there can be no doubt that the phrase "to fill with glory" refers to the manifest presence of God and not to physical splendor. We can therefore ask, In what

> way did the glory of the Second Temple surpass that of the
> First Temple? The answer is inescapable: The Messiah, the
> King of Glory, the very embodiment of the presence and
> power of God, visited that Temple.

We dealt with this objection in a different context in vol. 1, 2.1,
pointing out several compelling reasons that the references to the
Temple being *filled with glory* could not be explained with primary
reference to the *physical rebuilding* of the Temple with massive
amounts of silver and gold. Rather, Haggai's prophecy must ultimately
be understood as meaning that the Temple would be filled with *the
splendor of God's glorious presence*. Before expanding on this in more
depth, let's read the relevant verses in Haggai's prophecy:

> This is what the LORD Almighty says: "In a little while I will once more
> shake the heavens and the earth, the sea and the dry land. I will shake
> all nations, and the desired of all nations will come, and I will fill this
> house with glory," says the LORD Almighty. "The silver is mine and the
> gold is mine," declares the LORD Almighty. "The glory of this present
> house will be greater than the glory of the former house," says the LORD
> Almighty. "And in this place I will grant peace," declares the LORD
> Almighty.
>
> Haggai 2:6–9

How can we be sure the prophet is not simply declaring that the
Second Temple would be built more beautifully than Solomon's Temple? After all, the Hebrew word *kavod* can sometimes refer to wealth
and riches, as in Genesis 31:1: "Jacob heard that Laban's sons were
saying, 'Jacob has taken everything our father owned and has gained
all this wealth *[kavod]* from what belonged to our father.'" And the
context in Haggai 2 makes reference to the abundance of silver and
gold that God would send for the rebuilding of the Temple. What then
gives me the right to insist on a primarily *spiritual* interpretation to
this passage?

First, the Lord is making a specific comparison between the glory
of the First Temple and the glory of the Second Temple, and the
Scriptures are very clear about the nature of the glory of the First
Temple: The supernatural presence of God was there. The fire of God
was there. *That* was the glory of the First Temple (see 2 Chron. 7:1–4).
Second, God promises to "fill this house with glory," and the expres-
sion "fill with glory" always refers to the divine manifestation in the
Bible (see vol. 1, 2.1). Third, the Talmud and later Rabbinic litera-

ture noted that some of the most important elements found in the First Temple—some of the very symbols of the glory of God, I might add—were not found in the Second Temple, namely, the ark of the covenant, the divine fire, the Holy Spirit, the Shekhinah, the Urim and Thummim.[297] How then could it be said that the *glory* of the Second Temple would surpass that of the First when the Second Temple was devoid of the very manifest presence of God that *defined* the First Temple's glory? Fourth, the ancient Jewish sages could not agree on the meaning of the passage, some claiming that the glory would consist in the longer duration of the Second Temple (i.e., it lasted longer than the First Temple did; cf. b. Baba Bathra 3a). This argument, however, is so weak that even the sixteenth-century refutationist Isaac Troki—an arch opponent of Christianity—decisively refuted it, stating,

> Nor can we admit that the glory of the second temple consisted in its longer duration—a point discussed in the Talmud (Baba Bathra), for the Scripture makes no mention of the glory being attributable to the length of the time during which the temple was constructed or lasted. And even if the duration of the second temple had exceeded by double the time that of the first temple, the word *glory* could not have been assigned to this distinction.[298]

And if the promise was merely one of physical glory and splendor—which, as we have noted, falls far short of the description of being filled with God's glory—why then is an additional promise offered in Haggai 2:9, namely, that in the Second Temple God would appoint peace?[299] It is because the Lord is promising several things for the Second Temple: (1) It would be built with the riches of the nations; (2) it would be filled with the glory of God; and (3) the Lord would appoint peace there. So clear was this last word that Ibn Ezra actually raised the possibility that the promise of peace in Haggai 2:9 was *conditional*, the conditions being "if they will be completely righteous, as Zechariah said, and if they will diligently hearken and obey."

Ibn Ezra's interpretation reminds us of the interpretative problems faced by Rabbinic Judaism, since there are prophecies that were supposed to be fulfilled in the days of the Second Temple—Messianic prophecies of fundamental importance—but that were never fulfilled, according to the ancient rabbis (see vol. 1, esp. 2.1). Other prophecies were read as *possibilities*, since the Scriptures predicted that the Messiah would come on the clouds of heaven, exalted and glorious

(Dan. 7:13), and also declared that he would come riding on a donkey, meek and lowly (Zech. 9:9). According to the Talmud, if Israel was righteous and worthy, he would come on the clouds; if Israel was sinful and unworthy, he would come riding on a donkey. But the Bible did not say these were mere possibilities and only one of them would prove true; rather, they were inspired prophecies, both of which would prove true. First the Messiah came riding on a donkey (in point of fact, we were not worthy of his coming then); when we repent and welcome him back (thus becoming worthy to receive him as King), he will return in the clouds of heaven.

And it is Messiah's coming to the Second Temple that explains Haggai's prophecy. Something more wonderful than the divine fire would visit that place; something greater than the cloud of glory would be manifest there. The Son of God himself, King Messiah, the glorious Word made flesh, would come to that Temple, teaching, preaching, cleansing, refining, and working miracles. It would be the ultimate divine visitation, far greater than anything that took place in Solomon's Temple. The Second Temple was also the place of the outpouring of the Holy Spirit on Shavuot (the Feast of Weeks, or Pentecost), as recorded in Acts 2, as well as the place of miraculous healings through the Messiah's emissaries (see Acts 3; and note especially Acts 2:43; 5:12). Surely that Temple was filled with glory! And it was in the Second Temple that the one who gave his life as an offering to make peace between God and man, and between Jew and Gentile, came and offered peace (cf. also Luke 1:79; 2:14; 19:42; Acts 10:36).[300]

4.31. Zechariah 12:10 has nothing to do with Jesus.

> Although there are ambiguities in the Hebrew text, this passage clearly speaks of a time of national mourning in Israel over one slain, resulting in the spiritual cleansing of the nation (Zech. 12:10–13:1). One of the oldest Jewish interpretations of this passage, found in the Talmud, refers Zechariah 12:10 to the death of Messiah ben Joseph, the suffering Messiah of Jewish tradition. Why then should it surprise you that the New Testament interprets Zechariah 12:10 with reference to Yeshua?

Zechariah 12:10 is discussed in the Talmud in b. Sukkah 55a. The verse—read with a singular, not plural, subject—is first interpreted to mean that it is the evil inclination (i.e., the sinful tendency in man) that was slain, and the people wept when they saw how easily it could have been overcome. The second interpretation states that the people wept over Messiah son of Joseph who was slain fighting in the last great war (i.e., the last great *future* war) for his people, after which Messiah son of David asked God to raise him from the dead, and his request was granted. From this we learn two significant points: (1) The Hebrew was understood to be speaking of an individual person or thing, not of a plural subject (in other words, the one who was pierced through and slain, not those who were pierced through and slain); and (2) there was an ancient Jewish tradition interpreting the text in terms of a Messianic figure who died and then was raised from the dead.

Recently, both the Stone edition and the NJPSV translated Zechariah 12:10 with a plural subject: "They shall look toward Me because of those whom they have stabbed; they will mourn for him" *(Stone);*[301] and, "They shall lament to Me about those who are slain, wailing over them" (NJPSV).[302] But these interpretations are not reflected in some of the most ancient Jewish sources (cf. the Septuagint and the Talmud, b. Sukkah 52a; the Targumic rendering is similar to those just cited), nor are they a grammatically natural reading of the text, which is actually straightforward. It simply says, "They shall look to me whom (Hebrew, *'et 'asher*) they pierced, and they shall mourn over him."[303] Not surprisingly, the Stone edition has to change verbal objects in midstream ("because of *those* whom they have stabbed; they will mourn for *him,*" which is clearly contradictory), while the NJPSV must disregard the fact that the Hebrew in the second half of the sentence says *'alayw,* "over *him*" as opposed to "over *them*."[304] These translations, therefore, can safely be dismissed, leading us instead to two larger questions: (1) Are "they" looking to God or to the one pierced, or is God the one pierced, to whom they are looking? (2) What does the larger context say? Does it justify the Messianic interpretation?

In answer to the first question, it is clear that the mourners are turning to God, since he is the only one referred to in the first person throughout the chapter, beginning in verse 2, where the Lord declares, "*I* am going to make Jerusalem a cup that sends all the surrounding peoples reeling." Similar expressions are found in the following verses: verse 3, "*I* will make"; verse 4, "*I* will strike; *I* will keep; *I* will blind"; verse 6, "*I* will make"; verse 9, "*I* will set out to destroy"; and then in verse 10, "And *I* will pour out on the house of David and the inhabitants of Jerusalem a spirit of grace and supplication. They will look on *me,* the one they have pierced." It is perfectly clear, therefore, that the "me" in this verse is the Lord himself—as rendered in the Jewish translations cited above—suggesting the real possibility that the Hebrew text states that it is the Lord himself who was pierced. Read from a Messianic Jewish viewpoint, this makes perfect sense since, as we have demonstrated elsewhere (vol. 2, 3.1–3.3; above, 4.4 and 4.28), the Messiah is the very image of God, representing his fullness in bodily form on the earth. Thus, piercing the Messiah was equivalent to piercing the Lord, just as rejecting the prophets was equivalent to rejecting the Lord (see, e.g., 2 Chron. 36:15–16; for a related New Testament concept, see Matt. 10:14, 40).

How then do we explain the second half of Zechariah 12:10, which reads, "and they will mourn *for him* as one mourns for an only child, and grieve bitterly *for him* as one grieves for a firstborn son"? Either the text shifts from first person (lit., "look to me") to third person (lit., "mourn for him"), something that is not uncommon in biblical texts,[305] or we should follow the reading preserved in some Masoretic manuscripts, reflecting the tiniest variation in the Hebrew but resulting in a very different translation in English, namely, "they shall look *to him* whom they pierced."[306] If that reading is correct, then some of the traditional Jewish problems with the translation disappear, since the verse would not explicitly state the one pierced was the Lord himself, and there would seem to be no objection to the rendering of "they will look to him whom they pierced."

This leads, then, to the question of the larger context, and again we ask, Is the Messianic interpretation valid? The Talmudic interpretation, cited earlier, correctly follows the context of Zechariah 12, which speaks of an end-time battle over Jerusalem, culminating with a great victory for Judah and Jerusalem. Why then is there such great mourning (cf. 12:11–12a, "On that day the weeping in Jerusalem will be great, like the weeping of Hadad Rimmon in the plain of Megiddo. The land will mourn, each clan by itself, with their wives by themselves.")? According to the note in the Stone edition (which translated verse 10 as, "They shall look toward Me because of those whom they have stabbed"), the interpretation of Radak should be followed, namely, "The salvation will be so complete that people will be astonished if even one man is killed by the enemy." But there is a big problem here: Not only is the plural translation very questionable (namely, "those . . . stabbed"), but the interpretation suggested is contextually implausible, since the ones mourning are the ones who did the piercing! In other words, *they* are not mourning over what *someone else* did ("the enemy," according to *Stone*). *They* are one and the same![307]

Just look again at what the whole verse says: "And I will pour out on the house of David and the inhabitants of Jerusalem a spirit of grace and supplication. *They* will look on me, the one *they* have pierced,[308] and *they* will mourn for him as one mourns for an only child, and [*they* will] grieve bitterly for him as one grieves for a firstborn son." The Hebrew verbs are all third-person plural, and the subject of those verbs is clearly the same, namely "the house of David and the inhabitants of Jerusalem." So, the Scripture is saying that the Jewish people will be in mourning for one whom they pierced and killed, not for one of their own whom their enemies killed.[309] Again, I submit to you that this is the most natural and obvious meaning of the text in the Hebrew, and there is no good reason to reject it. Not only so, but it is the Messianic interpretation that makes contextual sense.

Looking once more at the larger context, we see that chapter 12 describes a final conflict between Jerusalem and the nations, one in which God delivers his people from their enemies. Yet the chapter ends with deep, national mourning, like the mourning over the death of a firstborn or only son, which leads to the first verse of chapter 13, "On that day a fountain will be opened to the house of David and the inhabitants of Jerusalem, to cleanse them from sin and impurity." *On that day*—the day of Jerusalem's deliverance and the day of her people's deep mourning—national atonement comes to Israel. Why? Because on that day, in their hour of greatest crisis, with all the world seemingly against them, the Jewish people will turn to God and cry out for salvation, realizing at that time that the one whom they thought was the cause of so many of their problems through the centuries (this despised Jesus Christ) was actually their Messiah, Yeshua, their only true hope, their deliverer. What a day that will be! How bitterly our people will mourn and grieve, and how wonderfully God will respond, cleansing his beleaguered people from all sin and guilt.

Before Yeshua's death, he wept over Jerusalem, wishing that the leaders of our people had recognized him and seeing the terrible consequences that would befall our nation because we rejected the Messiah (Luke 19:41–44). Listen carefully to his words: "O Jerusalem, Jerusalem, you who kill the prophets and stone those sent to you, how often I have longed to gather your children together, as a hen gathers her chicks under her wings, but you were not willing. Look, your house is left to you desolate. For I tell you, you will not see me again until you say, 'Blessed is he who comes in the name of the Lord'" (Matt. 23:37–39). In other words, you will not see me again until you welcome me as the Messianic King.[310]

And what is written in Zechariah 14:1–5? The Lord himself will come down and fight for his people, and *"on that day* his feet will stand on the Mount of Olives, east of Jerusalem, and the Mount of Olives will be split in two"* (14:4a). Yes, the Lord himself will come to earth, *to Jerusalem,* and deliver his people. When? On the day they look to him whom they pierced, on the day that national atonement comes to the people, on the day the Messiah—the Son of God—returns to earth![311]

So, rather than Zechariah 12:10 having nothing to do with Jesus, it has everything to do with him.[312]

4.32. Jesus fulfilled none of the Messianic prophecies!

> To the contrary, we know that Jesus is the Messiah because he fulfilled so many Messianic prophecies. The only real way to deny this is to claim that the many prophecies he clearly fulfilled are not Messianic, which is quite an impossible stretch.

To be perfectly candid, the first time I ever read this objection in a traditional Jewish book, I was absolutely shocked.[313] I was familiar with the claim that the authors of the New Testament fabricated the details of the life of Jesus to make it look as though he had fulfilled the Messianic prophecies. This is because his birth, life, death, and resurrection fulfilled so many prophecies and Messianic foreshadowings that anti-missionaries were forced to argue that Yeshua's life was almost "written to order." Thus, the argument ran, although it appears from the New Testament that he fulfilled many Messianic prophecies, in reality, he fulfilled none, since the events recorded never happened. This, of course, completely stretches the limits of credibility, for it suggests that the authors of the Gospels actually thought they could fool their contemporaries, who were themselves eyewitnesses of the Messiah's life, death, and resurrection. How absurd! (For further refutation of this extremely specious argument, see vol. 4, 5.14.)[314] It is another thing entirely, however, to claim that the life of Yeshua, as recounted in the New Testament writings, did not fulfill any Messianic prophecies. This objection certainly comes as a shock to the tens of thousands of Jewish believers in Jesus who came to faith in him *because of the Messianic prophecies*.

"But how do we know which prophecies really are Messianic?" you ask.

That is a good question to ask, but before answering it directly, let me draw your attention to several Rabbinic statements that point to the widespread nature of Messianic prophecy in the Scriptures. In a famous dictum of the Talmud it is stated, "None of the prophets prophesied except of the days of the Messiah" (meaning "the Messianic era," b. Sanhedrin 99a). This is in harmony with the statement of Yeshua's disciple Peter, who said, "All the prophets from Samuel on, as many as have spoken, have foretold these days" (Acts 3:24).

Writing in the twelfth century, Moses Maimonides stated that "this belief in the Messiah is in accordance with the prophecies concerning him, *by all the prophets, from our master Moses until Malachi, peace be unto them*."[315] Once again, we see the emphasis on the pervasive nature of the Messianic hope in the Hebrew Scriptures. It should come as no surprise, then, that the writers of the new covenant Scriptures saw references to the details of Jesus' life throughout the Hebrew Bible. We can summarize the main prophecies that Yeshua fulfilled (and is fulfilling) as follows:

- He was born where the prophet said he would be born (cf. Targum Jonathan, Rashi, and Radak on Micah 5:2[1]).
- He came into the world when the prophets said he would (according to the combined prophetic witness of Daniel, Haggai, and Malachi, along with hints found in the Talmud; see vol. 1, 2.1).
- He performed miraculous deeds of deliverance and healing, in accordance with the prophecies of Isaiah (Isa. 35:5–7; 49:6–7; 61:1–3).
- He was rejected by his own people, as was prophesied (Ps. 118:22; Isa. 49:4; 53:2–4).
- He suffered before his exaltation, as the prophets declared (Psalm 22; Isa. 52:13–15; Zech. 9:9).
- He died and then rose from the dead, according to the Scriptures (Isaiah 53; Psalms 16; 22).
- He has brought the light of God to the nations, as the prophets said he would (Isaiah 42, 49, 52)—so that countless millions of

people who were once "pagans" now worship the God of Israel through him.

• His last act, before he returns to Jerusalem in power and glory, will be to turn his people Israel back to him (Isaiah 49)—and it is this that he is now doing!

In addition to these major prophecies, the New Testament also points to lots of minor, specific fulfillments, along with allusions, foreshadowings, and midrashic (i.e., homiletical) applications of texts from the Tanakh, in keeping with Jewish interpretive methods of the day. Thus, James Smith can point to more than one hundred verses from the Hebrew Bible that are cited or alluded to in the New Testament with reference to Jesus and/or the events relating to his ministry. These include verses such as Isaiah 7:14, cited in Matthew 1:23 (see above, 4.3); Jeremiah 31:15, cited in Matthew 2:18; Psalm 78:2, cited in Matthew 13:35; Malachi 3:1, alluded to in Mark 1:2; Psalm 69:17, cited in John 2:17.[316] More specifically, Christian author Herbert Lockyer lists nineteen prophecies fulfilled in the death of Jesus alone, noting that he was to be betrayed by a friend, be sold for thirty pieces of silver, be forsaken by his disciples, be accused by false witnesses, be mocked and beaten, be pierced in his hands and feet, be crucified with thieves, pray for his persecutors, be the object of ridicule, have his garments gambled for, be deserted by God, agonize with thirst, commit himself to God, have his friends stand far off, be spared having his bones broken, be pierced, be hidden by darkness, be buried with the rich, and die a voluntary, substitutionary death.[317]

"But," you might say, "not all of these references can be called *Messianic prophecies*. Some of them are hardly Messianic, while others are hardly prophecies."

Actually, the New Testament authors, in keeping with the sentiments later expressed in the Rabbinic writings, saw the whole of the Hebrew Scriptures as pointing to King Messiah. Thus, they sometimes pointed to events in the history of Israel that found parallels in the life of Yeshua (see vol. 4, 5.2, on Matt. 2:15, citing Hos. 11:1), as well to events in the life of David that were paralleled in the Messiah's life (see 4.22 and 4.26). That means they did not only consider the clear evidence of the *prophecies,* but they also considered Israel's history to be prophetic in some sense as well.

"Exactly," you say. "That's my whole point. The New Testament is totally cavalier in its use of the Hebrew Bible and it can't be taken seriously."

I understand your point, but I reject it for two reasons: First, scholars who have carefully examined the usage of the Tanakh in the New Testament have noted that there is often great depth and insight in the New Testament interpretations. If you will simply review some of the points we have made in this volume (see, e.g., 4.1, 4.3, 4.23, 4.29), you will have to admit that there *is* real substance to the New Testament's usage of the Hebrew Bible. Second, compared to the Messianic interpretations of the Tanakh found in the early Rabbinic writings—some of which were composed more than five hundred years after the days of Yeshua and, ostensibly, could be expected to be more methodical and temperate—the New Testament authors were very sober and systematic. It is the Rabbinic writings that are often cavalier and noncontextual.

Alfred Edersheim, the learned nineteenth-century Jewish Christian scholar, summarized the Rabbinic data as follows: "The passages in the Old Testament applied to the Messiah or to Messianic times in the most ancient Jewish writings . . . amount in all to 456, thus distributed: 75 from the Pentateuch, 243 from the Prophets, and 138 from the Hagiographa, and supported by more than 558 separate quotations from Rabbinic writings. . . . The Rabbinic references might have been considerably increased, but it seemed useless to quote the same application of a passage in many different books."[318] What is the nature of some of these quotes? I will cite some representative examples, but as you read them, I would ask you to consider this one question: If the authors of the New Testament or contemporary Messianic Jews were applying these verses to Jesus as Messiah, would traditional Jews say that the verses were being twisted, misused, or taken out of context? The answer is self-evident.

Here, then, are some of the many examples listed by Edersheim:

- In the creation account, Genesis 1:2, it is stated that "the Spirit of God hovered over the face of the waters." This is explained to mean "the Spirit of the King Messiah," with reference to Isaiah 11:2 (see Genesis Rabbah 2:4, among other places).
- Through an extremely convoluted line of reasoning, the word for "generations" in Genesis 2:4—"These are the generations (Hebrew, *toledot*) of the heavens and earth"—is found to contain a hint of the six things the Messiah will restore to the earth (see Exodus Rabbah 30:3).

- Eve's words in Genesis 4:25 at the birth of her son Seth, "God has granted me another seed," are taken to refer to the Messiah, as if the text spoke of "a seed coming from another place" (Genesis Rabbah 23:5).
- Numbers 11:26 relates that Eldad and Medad, two Israelite elders, prophesied outside the camp. According to the Jerusalem Targum to this passage, their prophecy "is supposed to have been with regard to the war of the later days against Jerusalem and to the defeat of Gog and Magog by the Messiah."
- Ruth 2:14a reads, "And Boaz said unto her [Ruth], At mealtime come thou hither, and eat of the bread" (KJV). Midrash Rabbah Ruth to this passage contains what Edersheim rightly calls "a very remarkable interpretation." He points out, "Besides the application of the word 'eat,' as beyond this present time, to the days of the Messiah, and again to the world to come, which is to follow these days, the Midrash applies the whole of it mystically to the Messiah, viz. 'Come hither,' that is, draw near to the kingdom, 'and eat of the bread,' that is, the bread of royalty, 'and dip thy morsel in vinegar'—these are the sufferings, as it is written in Is. liii. 5, 'He was wounded for our transgressions.' 'And she sat beside the reapers'—because His Kingdom would in the future be put aside from Him for a short time, according to Zech. xiv. 2; 'and he reached her parched corn'—because He will restore it to Him, according to Is. xi. 4. R. Berachiah, in the name of R. Levi, adds, that the second Redeemer should be like the first. As the first Redeemer (Moses) appeared, and disappeared, and reappeared after three months, so the second Redeemer would also appear, and disappear, and again become manifest, Dan. xii. 11, 12 being brought into connection with it. Comp. Midr. on Cant. ii. 9; Pesik. 49 *a, b*. Again, the words, 'she ate, and was sufficed, and left,' are thus interpreted in Shabb. 113 *b*: she ate—in this world; and was sufficed—in the days of the Messiah; and left—for the world to come."[319]
- Ecclesiates 1:9 simply states, "What has been will be again, what has been done will be done again; there is nothing new under the sun." Edersheim notes that in the midrash to this verse, it is shown at great length that the Messiah would reenact all the miracles of the past.
- Many verses in the Song of Solomon are taken by that book's highly expansive Aramaic Targum to refer to the Messiah.

- Special attention should be given to b. Sanhedrin 96b–99a, the lengthiest and most focused Messianic discussion anywhere in the Talmud, cited at length by Edersheim for that very reason.[320] There is an extraordinary level of speculation among the sages quoted in this passage in terms of the times of the coming of the Messiah and the nature of the Messianic age, with many of the interpretations tied to specific verses. Thus, for example, in one section in which various proposals are being offered for the name of the Messiah, it is suggested that his name could be Chaninah, based on Jeremiah 16:13 ("So I will throw you out of this land into a land neither you nor your fathers have known, and there you will serve other gods day and night, for I will show you no favor [Hebrew, *chaninah*]."), while another suggestion is offered that the Messiah's name is Menachem son of Hezekiah, based on Lamentations 1:16 ("No one is near to comfort [Hebrew, *menachem*] me, no one to restore my spirit."). Similar examples—in the Talmud, Targum, and Midrash—could easily be multiplied.

In light of all this, I ask you once more: Whose interpretation of the Messianic texts is the more sober and systematic, the Jewish authors of the New Testament, or the Jewish authors of the Rabbinic texts? Clearly, it is the former.[321]

Believers in Jesus truly do have solid support for their conviction that he indeed fulfilled the Messianic prophecies, especially when comparison is made between Yeshua, our true Messiah, and some of the notable false Messiahs who gained widespread acceptance among Rabbinic leaders. How ironic it is that anti-missionaries accuse Messianic Jews of being unscholarly and uneducated when we claim that Jesus is the prophesied Messiah! There is quite a double standard here. Just look at the Messianic fervor that surrounded the warrior Bar Kochba, hailed as Messiah by Rabbi Akiva, the leading sage of his generation and one of the heroes of the Talmud. Yet Bar Kochba was not a teacher, or a miracle worker, or a peacemaker, nor was he born at the right time or in the right place. On what basis, then, was he hailed as the Messiah of the Scriptures? Or what were the Messianic credentials of the manic-depressive Shabbetai Svi, the massively popular false Messiah of the seventeenth century? What prophecies did he fulfill? Yet some of the greatest rabbis of his day became his followers based on his personal charisma coupled with some incredibly far-fetched mystical interpretations. Or what of the revered leader of the Lubavitcher Hasidic Jews, Menachem Mendel Schneerson, known as the Rebbe. Years after his death in 1994 his followers are *still* claiming that he was Messiah. On what scriptural basis? (See further vol. 1, 1.6 and 2.2.)

Yet followers of Yeshua are required to dot every *i* and cross every *t* in our interpretation of the Messianic prophecies—which we are still happy to do—while followers of the Rebbe (or in past generations, followers of Shabbetai Svi or Bar Kochba) can make Messianic claims for their leaders with virtually no straightforward biblical support at all. There is an unfair double standard here. In addition to this, antimissionaries can make a good case in the abstract ("When the Messianic prophecies are fulfilled, everyone will know it because there will be universal peace on earth," etc.), yet the Talmudic literature is far from clear on this subject, and as stated, false messiahs have appeared throughout Jewish history, sometimes gathering large followings, despite the fact that they fulfilled none of the key Messianic prophecies.[322]

A very sincere traditional Jew once told me that the burden of proof was on me if I claimed that Yeshua was the Jewish Messiah. Traditional Jews, he argued, had nothing to prove. I beg to differ, since our Messianic candidate has already fulfilled many clear and significant biblical prophecies, and he is the Jew through whom more people have come to worship God than any other Jew in history (multiplied a thousandfold!). And to this day, in his name, miracles still happen. Who do you say that he is?

4.33. Jesus fulfilled none of the *provable* Messianic prophecies!

> By "provable" Messianic prophecies, I assume you mean prophecies that refer to the Messiah bringing about an end to war and ushering in a universal golden age, or the Messiah regathering the exiles of Israel and rebuilding the Temple. But these are not the only provable Messianic prophecies, and there are some very important, provable prophecies of worldwide significance that Jesus—and only Jesus—has fulfilled, giving us every reason to expect that when he returns to earth, he will fulfill the rest.

I'll divide my answer into four parts: (1) provable prophecies fulfilled by Yeshua that no one else can ever fulfill, (2) provable prophecies fulfilled by Yeshua of a worldwide, indisputable nature, (3) provable prophecies that continue to be fulfilled, and (4) provable prophecies yet to be fulfilled.

1. Provable prophecies fulfilled by Yeshua that no one else can ever fulfill. The Tanakh gives clear indications that the Messiah had to come before the Second Temple was destroyed, since the prophets predicted that the Lord himself would visit that Temple, that its glory would be greater than the glory of the First Temple (Solomon's Temple), and that final atonement would be made before the Second Temple's destruction. (For an extensive discussion, see vol. 1, 2.1–2.2.) But that Temple was destroyed in 70 C.E., meaning that either the Messiah came right on schedule, almost two thousand years ago, setting in motion the plan of redemption and deliverance for Israel and the nations, or that there will never be a Messiah, since he failed to come at the appointed, prophesied time. I choose to believe the former.

Was there any Jewish figure other than Yeshua who fulfilled these time-dated prophecies? If it was not Yeshua, who then? And is there no significance to the Talmudic statement that "all the appointed times [lit., "ends," meaning the appointed times for the Messiah's coming] have passed and the matter is dependent only on repentance and good deeds" (b. Sanhedrin 97b)?[323]

In a sense, these are the most important of all the so-called provable prophecies, since they prove the trustworthiness of the ones who prophesied them as much as they prove the trustworthiness of the one who fulfilled them. In other words, how do we know that the end-time predictions of the prophets will really come to pass if their past, dated, already provable prophecies did not come to pass? Conversely, if their initial, now-past prophecies came to pass, we can be confident that their still-future prophecies will come to pass as well. Thus, we can say with assurance that since Yeshua has fulfilled the past prophecies, he will fulfill the future prophecies as well.

2. Provable prophecies fulfilled by Yeshua of a worldwide, indisputable nature. Messianic Jews point to many prophecies fulfilled by Jesus (see above, 4.32), but anti-missionaries respond by saying, "These cannot be *proven*." For example, we point out that the Messiah was born in Bethlehem, as Micah prophesied (see above, 4.4). Anti-missionaries respond by saying either "Prove it!" or "The Messiah could *still* be born in Bethlehem." We point out that his sufferings paralleled in detail those of the righteous sufferer of Psalm 22 (see above, 4.24). Anti-missionaries respond by saying either "Prove it!" or "Anyone could suffer those very things, and that does not make him the Messiah." But the problem arises for the anti-missionaries when we look at those prophecies pointing to the Messiah's world-wide influence, especially among the Gentile nations.

According to Genesis 49:10, the obedience of the peoples will be his; according to Isaiah 42:4, the islands will wait for his teaching; according to Isaiah 49:6, he would be a light to the nations, bringing salvation to the ends of the earth; according to Isaiah 52:15, kings will shut their mouths before him in worshipful adoration (see above, 4.1, especially for Gen. 49:10). Yeshua has fulfilled much of this and continues to fulfill this in dramatic fashion. More than one billion people—people of the nations, Gentiles, formerly without God and without hope—have come to worship and adore the God of Israel because of Yeshua's death and resurrection. This certainly proves something!

Name for me one other human being (let alone one other Jew) who has come anywhere near fulfilling these verses. There is none.[324] Therefore, we have confidence that we will see the totality of what is promised in these and related verses (namely, worldwide peace, the destruction of the unrepentant wicked, and the worldwide rule of God), through the one who came when the prophets declared he would come and did what the prophets said he would do.

Just consider how utterly absurd it would have seemed if as you stood at the foot of the cross as Yeshua suffered a torturous, igno-minious, shameful death, someone told you, "Two thousand years from now, this man will be the world's most famous Jew and world history will be divided into the years before his birth and the years after his birth. Hundreds of millions of people from all world reli-gions will forsake their idols and their dead traditions and will instead become followers of the God of Israel through him." Yet this is literal truth, without a hint of exaggeration. We dare not downplay the sig-nificance of this. And remember that it was in Psalm 22 that the world-wide impact of the Messiah's death and resurrection were foreshad-owed, the Scriptures plainly declaring that as a result of his deliverance from death, the Gentiles would turn to the one true God (see above, 4.24). This is *very* provable, and it has unfolded in the most supernat-ural ways imaginable (see vol. 1, 2.2), also pointing to the reality of his resurrection, a tremendously important topic that deserves sepa-rate discussion (see vol. 4, 5.15).

It is also important to remember that some of the same verses that prophesied the Messiah's acceptance by the Gentiles also prophesied his (temporary) rejection by his own Jewish people (see, e.g., Isa. 49:1–7; Isa. 52:13–53:12; note also the principle of Ezek. 3:1–7). Of course, someone could easily object to this and say, "The Jewish people have rejected many false Messiahs. Jesus' rejection by his own people can hardly be used as a proof of his true Messiahship." And there would certainly be truth to this objection. The simple fact that Jesus was rejected by the majority of our people and then embraced by (primarily) the Gentiles does not prove that he was the Messiah. However, *someone* has to fulfill those prophecies. There must be one Jew who would be rejected by his people, who would suffer and die and rise from the dead, whose name would be revered by Gentiles in every nation, who would turn multitudes back to the God of Abraham, Isaac, and Jacob, and who would then be received by his own brothers after the flesh.

Yeshua is that Jew, and it is no coincidence that today there are more Jews following him than at any time since the first century, perhaps numbering as high as two hundred thousand. When you add to all this the fact that he was born at the right time, in the right place, with the right lineage (see vol. 4, 5.10–5.12), there can be no question at all that he is our promised Messiah.

3. *Provable prophecies that continue to be fulfilled.* The prophetic Scriptures also indicated that the Messiah would perform miraculous deeds of healing and deliverance—opening blind eyes, making cripples whole, setting prisoners free from the bondage of sin—thus demonstrating that he was the anointed of the Lord, God's agent of mercy and restoration (see Isa. 35:1–7; 42:1–7; 49:5–6; 61:1–3).[325] The New Testament gives abundant testimony to these very miracles taking place throughout the ministry of Yeshua. Naturally, you could challenge this testimony and ask, "Who says these stories are true?" and I would grant you the validity of that challenge. Many ancient texts contain all kinds of accounts of extravagant miracles and death-defying miracle workers. This is actually the core of many mythological writings. How do we know that the New Testament writings are different?[326]

My answer might surprise you, but stay with me for a moment and I believe it will make perfect sense. The New Testament records not only that Jesus himself performed these miracles but that his followers also performed these supernatural acts. This served as a proof of the resurrection of the Messiah, which was also an event of extraordinary importance that was prophesied hundreds of years prior to his death. The Book of Acts records that when a man lame from birth was healed through Peter and John in the name of Yeshua, Peter explained to the crowds:

> Men of Israel, why does this surprise you? Why do you stare at us as if by our own power or godliness we had made this man walk? The God of Abraham, Isaac and Jacob, the God of our fathers, has glorified his servant Jesus. You handed him over to be killed, and you disowned him before Pilate, though he had decided to let him go. You disowned the Holy and Righteous One and asked that a murderer be released to you. You killed the author of life, but God raised him from the dead. We are witnesses of this. By faith in the name of Jesus, this man whom you see and know was made strong. It is Jesus' name and the faith that comes through him that has given this complete healing to him, as you can all see.
>
> Acts 3:12b–16

The Messiah not only died; he rose from the dead, sending the Holy Spirit down on his followers and thus empowering them to do the same things he did while on the earth.[327] If he was not truly the Messiah but rather was an impostor, and if he did not perform miraculous deeds by the power of the Spirit but rather by psychical or demonic power, his counterfeit miracles would have died with him. The New Testament records the exact opposite, demonstrating that he was indeed alive and well, continuing to heal and deliver through his earthly representatives.

"But," you say, "that still proves nothing. Why should I believe the account you just gave about the lame man? It's *still* taken from your New Testament."

Once again, you raise a good point. How do we know for sure that the witness of the New Testament is true? It is simply because Yeshua our Messiah is alive and not dead, appointed by God his Father to be the Lord of all (Acts 2:36; 10:36)—which means that he is *still* performing miracles of healing and deliverance for those who call on his name.

I am not claiming that those who follow the Messiah are exempt from hardship and pain, that they are never sick, that they do not die in accidents and natural disasters, that they can simply snap their fingers and receive a miracle, that they are never frustrated by the mystery of unanswered prayer. Not at all. Nor am I saying that other religious groups—and even nonreligious groups—have no claims of contemporary miracles. I am simply saying this: (1) The biblical prophets declared that certain miracles would characterize the ministry of the Messiah on the earth; (2) Yeshua performed those very miracles; and (3) he is still performing them today. For many of my fellow Jewish followers of Jesus, it was not an eloquent argument that persuaded them that he was truly the Messiah, nor was it a study of the Messianic prophecies (although many Jews do, in fact, come to know him through these very texts). Rather, it was the fact that in Jesus, they encountered the reality of the one true God. They experienced God for themselves, either in deep conviction of personal sin and guilt, followed by liberating and transforming forgiveness, or in an undeniably supernatural path that led straight to the Lord, or through a miraculous healing or deliverance when they called on Yeshua's name.[328] In many cases, it was only after experiencing "new birth" and being persuaded beyond a doubt that Jesus was our Messiah and King that these men and women began to engage in serious discussion with rabbis or anti-missionaries, going back to the Scriptures and discovering to their delight that Jesus is the one spoken of by Moses and the Prophets and the Psalms.[329]

Lest you downplay the importance of personal experience, the Torah emphasizes the importance of each generation having its own encounter with God (see Deut. 5:1–4; 11:1–7), and the psalmist took it as a sign of divine judgment when there were no signs and wonders among the people (Ps. 74:1–9). And what is true for the nation as a whole was true for individuals: God did not want his people to have a merely theoretical knowledge of him, simply knowing *about* him. He wanted them to *know him*. This, in fact, is one of the clearly expressed goals of the new covenant, prophesied by Jeremiah, as it is written, "'They will all know me, from the least of them to the greatest,' declares the LORD. 'For I will forgive their wickedness and will remember their sins no more'" (Jer. 31:34b). Note also the related prophecy of Ezekiel: "I will give you a new heart and put a new spirit in you; I will remove from you your heart of stone and give you a heart of flesh. And I will put my Spirit in you and move you to follow my decrees and be careful to keep my laws" (Ezek. 36:26–27).

Do *you* know him? Have all your sins and wicked deeds been forgiven? Has the old heart of stone been replaced by a heart of flesh? Does God's Spirit really live in you? If you say, "But that is reserved for the Messianic age!" I reply, "But the Messianic age has already begun!" This too is provable—and of great importance, since in the end, everything comes down to your relationship with God and the condition of your own soul. These weighty issues are ultimately personal matters between you and him. You will stand alone before God when you give account for your life, and only you can decide how you will respond to his Word today, while you are alive and breathing.

The prophet Joel declared that God would pour out his Spirit on all flesh, a promise that began its journey to fulfillment in Acts 2:1–21, fifty days after the resurrection of the Messiah on the biblical Feast of Weeks (Shavuot, or Pentecost).[330] Joel then declared, "And everyone who calls on the name of the LORD will be saved" (Joel 2:32a[3:5a]), a text quoted several times in the New Testament with reference to Yeshua (e.g., Rom. 10:13). This too is a provable prophecy!

So, if you recognize your need for forgiveness and mercy; if you understand that God is holy and you are not; if you understand that he desires to deliver you from every bondage and addiction—physical, emotional, and spiritual—and remake you in his image; if you are ready to surrender your life and will to his service, becoming part of his family; if you are considering whether Jesus is really the Messiah, the anointed of the Lord, then call out to God in his name, asking him to save you from your uncleanness and guilt, putting yourself completely in his hands. He will answer from heaven!

4. Provable prophecies yet to be fulfilled. What then of the Messianic prophecies that remain to be fulfilled, such as Isaiah 2:1–5 and Isaiah 11:1–9, which predict universal peace? The answer is obvious: The one who *already fulfilled* every provable prophecy that had to be fulfilled up until this time is the one who will fulfill the rest. Certainly, this is the only reasonable, logical, and scripturally consistent answer. It is no mystery, then, who this Messiah will be that will come with the clouds of heaven. He will be the one who was despised and rejected by his own people, the one who became a light to the nations, and the one who will *return* and establish his Father's kingdom in Jerusalem.

4.34. Even modern Christian scholars reject the so-called Old Testament proof texts about Jesus. Just check most modern Christian Bible commentaries and translations.

> Those "Christian" scholars who reject the so-called proof texts to which you refer are the very same scholars who reject any clear expectation of a Messiah of any kind—Jewish or Christian—in the Hebrew Scriptures. Their findings

are just as incompatible with traditional Judaism as they are with traditional Christianity. On the other hand—and you might find this interesting—most of these very same scholars fully recognize the New Testament methods of interpreting the Hebrew Scriptures as thoroughly Jewish, in keeping with the style of the Dead Sea Scrolls and later Rabbinic writings, except often more sober! In any case, the real issue is not whether these scholars believe that Jesus is the prophesied Messiah of the Tanakh. The issue is: Is Jesus, in fact, that prophesied Messiah?

The point of this objection is not whether or not Jesus is the Messiah spoken of in the Hebrew Bible; the point is whether or not Christian scholars believe that he is. The answer is really quite simple: Christian scholars who accept the New Testament as the inspired, infallible Word of God believe that Jesus fulfilled the Messianic prophecies; Christian scholars who reject the New Testament as the inspired, infallible Word of God are not in agreement on this. But they are not in agreement on many other issues that most Christians consider to be fundamentals of the faith (such as the Messiah's virgin birth, his literal resurrection from the dead, salvation being found only in him, etc.), and thus they separate themselves from the vast majority of Christian believers through the centuries. Some would say that in a certain sense, they are "Christian" in name only, since they deny the foundations of "Christianity."

It's also interesting to note that these same scholars who reject the New Testament as the inspired, infallible Word of God also reject the Hebrew Scriptures as the inspired, infallible Word of God. And many of them reject the idea that Jesus fulfilled the Messianic prophecies simply because they don't believe the prophets actually prophesied about a Messiah! So, their problem is not necessarily with Yeshua; their problem is with a whole different set of beliefs.

A similar situation can be found in Judaism. Reform Jews deny the binding authority of the Torah; they deny the verbal inspiration of the Five Books of Moses; they deny that Moses wrote the Five Books; they deny that there was an oral law going back to Moses; they deny that there will be a literal Messiah who will reign on the earth. The list could easily be multiplied, but the bottom line is this: Jewish scholars who are fundamentalist believers—representing the minority of those who teach at Jewish seminaries and institutes of higher learning in America—literally believe all these things which liberal

Jewish scholars—representing the majority of Jewish professors in America—reject.

What does this prove? Simply that "believers" hold to one set of beliefs and "nonbelievers" don't hold to those beliefs. So, believing Christian scholars believe that Jesus fulfilled the prophecies, and liberal (or nonbelieving) Christian scholars don't. Therefore, the objection raised here is factually untrue and really proves nothing.

More importantly, there are many learned Christian scholars, some of whom are recognized authorities in the Hebrew Bible, the Hebrew language, biblical interpretation, Semitic studies, and even Rabbinic literature, who believe that Yeshua fulfilled the Messianic prophecies and that the New Testament authors rightly interpreted the prophecies of the Tanakh. This is true of the current generation of scholars, and it has been true for hundreds of years. Again, this does not prove that Yeshua *is* our promised Messiah, but it does prove that your objection is untrue and that many sincere, learned people find ample evidence to support their faith in Jesus (see vol. 1, 1.12).

Thus, it is not surprising that conservative Christian and Messianic Jewish commentaries on the Bible continue to hold to the view that Yeshua fulfilled the Messianic prophecies; conservative Christian and Messianic Jewish studies on the Messianic prophecies themselves continue to support that same view; and the most widely used modern Christian translations of the Bible continue to translate the original texts in harmony with the view that Jesus fulfilled the prophetic Scriptures. (The most widely used modern Christian versions of the Bible are the New International Version, the New American Standard Bible, and the New King James Version, all of which support the position I am taking here.) Of course, this does not prove that these commentaries, special studies, or Bible translations are correct. It simply proves that the objection raised here is not true.

What *is* interesting is that many of the same liberal scholars who deny the verbal inspiration of the Bible *do* recognize the Jewishness of the New Testament texts and the need to interpret these texts against the Jewish background of the day. Thus, while they may not actually believe that a given prophet delivered a specific prophecy about the Messiah—and consequently, they do not believe that Yeshua specifically fulfilled that prophecy—they often feel that the New Testament author who cited that prophecy was following normal Jewish/Rabbinic patterns of interpretation, as reflected in the

Talmud, Targums, and Midrash. In other words, just as the Talmudic rabbis interpreted the Hebrew Bible, so also did the authors of the New Testament, almost all of whom were Jews. What is even more interesting is that some recent scholarly studies have demonstrated that the (Jewish) methods of interpretation reflected in the New Testament are more sober and biblically consistent than those of the (Jewish) Dead Sea Scrolls and later Jewish literature (meaning classical Rabbinic literature). (For more on this, see vol. 4, 5.1.)

So, we return to where we started. The question is not, Which scholars believe Jesus is the promised Jewish Messiah? The question is, What do the prophecies say? As we have indicated clearly in answering the objections in this volume, the prophecies point to him.

4.35. Jesus cannot be the Messiah because the Messiah was to be a reigning king, whereas Jesus was despised, rejected, and crucified.

> The prophetic Scriptures indicate that first the Messiah would suffer and then he would reign. This is exactly what happened: Jesus-Yeshua—who is one of us and has identified himself totally with us—joined us in our suffering, rejection, and pain. We have suffered torture and death; he too was tortured and killed. We have been mocked, maligned, and misunderstood; to this day, he is the butt of ugly jokes and a common curse on people's lips. (When people get angry, they don't yell, "Moses!" or "Buddha!" or "Muhammad!" but "Jesus Christ!") But whereas we have often suffered because we were guilty, he suffered because he was innocent—and he did it for us. Therefore, Jesus was and is the perfect Messiah for us, the ideal Savior for a despised and rejected people.

We have addressed this objection elsewhere (see vol. 1, 2.1 and vol. 2, 3.23), demonstrating that the Hebrew Bible pointed to a suffering-then-reigning Messiah, while many Jewish traditions also spoke of a suffering Messiah. Recently, some prominent biblical and Semitic scholars, Israel Knohl of the Hebrew University in Jerusalem and Michael Wise of the University of Chicago's Oriental Institute, have argued that *even before the time of Jesus*, there was a Jewish belief in a suffering Messiah, something which scholars have debated for many decades.[331] In all probability, the proposals of Wise and Knohl will stir further scholarly debate and dialogue in the decades to come, and without a doubt, their proposals will be considered correct by some and unsupportable by others.

What is much more clear is the testimony of Scripture, including the following biblical testimony:

- According to Isaiah 52:13–15, a passage widely recognized as a Messianic prophecy in traditional Jewish circles (see above, 4.6–4.8), the servant of the Lord would suffer terrible humiliation before being highly exalted and raised up. The following chapter in its entirety (53:1–12) spells this out in detail.

- According to Zechariah 9:9–10, the king whose reign will extend over the entire earth will come meek and lowly, riding on a donkey. (According to Rashi and b. Sanhedrin 98a, this is King Messiah.)

- According to Zechariah 12:10, cited once as a Messianic prophecy in the Talmud, the Messiah will be pierced and killed. Zechariah 13:7 also prophesies that the shepherd—a highly significant figure—will be smitten, causing the sheep to be scattered (see above, 4.31).

- According to Psalm 118:22 (a psalm with strong Messianic implications), the stone rejected by the builders will become the capstone. This is in keeping with the biblical pattern in which *the Lord himself* was a stone of stumbling to his people. See Isaiah 8:12–15, where it is declared that the Lord "will be a sanctuary; but for both houses of Israel *he will be a stone that causes men to stumble and a rock that makes them fall. And for the people of Jerusalem he will be a trap and a snare. Many of them will stumble; they will fall and be broken, they will be snared and captured*" (Isa. 8:14–15). Note also Isaiah 28:16–19, where the Lord says, "See, I lay a stone in Zion, a tested stone, a precious cornerstone for a sure foundation; the one who trusts will never be dismayed" (v. 16)—yet for the ungodly in Jerusalem, that stone would mean judgment (vv. 17–19). Thus, we see that just as God himself was both the rock of salvation and the rock of offense for his people, being rejected by the majority during biblical times, the same pattern holds true for the Messiah.

I pointed out when addressing the question of the Holocaust (vol. 1, 2.10), that Yeshua is the Messiah we need, our ideal representative. Would we rather have someone who was only a lofty king who exercised total authority, a royal figure who could not possibly relate to the sting of public rejection and ridicule, who had never tasted the humiliation of being stripped and beaten by taunting soldiers and had never been challenged, never misunderstood, never slandered, never repaid with evil for doing good? Is that the kind of Messiah we want? Or do we want a Messiah who suffers and then reigns, who dies and then lives again, who gives himself for us long before we give ourselves for him? The choice should be obvious.

In this light, the New Testament Letter to the Hebrews explains as follows:

> Since the children have flesh and blood, he too shared in their humanity. . . . For surely it is not angels he helps, but Abraham's descendants. For this reason he had to be made like his brothers in every way, in order that he might become a merciful and faithful high priest in service to God, and that he might make atonement for the sins of the people. Because he himself suffered when he was tempted, he is able to help those who are being tempted.
>
> Hebrews 2:14, 16–18

> Therefore, since we have a great high priest who has gone through the heavens, Jesus the Son of God, let us hold firmly to the faith we profess. For we do not have a high priest who is unable to sympathize with our weaknesses, but we have one who has been tempted in every way, just as we are—yet was without sin. Let us then approach the throne of grace with confidence, so that we may receive mercy and find grace to help us in our time of need.
>
> Hebrews 4:14–16

Messiah our King is also Messiah our High Priest—just as the Scriptures foretold. It could not be any other way.

And look at the worldwide reign of Jesus the King over the lives of countless tens of millions from every nation under the sun. They give him their total allegiance and loyalty. His reign is far, far greater and more influential than the reign of any Davidic king—including David himself—and this is only the beginning.

4.36. Jesus cannot be the Messiah because the Messiah had to rebuild the Temple, yet the Temple was standing in Jesus' day.

> There is a fatal flaw to your objection, since we know for a fact that many religious Jews in Jesus' day were expecting the coming of the Messiah in their lifetimes. This means they were not expecting the Messiah to rebuild the Temple; the Temple was already standing! As for the prophecies in the Hebrew Scriptures associating the rebuilding of the Temple with the work of the Messiah, we should point out that these prophecies were delivered during the time of the Babylonian exile and pointed to the rebuilding of the Second Temple—and that Temple was destroyed more than nineteen hundred years ago. This means that we must reinterpret these passages if we are to apply them to a future rebuilding of the Temple. In that case, it can be argued that these prophecies await the return of the Messiah, when he will establish his kingdom on the earth and build the Third Temple.

It is a widely held principle of traditional Judaism that the Messiah will rebuild the Temple. In fact, according to Maimonides, this is how the Messiah will be recognized:

> If a king will arise from the House of David who is learned in Torah and observant of the miztvot [commandments], as prescribed by the written law and the oral law, as David, his ancestor was, and will compel all of Israel to walk in [the way of the Torah] and reinforce the breaches [in its observance]; and fight the wars of God, we may, with assurance, consider him the Messiah.[332]
>
> If he succeeds in the above, builds the Temple in its place, and gathers the dispersed of Israel, he is definitely the Messiah.[333]

This scenario, however, is not universally held to by traditional Jews, as explained in the commentary to the above translation, where it is noted that

> The Rambam's [i.e., Maimonides'] source is the Jerusalem Talmud, Megillah 1:11 and Numbers Rabbah 13:2. By contrast, Rashi and *Tosafot* (Sukkah 41a) and Midrash Tanchuma, Pekudei, maintain that the third Temple is "the sanctuary of God, established by Your hands."

It is already completely built and is waiting in the heavens to be revealed.[334]

So, both the traditional Jewish sources (the Talmudic and midrashic writings) and the leading Rabbinic authorities (Rashi and Rambam) differ over this question. Nonetheless, it is understandable why the belief that the Messiah will be the one to rebuild the Temple in Jerusalem would be psychologically powerful since: (1) The destruction of the Temple in 70 C.E. was a devastating national tragedy, deeply affecting the psyche of the Jewish people. Since the Temple was destroyed over nineteen hundred years ago, it would seem that only a figure as great as the Messiah could rebuild it. (2) Traditional Jews pray three times daily for the rebuilding of the Temple, just as they pray for the Messianic era of redemption to come. This great event, then, plays a large role in the hopes of many of our people, and the longer the Temple remains in ruins, the more its restoration will seem to be a cosmic, end-time event associated with the work of the Messiah. Many Christians also believe that there will be a restored Temple in the Messianic era, although it is by no means a central doctrine and there is widespread disagreement on this subject among followers of Jesus (see vol. 2, 3.17).

The questions we must address here are: What does the Tanakh teach about the Messiah's role in the rebuilding of the Temple? And if the Messiah is to build a literal Temple in Jerusalem, when will this take place?

Given the importance placed on this subject by Maimonides—writing more than one thousand years after the time of Jesus—you might find it surprising to learn that there are very few Messianic prophecies in the Hebrew Scriptures that say anything about the rebuilding of the Temple, and those few that speak of it seem to be pointing to the rebuilding of the *Second Temple* in the sixth century B.C.E. The prophet Isaiah did not say a word about a restored or rebuilt Temple, nor did he link any such concept to the Messianic hope. He did speak of Messianic subjects such as the regathering of the Jewish exiles from the nations (Isa. 11:10–11), the abolition of war from the earth (Isa. 2:1–4; 11:1–9), the atoning death of the Messiah (Isa. 53:4–6), and salvation coming to the Gentile nations, all of whom would come to the house of the Lord in Jerusalem (Isa. 2:1–4; see also 19:16–25; 42:1–7; 49:5–7). But there is nothing at all about part of the Messiah's mission being the rebuilding of the Temple, let alone it's being a major part of his mission.[335]

Jeremiah, who lived to see the Temple's destruction in 586 B.C.E., has a number of key prophecies about the restoration of Jerusalem, including promises that the sounds of joy will once again be heard there—sounds of the bride and bridegroom, sounds of dancing and celebration—and that sacrifices will again be offered to the Lord (e.g., Jer. 33:10–11; see also vol. 2, 3.17). But there is no mention of the Temple's restoration, nor is there any explicit connection between the Temple and the Messiah anywhere in the book. Similar statements could be made concerning every one of the remaining prophetic books except Zechariah and Ezekiel. This is true for two reasons: (1) Some of the prophets lived during the days of the First Temple (such as Hosea, Amos, Isaiah, and Micah), while others lived during the days of the Second Temple (Malachi), therefore the rebuilding of the Temple was hardly an issue for any of these prophets. Rather, their issue was God's visitation at his Temple (see, e.g., Mal. 3:1–5). Thus, in Yeshua's day many Jewish people were expecting the Messiah to come to the Temple (which had been standing for more than five hundred years) rather than rebuild it. (2) The rebuilding of the Temple was *not* the primary work of the Messiah. Rather, his role was first to make atonement for his people as a priestly King, offering forgiveness and redemption to Israel and the nations, and then, through his redeemed people, to extend his kingdom throughout the world until he would return to earth and establish a reign of universal peace. At that time, if at all, the issue of a rebuilt Temple in Jerusalem would be a factor. Thus, *if* part of the Messiah's mission was to rebuild the Temple, it would be the tail end of his mission rather than the beginning (or even central) part of it.

As for the lengthy Temple prophecies of Ezekiel, studied in vol. 2, 3.17, it is important to observe that the prophet does not give any hint whatsoever that the Messiah will build this Temple, simply mentioning that "the prince" will worship there (see Ezekiel 44–46). In fact, Ezekiel doesn't say that anyone will build it. Rather, he is shown in a vision the fully built, glorious Temple of the Lord.

Where then are the alleged prophecies that the Messiah will build the Temple? They are found in only *one book* of the Hebrew Scriptures, and the passages in question are by no means a clear declaration that the Messiah will one day build a literal Third Temple in Jerusalem. In fact, Rashi believes there is nothing Messianic about the verses in question and that the prophecies refer exclusively to events that took place more than twenty-five hundred years ago. Let's look carefully at the relevant texts in the Book of Zechariah.

In the first half of Zechariah, there are two anointed leaders spoken of by the prophet—Joshua, the high priest, and Zerubbabel, the governor of Judah and a descendant of David (see Zech. 3:8; 4:1–14; 6:9–15). Both of these men serve as prototypes of "the Branch," a well-known Messianic title (Zech. 3:8; 6:12; Jer. 23:5; 33:15; cf. also Isa. 11:1),[336] and both of them were key players in the rebuilding of the Temple (the Second Temple) after the Babylonian exile (see the Books of Haggai and Ezra). But of Zerubbabel it is said, "The hands of Zerubbabel have laid the foundation of this temple; his hands will also complete it. Then you will know that the LORD Almighty has sent me to you" (Zech. 4:9). This seems to be fairly straightforward in meaning, reiterating the major role that Zerubbabel would play in the Temple's restoration.

The longer oracle, found in Zechariah 6:9–15, is more open to Messianic interpretation:

> The word of the LORD came to me: "Take silver and gold from the exiles Heldai, Tobijah and Jedaiah, who have arrived from Babylon. Go the same day to the house of Josiah son of Zephaniah. Take the silver and gold and make a crown, and set it on the head of the high priest, Joshua son of Jehozadak. Tell him this is what the LORD Almighty says: 'Here is the man whose name is the Branch, and he will branch out from his place and build the temple of the LORD. It is he who will build the temple of the LORD, and he will be clothed with majesty and will sit and rule on his throne. And he will be a priest on his throne. And there will be harmony between the two.' The crown will be given to Heldai, Tobijah, Jedaiah and Hen son of Zephaniah as a memorial in the temple of the LORD. Those who are far away will come and help to build the temple of the LORD, and you will know that the LORD Almighty has sent me to you. This will happen if you diligently obey the LORD your God."

This time, it is not Zerubbabel who is singled out but rather Joshua, seated as a royal priest, a prototype of "the man whose name is the Branch." What a fitting picture this is of Yeshua, our King and our great High Priest! (See above, 4.1 and 4.29, and more fully, vol. 1, 2.1.) But what exactly does this prophecy mean? How and when will this man called the Branch build the Temple of the Lord, and who are those who will come from "far away" and help build the Temple? I believe there are three possible answers to these questions, none of which exclude Jesus in the least.

The first possibility is on a purely historical level: Both Joshua and Zerubbabel were involved with the building of the Second Temple, and so their *historical actions* serve as types and shadows of *things to come*. It is true that Rashi sees no prophetic significance to these passages, stating, "Some interpret this [namely, the reference to "the Branch" in 6:12] as referring to the King Messiah but the entire context deals with the [time of the] Second Temple." And if that is the case, then that would mean that *there is not a single prophecy in the Tanakh predicting that the Messiah would build a future Temple*— thereby undermining this entire objection. Nonetheless, the Messianic imagery in the Hebrew Bible associated with the Branch is too clear to be denied, and it is also clear that Joshua and Zerubbabel serve as Messianic prototypes, the former as the (royal) high priest, the latter as the ruling son of David.[337] In light of this, I do not believe that Zechariah is speaking only of events that would take place in his lifetime but that he is delivering Messianic prophecies here as well. This would indicate that the literal building of the Second Temple by Joshua and Zerubbabel, the two Messianic prototypes, foreshadows the building of another Temple by the Messiah. But what kind of Temple will he build?

The second possibility is that this passage in Zechariah 6 is foretelling the building of a spiritual Temple, a house of the Lord made up of people, not wood and stones. This is a rich spiritual image that is found frequently in the New Testament writings, and it is an interpretation that makes very good sense when you consider the context. You see, the building of the Second Temple was already well under way when Zechariah delivered his prophecy, and it was the building of *that* Temple that was in view.[338] To think otherwise would be totally illogical, since there would be no way in the world that anyone hearing the prophecy would be thinking about building *another* Temple somewhere in the distant future. They were expending all their energies on building *that* Temple, the prophets were encouraging them to build *that* Temple (see Haggai 1–2; Ezra 5:1–2), and all their hopes and aspirations were caught up with *that* Temple.[339] How strange it would be for a prophet to bring a word of encouragement that "the Branch" (meaning the Messiah) would build a future Temple when the present Temple was not even fully rebuilt, let alone rebuilt, destroyed, and left in ruins for millennia. Hardly! This would be similar to someone standing in Japan during the early stages of the rebuilding of Hiroshima after World War II and prophesying that the city would be restored—but actually meaning that after it was rebuilt in the mid-twentieth century, it would be destroyed again hundreds of years later, then lie in ruins for more than a thousand years, then one day be restored.

Looking back at Zechariah's prophecy, then, it could be argued that the building of the physical Temple in Jerusalem by Joshua and Zerubbabel, both of whom were Messianic prototypes, foreshadows the building of a spiritual Temple by the Messiah himself. As we noted in vol. 2, 3.17, the new covenant Scriptures do not emphasize a holy building inhabited by God but rather a holy people inhabited by God. Here are two of the key references:

> Don't you know that you yourselves are God's temple and that God's Spirit lives in you? If anyone destroys God's temple, God will destroy him; for God's temple is sacred, and you are that temple.
>
> 1 Corinthians 3:16–17

> As you come to him, the living Stone—rejected by men but chosen by God and precious to him—you also, like living stones, are being built into a spiritual house to be a holy priesthood, offering spiritual sacrifices acceptable to God through Jesus [the Messiah].
>
> 1 Peter 2:4–5

What is especially interesting about this "spiritual Temple" concept is that its origins are found in the Tanakh, where the Lord declared that he would dwell in the midst of his people, just as he had promised to dwell in the midst of the Tabernacle/Temple (see vol. 2, 3.1–3.2). And so, when Paul (whose Hebrew name was Saul) exhorted Gentile followers of the Messiah to live as holy temples of the Lord, he backed up his exhortation by weaving together several passages from the Hebrew Bible:

> What agreement is there between the temple of God and idols? For we are the temple of the living God. As God has said: "I will live with them and walk among them, and I will be their God, and they will be my people" [see Lev. 26:12; Jer. 32:38; Ezek. 37:27]. "Therefore come out from them and be separate, says the Lord. Touch no unclean thing, and I will receive you [see Isa. 52:11; Ezek. 20:34, 41]. I will be a Father to you, and you will be my sons and daughters, says the Lord Almighty" [see 2 Sam. 7:14; 7:8]. Since we have these promises, dear friends, let us purify ourselves from everything that contaminates body and spirit, perfecting holiness out of reverence for God.
>
> 2 Corinthians 6:16–7:1

We should also point out that these quotes deepen the spiritual meaning of the verses cited within them. That is to say, the Lord promised his obedient people that his dwelling place would be in their midst (see, e.g., Lev. 26:12, referred to in the passage cited above), meaning that there would be a literal building, in a real geographical location in the land of Israel, in which God would manifest his glory. This also means that, due to its geographical location in one place in the land, few people would have regular access to this building, and therefore they would rarely, if ever, experience the reality of God's presence in their midst. With the coming of the Messiah into the world, all of God's people are indwelt by his Spirit—both individually and corporately—and now communion and fellowship with the Lord can be experienced directly and universally by one and all. This is in keeping with Ezekiel's prophecy to his Jewish people scattered among the nations:

> For I will take you out of the nations; I will gather you from all the countries and bring you back into your own land. I will sprinkle clean water on you, and you will be clean; I will cleanse you from all your impurities and from all your idols. I will give you a new heart and put a new spirit in you; I will remove from you your heart of stone and give you a heart of flesh. And I will put my Spirit in you and move you to follow my decrees and be careful to keep my laws. You will live in the land I gave your forefathers; you will be my people, and I will be your God.
>
> Ezekiel 36:24–28

Is the picture becoming more clear? This spiritual Temple is being built every day, as more and more people—both Gentiles and Jews—turn to the God of Israel through Yeshua the Messiah. And this Temple will be complete when Ezekiel's prophecy comes to pass and the Jewish people en masse are cleansed, renewed, and indwelt by the Spirit.

This spiritual concept also sheds light on the final verse of Zechariah 6, where it is stated, "Those who are far away will come and help to build the temple of the LORD" (v. 15a). In its immediate context, this could refer to men like Heldai, Tobijah and Jedaiah (all mentioned in Zechariah 6) who were exiles who had returned from Babylon. Such an interpretation is common.[340] However, if Joshua and Zerubbabel serve as earthly prototypes of coming spiritual realities, could it be that the Jewish exiles returning to Jerusalem are prototypes of the Gentile nations—all of whom are, in a sense, spiritual exiles—turning to the Lord? And could it be that just as the exiles came from far away and helped build the physical Temple in Jerusalem, these converted Gentiles will come from far away (both geographically and spiritually) and help build the worldwide spiritual Temple?[341]

We know that the prophets declared that the Gentile nations would come streaming to Jerusalem in the Messianic age to learn the ways of the Lord (see esp. Isa. 2:1–5; Mic. 4:1–3; cf. also Isa. 19:18–25), and we also know that Malachi prophesied that the Lord's name would be revered among the nations. As it is written in Malachi 1:11, "'My name will be great among the nations, from the rising to the setting of the sun. In every place incense and pure offerings will be brought to my name, because my name will be great among the nations,' says the Lord Almighty." But what is meant by the promise that "in every place incense and pure offerings will be brought to my name"? Will this be literally fulfilled, with offerings and incense being brought to the Lord from every location on the globe, or will the worshipers from every nation offer praise and prayer and adoration and service to the Lord, part of their spiritual ministry to God, part of their building a Temple fit for his dwelling?

Paul seems to give credence to the latter view, reminding Gentile followers of the Messiah that at one time they were "separate from [Messiah], excluded from citizenship in Israel and foreigners to the covenants of the promise, without hope and without God in the world. But now in [Messiah] Jesus you who once were *far away* have been brought near through the blood of [Messiah]" (Eph. 2:12–13). He then explains that Jesus "came and preached peace to you who were *far away* and peace to those who were near. For through him we both have access to the Father by one Spirit" (Eph. 2:17–18). And this leads to his final statement:

> Consequently, you are no longer foreigners and aliens, but fellow citizens with God's people and members of God's household, built on the foundation of the apostles and prophets, with Christ Jesus himself as the chief cornerstone. In him the whole building is joined together and rises to become a holy temple in the Lord. And in him you too are being built together to become a dwelling in which God lives by his Spirit.
>
> Ephesians 2:19–22

So then, those who were "far away" *did* come and help build the Temple of the Lord, with the Branch himself being the cornerstone and chief architect, thus fulfilling the prophecy of Zechariah (cf. also Isa. 57:15–19). Certainly, this interpretation deserves consideration and is a fitting complement to the earthly Temple imagery found in that prophetic book. It also makes sense when you realize that when the Messiah came into the world almost two thousand years ago, the Second Temple was still standing, having been elaborately beautified by Herod. The building of *that Temple* was obviously not in question. In fact, one of Yeshua's most unpopular pronouncements was that that glorious, imposing Temple would be totally destroyed! Yet, in the providence of God, before the earthly Temple in Jerusalem was demolished, a worldwide spiritual Temple consisting of redeemed Jews and Gentiles was being built.

Having said all this, there is still the third possibility that our Messiah will rebuild a physical Temple in Jerusalem when he returns to earth to destroy the wicked and establish his Father's kingdom. As I stated previously, this view is held to by some Christians, who see this as the culmination of God's promises to the house of Israel. If that is the case, then we can be sure that when Yeshua sets his feet on the Mount of Olives (see Zech. 14:1–5) and brings cleansing to the land (see Zech. 12:10–13:1), he will soon order the building of the final Temple (or else, in keeping with some traditional Jewish thought, that Temple will descend to earth).

Certainly, this is a subject for speculation. But one thing is sure: If there is to be a final glorious Temple to be built by the Messiah himself, we know who that Messiah will be!

What then do we make of the description of the Messiah outlined by Maimonides? There is no doubt but that he missed the mark, painting a picture of the Messiah that (1) would be in agreement with Rabbinic Judaism and (2) would rule out Yeshua as a candidate. And so after stating that all the prophetic books make mention of "this matter" (meaning the matter of the Messiah),[342] he immediately downplays the miracles of the Messiah—despite the fact that the prophets explicitly associated miraculous acts with the Messianic age (see, e.g., Isa. 35:5–7)—by stating, "One should not presume that the Messianic King must work miracles and wonders, bring about new creations within the world, resurrect the dead, or perform other similar deeds. This is definitely not true."[343] As explained in the commentary of Rabbi Eliyahu Touger, "The identity of the Messiah will not be determined by miracles and wonders, but rather, as explained in the following Halachah [legal statement], by his ability to lead the Jewish people to a more complete observance of Torah and Miztvot"[344]—meaning both the written and the oral law, as cited at the beginning of this objection. Maimonides even goes so far as to say that David himself observed both the written and the oral law, whereas the truth is that no one ever heard of such a thing as an authoritative "oral law" until more than one thousand years after the time of David.[345]

Yet there is more. Not only did Maimonides fashion the Messiah after the image of a great rabbi or Torah sage;[346] he also made it clear that anyone claiming to be the Messiah who died could not be the Messiah. Thus, speaking of the false messiah Bar Kochba (who died in the war against Rome in 135 C.E.), he writes that Rabbi Akiva "and all the Sages of his generation considered him to be the Messianic King until he was killed because of sins. Once he was killed, they realized that he was not [the Messiah]. The Sages did not ask him for signs or wonders."[347] This, then, would clearly exclude Jesus, who did work signs and wonders and who did die. The only problem with this exclusion is that Jesus performed signs and wonders in keeping with the prophetic promises and in fulfillment of his liberating Messianic role.[348] And he not only died, he rose from the dead—also in keeping with the prophetic Scriptures (see above, 4.13–4.14 and 4.23–4.24). Unfortunately, Maimonides failed to see the priestly role of the Messiah, of making atonement for the sins of Israel and the world, and the prophetic role of the Messiah, of bringing a message from heaven in the power of the Spirit.[349] It is also unfortunate to realize that for more than eight hundred years, most observant Jews have been more familiar with the Maimonidean description of the Messiah than with the biblical description, actually believing that his description *is* the biblical one. It behooves us to set the record straight.

4.37. The only true prophecy about Jesus in the Hebrew Scriptures is found in Zechariah 13:1–6—a passage dealing with false prophets. It even makes explicit reference to his crucifixion!

Actually, the passage of which you speak has nothing whatsoever to do with Jesus. To be sure, you are right in saying it is a prophecy about false prophets, but it makes no reference to crucifixion—the Hebrew actually speaks of wounds on the false prophet's back, not on his hands. The only references to the Messiah in this passage of Scripture are in the powerful, God-centered, repentance-based pas-

> sages that come before and after Zechariah 13:1–6. So, you
> have failed to recognize the true references to the Messiah
> in Zechariah 12–14 and have focused on the one passage
> that does not apply to him.

Now, I must admit that some Messianic Jews and Christians have been their own worst enemies here, getting excited about some English renderings of Zechariah 13:6 ("And one shall say unto him, What are these wounds in thine hands? Then he shall answer, Those with which I was wounded in the house of my friends." [KJV]) and immediately saying to themselves, "That's Jesus! That's a prophecy about Jesus!" Consequently, they have used this verse as a Messianic proof text, giving the anti-missionaries something embarrassing and erroneous to expose. This passage has nothing to do with Yeshua, and it is not Messianic in any sense of the word.

The context is quite clear, referring to a time of national cleansing in Israel's future when false prophets will be exposed (see Zech. 13:1–2, "'On that day a fountain will be opened to the house of David and the inhabitants of Jerusalem, to cleanse them from sin and impurity. On that day, I will banish the names of the idols from the land, and they will be remembered no more,' declares the LORD Almighty. 'I will remove both the prophets and the spirit of impurity from the land.'"). That time has not yet come; so it cannot apply to Yeshua's crucifixion two thousand years ago. As we continue reading, we see that Zechariah 13:3 provides further evidence that the text cannot refer to Jesus. It states: "And if anyone still prophesies, his father and mother, to whom he was born, will say to him, 'You must die, because you have told lies in the LORD's name.' When he prophesies, his own parents will stab him." This doesn't work either, since Jesus' parents didn't stab him! And how in the world could Zechariah 13:5 be applied to Jesus ("He will say, 'I am not a prophet. I am a farmer; the land has been my livelihood since my youth.'"), when Jesus earned his livelihood as a carpenter?

Of course, you might still ask, "What about verse 6, where the King James Version speaks of 'wounds in thine hands,' and anyone who can read Hebrew can see that this translation is accurate. That certainly seems to apply to Jesus—especially when the one speaking says he received the wounds in the house of his friends!"

Actually, that is *not* what the Hebrew says. In fact, no less a Hebrew authority than H. L. Ginsberg concluded that the Hebrew actually meant "on your back" (literally, "between your shoulders").[350] He demonstrated this in an article published in 1978, basing his conclusions on examples from the Ugaritic language (discovered in 1929 in Syria) and from the Tanakh itself. This helps to explain why the NJPSV, of which Ginsberg was the editor primarily responsible for the translation of the Prophets, rendered Zechariah 13:6, "And if he is asked, 'What are those sores on your back?' he will reply, 'From being beaten in the homes of my friends.'"[351] (Note again that the Hebrew says *"between* your hands/arms" and not *"on* your hands/arms.")

What makes this wrong interpretation all the more tragic is the fact that there are several very important Messianic passages surrounding Zechariah 13:1–6, which apply clearly and powerfully to Jesus, but these passages have been totally missed by the anti-missionaries. I speak of Zechariah 12:10–14, referring to Israel's repentance when they look at the pierced Messiah (see above, 4.31, and also 4.4); 13:7–9, speaking of the betrayal and smiting of the shepherd-Messiah, causing the flock to be scattered (for discussion of the Messiah's closeness to God, spoken of in v. 7, see 4.4); chapter 14 in its entirety, with specific reference to the Messiah's return (Zech. 14:4 says that his feet will touch the Mount of Olives when he comes to fight for his people; see again 4.4) and all nations coming to Jerusalem to celebrate the Feast of Tabernacles.

I encourage you not to be misinformed about the meaning of Zechariah 13:1–6—a passage that promises the exposure and eradication of false prophets in the land and that cannot possibly be applied to Yeshua in any way—and not to overlook the other glorious prophecies in Zechariah 12–14 pointing to the suffering, death, and return of the Messiah, so clearly referring to Jesus.

4.38. Paul claimed that the Hebrew Scriptures prophesied the resurrection of the Messiah on the third day. Nowhere in our Bible is such a prophecy found.

Paul's exact words are: "For what I received I passed on to you as of first importance: that Messiah died for our sins according to the Scriptures, that he was buried, that he was raised on the third day according to the Scriptures . . ." (1 Cor. 15:3–4). As a Jew schooled in the Scriptures from his childhood, Paul was not thinking of just one passage but of several passages that pointed to the Messiah's resurrection on the third day. And remember: Paul was not trying to "pull a fast one" on anybody! And no one had pulled a fast one on him either. This is the tradition he received, and if someone taught him something that was not in his Bible, he would have known it immediately. In fact, when we study the Tanakh, we see that the third day is often the day of completion and climax—and so it was with the Messiah's death and resurrection!

We should first look at some prophecies that make reference to restoration—or rescue from death—on the third day.

- Hosea 6:1–2 states, "Come, let us return to the LORD. He has torn us to pieces but he will heal us; he has injured us but he will bind up our wounds. After two days he will revive us; on the third day he will restore us, that we may live in his presence." This is a word given to Israel as a whole, but the sequence is there: full restoration on the third day![352]

- According to Genesis 22:4, it was on the third day that Abraham arrived at Mount Moriah and prepared to sacrifice his son Isaac—that important event known in later Rabbinic tradition as the Akedah, "the binding (of Isaac)"—an event seen as a Messianic foreshadowing by the rabbis (see above, 4.1). In similar fashion, the Letter to the Hebrews notes, "Abraham reasoned that God could raise the dead, and figuratively speaking, he did receive Isaac back from death" (Heb. 11:19)—and this took place on the third day.

- This was the time set for the miraculous healing of King Hezekiah, who as a son of David serves as somewhat of a Messianic prototype (cf. also b. Sanhedrin 94a, 98a): "Go back and tell Hezekiah, the leader of my people, 'This is what the LORD, the God of your father David, says: I have heard your prayer and seen your tears; I will heal you. On the third day from now you will go up to the temple of the LORD' " (2 Kings 20:5; cf. also v. 8).

- Jonah was in the belly of the fish for three days (a deathlike experience, to be sure!—cf. Jonah 2:1–9) before being spit out on dry land, and hence saved from his watery tomb (Jonah 1:17; 2:10). Jesus himself makes reference to this event in the context of his death and resurrection (see, e.g., Matt. 12:40).

Elsewhere in the Tanakh, it is striking to see how often the third day has special significance:

- God told the children of Israel assembled at Mount Sinai to be ready for the third day "because on that day the LORD will come down on Mount Sinai in the sight of all the people" (Exod. 19:10).
- After calling the people to fast for three days for divine intervention to save her Jewish people from annihilation, on the third day, Esther stood before the king and appealed for mercy (Esther 5:1).
- The building of the Second Temple was completed on the third day of the month of Adar (Ezra 6:15).
- On the third day after Joseph interpreted the dreams of two of his fellow prisoners—both of whose dreams included a symbolic "three"—one of the men was hung and the other man restored to his former position (Gen. 40:1–23).
- Sacrifices left until the third day could no longer be eaten but were to be wholly consumed by the altar's flames (Lev. 7:17–18; 19:6–7).
- It was on the third day—and in the third battle—that the Israelites defeated their Benjamite brothers in battle (see Judges 20, esp. 20:30).
- After three days the Israelites crossed the Jordan—by the miraculous intervention of God (Josh. 1:11; 3:2).[353]

Based on this biblical data, the German biblical scholar Roland Gradwohl argued that "'three days' is a stereotyped phrase used by the Old Testament in describing a situation when something will be fulfilled or completed within a useful and reasonable time. . . . The 'third day' is used to describe the moment when an event attains its climax."[354] Another German scholar, K. Lehmann, wrote an entire volume on the subject of resurrection on the third day, pointing to passages such as Exodus 19:11, 16; Genesis 22:4; 2 Kings 20:5; Esther 5:1; Hosea 6:2 (all cited above) as evidence that the third day was associated with special divine activity, something that caught the attention of the ancient rabbis as well.[355] These insights, coupled with some key verses about restoration, salvation, or rescue from death on the third day, give Paul the right to say that the Messiah rose from the dead on the third day according to the Scriptures. There would have been no day more suitable than this, from the viewpoint of the Word of God.[356]

4.39. I can find prophecies in the Bible that point to Muhammad just as easily as you can find prophecies that point to Jesus. That's because all of your so-called proofs are either distortions, make-believe creations, or Jewish midrash—free, homiletical interpretations—of the worst kind.

> Really? Then why didn't the Muslims find Muhammad everywhere in the Hebrew Bible? Why did they have to completely rewrite their own version of the Scriptures (i.e., the Koran) instead of referring back to the Hebrew Bible—the Word of God accepted by both Christians and Jews? And where does the Tanakh point to Muhammad's place of birth, or the time of his coming, or the manner of his death, or his alleged ascension to heaven? (Remember, the Hebrew Scriptures point to the place of Yeshua's birth, the time of his coming, the manner of his death, and his resurrection!) I also remind you that modern scholars—both Jewish and Christian—recognize that the authors of the New Testament were highly sophisticated in their interpretive techniques (see vol. 4, 5.1). Sorry, but you'll have to do better. Objections like this are hardly worthy of the name.

I want to appeal to you, Jewish reader, in the words of the Lord as spoken through the prophet Isaiah: "Come now, let us reason together" (Isa. 1:18a). Can I ask you to hear me out?

Maybe you've had many objections to the Messiahship of Jesus, believing that he really didn't fulfill the Messianic prophecies. But now you've seen each of these objections answered, systematically and comprehensively. Still, you're hesitant to believe. After all, generations of our people have rejected Jesus as Messiah, and it has only been a small Jewish minority that has acknowledged him as our promised Redeemer and King. But what if the minority is right? This would not be the first time such a thing has happened in our history! And what if God has not given us eyes to see and ears to understand until this day? What if now, in this day, the light is beginning to dawn, and little by little, more and more of our people are putting their faith in Yeshua as God's anointed one? What if this very thing was prophesied in the new covenant Scriptures? Well, it is!

The Jewish teacher Saul of Tarsus (known to most of the world as the apostle Paul) explained to Gentile followers of Jesus who were living in Rome that "Israel has experienced a hardening in part until the full number of the Gentiles has come in" (Rom. 11:25). In other words, for the better part of two thousand years, most of our Jewish people have experienced a degree of spiritual blindness when it comes to recognizing the Messiah. This is similar to what happened to our people when the nation of Israel came out of Egypt: We saw God's miracles, we heard God's voice, but we really didn't understand. As Moses said to that generation, "But to this day the LORD has not given you a mind that understands or eyes that see or ears that hear" (Deut. 29:4). And then the light went on, and God opened the eyes of a nation. At last they saw and understood!

This will happen again to the people of Israel before the Messiah returns. As Paul explained to the Roman believers, "the full number of Gentiles [will] come in" (meaning that a vast number of Gentiles from every tribe and language and people will turn to God and put their faith in Yeshua), and then "all Israel will be saved, as it is written: 'The deliverer will come from Zion; he will turn godlessness away from Jacob. And this is my covenant with them when I take away their sins'" (Rom. 11:26–27, citing Isa. 59:20–21). There will be a mass turning of the Jewish people to Yeshua the Messiah, and just as there has been a national, Jewish rejection of Jesus, there will be a national, Jewish acceptance of Jesus.

You see, many of our forefathers were guilty of rejecting Yeshua the Messiah when he came—despite his miracles, despite his sinless character, despite his atoning death, despite his glorious resurrection. And this set the pattern for the generations to come, as the children followed in the footsteps of their fathers, rejecting Yeshua because "Jews don't believe in Jesus." To make matters even worse, many hypocritical Gentiles who claimed to be Messianic believers (= Christians) were terrible examples, living compromised lifestyles and even persecuting Jews who didn't believe in Jesus. This only confirmed to our Jewish people that this Jesus was not for them.

Yet in spite of all this, there has always been a remnant of our people who have rightly recognized our Messiah, sometimes numbering more than one hundred thousand Jews in a generation. That is the case today, and the number of Jews who believe in Jesus is rising every year, even among the Orthodox and ultra-Orthodox. And in direct parallel to this is the ever-increasing number of Gentiles who are genuinely turning to Jesus—and I mean genuinely. (One of the clearest signs that these Gentiles are becoming true followers of Jesus is the fact that many of them are deeply devoted to the people of Israel, praying for them, fasting for them, supporting them in the Land, and standing with them when much of the world stands against them.)

Now the time has come for us to stop and think. Could it be that this Jesus Christ is really Yeshua our Messiah? Could it be that we have been wrong in rejecting him as our anointed leader? Could it be that now, in our generation, that great turning back will begin to take place, and our eyes will be opened en masse? I close this volume with A PLEA TO THE JEWISH COMMUNITY TO RECONSIDER THE POSSIBILITY THAT YESHUA (JESUS) OF NAZARETH IS OUR PROMISED MESSIAH AND REDEEMER. Consider the facts:

- *No other worthy Messianic candidates have arisen in the last two thousand years.* The positive world influence of Yeshua the Jew totally dwarfs the positive world influence of every other alleged Messianic candidate, including the most recent candidate, Menachem Schneerson, the Lubavitcher Rebbe.

- *Yeshua fulfilled the essential prophecies that had a definite time frame and that had to be completed before the Second Temple was destroyed.* This is not a matter of speculation. It is a matter of historical fact. And since he fulfilled the past prophecies (coming as our great High Priest, making atonement for our sins), we can be sure that he will fulfill the future prophecies (reigning as the worldwide King and bringing peace to the earth).

- *He identifies with us in our suffering.* For most of our history, we have been cast out, despised, rejected, and misunderstood. That is a picture of our Messiah too! Yeshua is the ultimate example of the suffering, persecuted Jew. He is not only one *of* us; he is one *with* us.

- *More than one hundred thousand Jews around the world recognize Yeshua as the Messiah, including a rapidly growing underground movement of Orthodox and Hasidic Jews who are convinced by the Scriptures that he is the one.* Messianic Jews can no longer be ignored or disregarded, and we are merely the firstfruits of something much larger—the national turning of Israel to our Messiah and King.

- *Every day, thousands of people around the world are coming to the God of Israel through Yeshua.* The fullness of the Gentiles *is* coming in, and on the heels of that, all Israel shall be saved. So it is written, and so it shall be.

And so I appeal to my Jewish people to take time to reconsider the Messianic claims of Yeshua of Nazareth. And I appeal to every individual Jew reading this book to seek God, study the Scriptures, put all biases and fears aside, and decide for yourself: Who is this man Jesus? This is a question you can't avoid.

I leave you with the words of Isaiah. Of whom does the prophet speak?

> See, my servant will act wisely;
>   he will be raised and lifted up and highly exalted.
> Just as there were many who were appalled at him—
>   his appearance was so disfigured beyond that of any man
>   and his form marred beyond human likeness—
> so will he sprinkle many nations,
>   and kings will shut their mouths because of him.
> For what they were not told, they will see,
>   and what they have not heard, they will understand.
>
> Who has believed our message
>   and to whom has the arm of the Lord been revealed?
> He grew up before him like a tender shoot,
>   and like a root out of dry ground.
> He had no beauty or majesty to attract us to him,
>   nothing in his appearance that we should desire him.
> He was despised and rejected by men,
>   a man of sorrows, and familiar with suffering.
> Like one from whom men hide their faces
>   he was despised, and we esteemed him not.
>
> Surely he took up our infirmities
>   and carried our sorrows,
> yet we considered him stricken by God,
>   smitten by him, and afflicted.
> But he was pierced for our transgressions,
>   he was crushed for our iniquities;
> the punishment that brought us peace was upon him,

and by his wounds we are healed.
We all, like sheep, have gone astray,
    each of us has turned to his own way;
and the Lord has laid on him
    the iniquity of us all.

He was oppressed and afflicted,
    yet he did not open his mouth;
he was led like a lamb to the slaughter,
    and as a sheep before her shearers is silent,
    so he did not open his mouth.
By oppression and judgment he was taken away.
    And who can speak of his descendants?
For he was cut off from the land of the living;
    for the transgression of my people he was stricken.
He was assigned a grave with the wicked,
    and with the rich in his death,
though he had done no violence,
    nor was any deceit in his mouth.

Yet it was the Lord's will to crush him and cause him to suffer,
    and though the Lord makes his life a guilt offering,
he will see his offspring and prolong his days,
    and the will of the Lord will prosper in his hand.
After the suffering of his soul,
    he will see the light of life and be satisfied;
by his knowledge my righteous servant will justify many,
    and he will bear their iniquities.
Therefore I will give him a portion among the great,
    and he will divide the spoils with the strong,
because he poured out his life unto death,
    and was numbered with the transgressors.
For he bore the sin of many,
    and made intercession for the transgressors.

Isaiah 52:13–53:12

Appendix

"You don't know what you're talking about!"

"You're completely misinterpreting Isaiah!"

"This verse has absolutely *nothing* to do with your Jesus! The fact is, it's not even a Messianic prophecy!"

"As for the *real* Messianic prophecies, Jesus fulfilled none of them."

Have you ever had these arguments thrown out at you? Do you know how to answer them? Here are some important keys and principles that will help you to see that, in fact, Yeshua fulfilled the prophecies of the Hebrew Scriptures.

1. Messianic prophecies are not clearly identified as such.

There is not a single verse in the entire Hebrew Bible that is specifically identified as a Messianic prophecy. Nowhere do the Scriptures say, "The next paragraph contains a prediction of the Messiah!" Thus, whether or not one accepts a certain passage as Messianic depends largely on how one understands the person and work of the Messiah.

For example, if someone believes that the Messiah will be a king who will bring peace to the earth, he will probably interpret Isaiah 11 as a Messianic prophecy. But he will not interpret Isaiah 53 in a Messianic way *because it does not fit his preconceived notion of what the Messiah will do*. And so, when we point to Isaiah 53, he will confidently say to us, "But that is not a Messianic prophecy!"

How can we answer his argument? Just ask a simple question: "Who says Isaiah 53 is *not* Messianic while Isaiah 11 *is* Messianic? Who says your interpretation is right?" In other words, help him to see that his understanding of Messianic prophecy is based on *traditional bias* as opposed to *objective scriptural truth*. Thus, rather than being put on the defensive (isn't this where we often end up?), we can challenge his objectivity. Maybe it is he who has brought preconceived notions to the text. If he is open to dialogue, you can take things a step further and ask, "Are you sure your picture of the Messiah is correct? Maybe you are missing some of the pieces to the puzzle! How do you know that Messiah hasn't already come?" And from there you can show him the way!

2. The Messianic hope in Israel developed gradually.

This helps explain why Messianic prophecies were not clearly identified as such: They were not initially understood as referring to *the Messiah*. Also, the Hebrew word *mashiach* (Messiah), which literally means "anointed one," almost never refers to *the Messiah* in the Hebrew Bible. Instead, it refers to the anointed king (like Saul or David), the anointed high priest (like Aaron), or even an "anointed" (chosen) foreign ruler (like Cyrus).

Let's apply this to the Messianic hope in Israel. David was a great king, a *mashiach* of the Lord; so was his son Solomon, who had a wonderful reign of peace. Many of the Psalms were written for them or about them: among others, Psalm 72, which is a prayer for Solomon; Psalm 2, which celebrates the coronation of the king; and Psalm 45,which commemorates the royal wedding ceremony. And when all was well, God's people recognized no need for *the Messiah*.

But when Israel's kings began to fail, when there were no more Davids or Solomons, and when the Jewish people were exiled from the Land, they began to realize their need for a special *mashiach*, supernaturally anointed by God. And what do you think happened when they went back and reread the Psalms? They began to see the Messianic significance of the verses! They recognized, for example, that Psalm 2, which prophesied *the worldwide dominion* of the Lord's anointed, was *not* fulfilled by David, Solomon, or any other king. Only *the Messiah* could fulfill this prophecy. And so, little by little, they began to understand the Messianic hope.

3. Many biblical prophecies are fulfilled gradually.

This key principle applies to *all types* of prophecy, whether Messianic or not. This is implied by the word "fulfill": The prophet's words had to be "filled up to the full" to be "fulfilled."

Ezekiel, *living in Babylonian exile*, prophesied that his people would return from their captivity. The fulfillment *began* in 538 B.C.E., when the first group of exiles returned to Judah; it has *continued* in the twentieth century with the return of the Jewish people to the Land; and it *will reach fulfillment* when Jesus comes back and gathers his scattered people from every corner of the globe. Over twenty-five hundred years and this prophecy is still being fulfilled!

Now let's look at a Messianic prophecy. Zechariah prophesies that when Israel's King comes, he will be "righteous and having salvation, gentle and riding on a donkey. . . . His rule will extend from sea to sea and from the River to the ends of the earth" (Zech. 9:9–10). If you show this to a rabbi, he will probably say, "It's clear that Jesus hasn't fulfilled it!"

How should you respond? Simply explain to him that the prophecy *is presently being fulfilled* (i.e., it is in the ongoing process of fully coming to pass): Jesus *came* as the prophet foretold, "righteous and having salvation, gentle and riding on a donkey"; *every day* the number of individuals over whom he reigns as king continues to increase (countless millions from every country!); and *in the future,* when he returns, he will completely establish his rule.

4. The prophets saw the Messiah coming on the immediate horizon of history.

Have you ever stood on top of a mountain and looked across to another mountain peak? The mountains appear to be next to each other, even though there is a huge valley in between. It is the same with biblical prophecy. *The prophets saw the future through a telescope.* Things far away in time appeared close. They did not realize that centuries would come and go between their initial prediction and its actual fulfillment. In fact, to the prophets, the expression "at the end of days" could have meant "right around the corner"!

This principle is important to understand with regard to Messianic prophecy because we are often accused of taking a verse "out of context." We are told, "That prophecy applied to Isaiah's day twenty-seven hundred years ago. It certainly does not refer to Jesus!" But did it *really* apply to Isaiah's day, or was it an example of prophecy being telescopic? Did Isaiah see the coming of the Messiah (i.e., a great deliverer) *in the context of his very own day?*

Let's look at Isaiah 9:1–7 (8:23–9:6 in some Bibles), where it is predicted that the yoke of the enemy (i.e., Assyria) would be broken by the son of David *who was already born.* And this son of David would have an everlasting kingdom of peace. When was Assyria crushed? Twenty-six hundred years ago. Who was born shortly before that time? Hezekiah. Did he *fulfill* the prophecy? Obviously not! But the prophet saw the coming of the future Davidic ruler as if it were about to happen in his very own day.

Watch carefully for prophecies like this, since they are extremely common. In fact, this key to prophetic interpretation is really a summary of the first three principles just given. If you go back and read them again, things will begin to fall into place for you.

5. It is important to read every prophecy in its overall context in Scripture.

Do the writers of the New Testament take Old Testament verses out of context, or are they faithful to the meaning of the text? In Matthew 1:23, Isaiah 7:14 is applied to the birth of Jesus ("The virgin [or maiden] will be with child and will give birth to a son, and they will call him Immanuel"). But is this quotation faithful to Isaiah? How can Matthew apply *a sign given to King Ahaz in about 734 B.C.E.* to the birth of Yeshua over seven hundred years later? How could this be a relevant sign?

Consider the context of Isaiah chapters 7–11. Judah was being attacked by Israel and Aram. These nations wanted to replace Ahaz, who represented the house of David (see Isa. 7:2, 13), with their own man named Ben Tabeel. *This would mean the end of Davidic rule in Judah.* Yet when Ahaz would not ask God for a sign, God gave him his own: A child named Immanuel (meaning "God is with us") would be born, and within a few years, before the child was very old, Judah's enemies would be destroyed.

Who was this Immanuel? Obviously a child to be born to the house of David in place of faithless Ahaz. This child would be a token of the fact that God was with his people. (In other words, good news for the nation and bad news for Ahaz!) But is this Immanuel's birth ever mentioned in the Book of Isaiah? No! In fact, the birth of Isaiah's son Maher-Shalal-Hash-Baz in Isaiah 8:1–4 *seems to take its place as a time setter* (read Isaiah 7:14–16 and 8:3–4; before Maher-Shalal-Hash-Baz would be very old, Judah's enemies would be destroyed—just what was said about Immanuel!).

What happened to Immanuel? Nothing is clearly said. But what is clearly said in Isaiah 9:6–7 (9:5–6 in some Bibles) and 11:1–16 is that there will come forth a rod from Jesse (David's father) who will rule the nations in righteousness.

And this was Matthew's context! He was reading Isaiah 7–11 in full! Thus, he quotes Isaiah 7:14 in Matthew 1:23; Isaiah 9:1–2 (8:23–9:1 in some Bibles) in Matthew 4:15–16; and he alludes to Isaiah 11:1 in Matthew 2:23 (the Hebrew word for "Nazarene" resembles the Hebrew word for "branch").

Was anyone born in Isaiah's day that began to fulfill the Immanuel prophecy? We simply do not know. But of this we can be sure: Jesus, the ideal King from the house of David, and clearly the subject of the Messianic prophecies in Isaiah 9 and 11, is Immanuel—God with us— in the fullest sense of the word!

6. The Messiah was to be both Priest and King.

Everyone who believes in the Messiah accepts the *royal* prophecies of the Scriptures as referring to Messiah the King. But what about the predictions of *suffering?* What do *these* verses have to do with the Messiah?

Here is an important answer! *The prophecies of suffering and death point to the priestly ministry of the Messiah, since it was the duty of the high priest to intercede for his people and make atonement for their sins.*

Did you know that in the first century of this era there was widespread belief in the coming of a *priestly* Messianic figure as well as a *royal* Messianic figure? This belief was almost correct. There *was* to be a priest and there *was* to be a king, only these two figures were one! According to Psalm 110, the Davidic ruler was to be both priest and king. In Zechariah 6, *the crown* is placed on the head *of the high priest* named Joshua (he is also called *Yeshua* in Ezra and Nehemiah!), who is then referred to as "the Branch," a Messianic title!

Thus, it is clear that the Messiah would have a dual role: As High Priest he would take his people's sin on himself and intercede for them; as King he would rule and reign. Because traditional Judaism has largely forgotten the Messiah's priestly work, it has not always recognized key passages in Isaiah as referring to him.

7. The Messiah is the ideal representative of his people.

In ancient Israel, the king and his people were one. As the kings of Israel went, so went the nation. The people saw themselves represented in their head.

How does this apply to the Messiah? First, the history of Israel paralleled the life of Jesus. For example, when Moses was born, Pharaoh was trying to kill Israelite baby boys. Also, both the nation of Israel and Jesus spent their early years in Egypt. (*That* is why Matthew quotes Hosea 11:1 in Matthew 2:15! Compare also Matthew 2:20 with Exodus 4:19.)

And because the Messiah was the ideal representative of his people, *he fulfills the words of the Psalms.* Thus, Psalm 22, the psalm of the righteous sufferer whom God wonderfully delivers, is not at all identified as a Messianic prophecy. Yet to any impartial reader, it is clear that both the depth of suffering described as well as the universal effects of the deliverance can refer only to Jesus, the ideal righteous Sufferer, the representative King, the one greater than David. Therefore, the New Testament writers often see the Psalms as containing Messianic prophecies, since the Messiah is seen as their ultimate, representative subject.

How can you put all these principles together? Every time you see a Messianic prophecy quoted in the New Testament, look it up in the Old Testament and read the whole section from which it is taken (this could be a paragraph, a chapter, or even more). Then try and see which of the interpretive keys presented here explains the quote. Remember, often several principles are at work together!

Not only will you enrich your understanding of the Word, but you will learn to appreciate how wonderfully God has woven together the prophecies of the Messiah's coming.

And *then* what should you do? Share your discoveries with an interested Jewish friend!

Notes

1. Maimonides follows the traditional Jewish interpretation of Numbers 24:17–18, understanding the text to refer to both David and the Messiah: "'I see him, but not now'—this refers to David; 'I perceive him, but not in the near future'—this refers to the Messianic King; 'A star shall go forth from Jacob,'—this refers to David; 'and a staff shall arise in Israel'—this refers to the Messianic King; 'crushing all Moab's princes'—this refers to David, as [2 Sam. 8:2] relates: 'He smote Moab and measured them with a line;' 'dominating all of Seth's descendants'—this refers to the Messianic King regarding whom [Zech. 9:10] prophesies: 'He will rule from sea to sea.' 'Edom will be demolished'—this refers to David, as [2 Sam. 8:6] states 'Edom became the servants of David;' '[Seir] will be destroyed'—this refers to the Messianic King, as [Obad. 1:21] prophesies: 'Saviors will ascend Mount Zion [to judge the mountain of Esau].'" See Rabbi Eliyahu Touger, ed. and trans., *Maimonides, Mishneh Torah: Hilchot Melachim U'Milchamoteihem, Laws of Kings and Their Wars* (Brooklyn: Maznaim, 1987), 226–28, rendering Maimonides' Laws of Kings and Their Wars 11:1. Although the commentary supplied by Touger points to David as "the epitome of a Jewish king [who] led the Jewish people to a much more complete observance of Torah and Mitzvot" (226), it is clear that the text in Numbers 24 speaks only of the military triumphs of the prophesied leader, not his qualities as a Torah teacher. Thus, we see a twofold Rabbinic eisegesis here (that is, reading one's own ideas into the biblical text): (1) the reference to two leaders (David and the Messiah) rather than one (who could well be a prototype of the Messiah), and (2) the reference to David as a Torah leader rather than as a military leader. Targum Onkelos uses the term *meshicha'* (the Aramaic equivalent to Hebrew *mashiach*) twice in the entire Torah, Genesis 49:10 and Numbers 24:17; for Genesis 49:10, see below, end of 4.1.

2. If as a Jew you have a problem with this comparison, seeing that the Akedah is "your story" and I am using it to point to Jesus, I remind you that the Akedah in the Bible is my story too—as a Jewish follower of Yeshua the Jew and as one reading my sacred Scriptures. In applying it to the Messiah, I am only doing what the ancient rabbis also did: taking an important account from our Scriptures and using it to illustrate a central theological truth. With regard to the significance of the Akedah in traditional Judaism, note the following petition, recited daily (except on the Sabbaths and festivals) by Rabbinic Jews: "Remember on our behalf—O Lord, our God—the love of the Patriarchs, Abraham, Isaac and Israel, Your servants; the covenant, the kindness, and the oath that You swore to our father Abraham at Mount Moriah, and the Akeidah, when he bound his son Isaac atop the altar, as it is written in Your Torah" (Genesis 22:1–19 follows and is also read on the Sabbaths and festivals, when the preceding

petition is omitted; see *The Complete Art Scroll Siddur,* translated with an anthologized commentary by Rabbi Nosson Scherman [Brooklyn: Mesorah, 1987], 23). After the reading from Genesis 22, the following petition is offered up (reproduced only in part here because of its length): "Master of the universe! . . . Just as Abraham our fore-father suppressed his mercy for his only son and wished to slaughter him in order to do Your will, so may Your mercy suppress Your anger from upon us and may Your mercy overwhelm Your attributes. May You overstep with us the line of Your law and deal with us—O LORD, our God—with the attribute of kindness and the attribute of mercy" (ibid., 25).

3. A well-known midrash in the Talmud (b. Sanhedrin 89b) amplifies God's dia-logue with Abraham, heightening the tension of the narrative. When God told Abra-ham to take his son, he replied, "I have two sons" (meaning Isaac and Ishmael). The Lord then said, "Your only one," to which Abraham countered, "This one is the only son of his mother and that one is the only son of his mother." God then clarified fur-ther, explaining, "Whom you love," and Abraham replied, "I love them both!" It was then that the Lord said, "Isaac," putting an end to the interaction. The ensuing dia-logue between Satan and Abraham (an insightful Talmudic fiction; b. Sanhedrin 89b) has some acute spiritual insights, brought out by the later commentators (conveniently collected in the Schottenstein edition of Art Scroll [Brooklyn: Mesorah, 1995], 89b[3-4]).

4. For relevant literature on the Akedah and the Messiah, see Louis A. Berman, *The Akedah: The Binding of Isaac* (Northvale, N.J.: Aronson, 1997); and Aharon (Ronald E.) Agus, *The Binding of Isaac and Messiah: Law, Martyrdom, and Deliverance in Early Rabbinic Religiosity* (Albany: State Univ. of New York Press, 1988). See also the clas-sic work of Shalom Spiegel, *The Last Trial: On the Legends and Lore of the Command to Abraham to Offer Isaac as a Sacrifice: The Akedah,* translated with an introduction by Judah Goldin (repr., Woodstock, Vt.: Jewish Lights, 1993).

5. Some scholars have also pointed out that Moses was not recognized the first time he sought to deliver his people Israel from Egypt but only the second time, after many years (Exod. 2:11–14; see also Acts 7:25: "Moses thought that his own people would realize that God was using him to rescue them, but they did not."). For more on the concept of a rejected-hidden-revealed Messiah, cf. Raphael Patai, *The Messiah Texts* (Detroit: Wayne State Univ., 1979), xxx–xxxv. For additional thoughts on the parallels between Joseph and Jesus, see vol. 2, 3.24.

6. The term *scapegoat* is derived from the words "escape goat," since it escaped into the wilderness. For recent studies on the Hebrew phrase *la'az'azel,* which lies behind the scapegoat concept, cf. Jacob Milgrom, *Leviticus 1–16: A New Translation with Intro-duction and Commentary,* Anchor Bible (New York: Doubleday, 1991), 1020–21.

7. See b. Zevahim 68b for additional, relevant discussion; cf. also b. Moed Katan 28a.

8. The word *Tanakh,* which is an acronym for *Torah* (= Law of Moses), *Nevi'im* (= Prophets), and *Ketuvim* (= Writings, the most prominent part of which is the Psalms), reflects this same threefold division of the Hebrew Scriptures.

9. Merrill C. Tenney, "John," in the *Expositor's Bible Commentary* (Grand Rapids: Zondervan, 1979), 9:48 (henceforth cited as *EBC*). See also Ronald B. Allen, "Num-bers," *EBC,* 2:878–79. For a different perspective, cf. Baruch A. Levine, *Numbers 21–36: A New Translation with Introduction and Commentary,* Anchor Bible (New York: Dou-bleday, 2000), 85–90.

10. According to Albert Barnes, "The points of resemblance between his being lifted up and that of the brass serpent seem to be these: (1) In each case those who are to be

benefited can be aided in no other way. The bite of the serpent was deadly, and could be healed only by looking on the brass serpent; and sin is deadly in its nature, and can be removed only by looking on the cross. (2) The mode of their being lifted up. The brass serpent was in the sight of the people. So Jesus was exalted from the earth raised on a tree or cross. (3) The design was similar. The one was to save the life, the other the soul; the one to save from temporal, the other from eternal death. (4) The manner of the cure was similar. The people of Israel were to look on the serpent and be healed, and so sinners are to look on the Lord Jesus that they may be saved" (commenting on John 3:14; see *Barnes' Notes on the New Testament* (Electronic Edition, STEP Files, Copyright 1999, Parsons Technology).

11. Cited by Risto Santala, *The Messiah in the New Testament in the Light of the Rabbinical Writings,* trans. William Kinnaird (Jerusalem: Keren Ahvah Meshihit, 1992), 133.

12. Scholars have debated for years whether prophecy completely ceased in the years between the Hebrew Bible and the New Testament writings or whether it simply decreased and played a less prominent role. For recent discussion and relevant bibliography, cf. the following two articles: Frederick E. Greenspahn, "Why Prophecy Ceased," *Journal of Biblical Literature* 108 (1989): 37–49; and Benjamin Sommer, "Did Prophecy Cease? Evaluating a Reevaluation," *Journal of Biblical Literature* 115 (1996): 31–37.

13. For discussion of relevant sources from the Dead Sea Scrolls and early Samaritan literature, cf. N. A. Dahl, "Messianic Ideas and the Crucifixion of Jesus," in James H. Charlesworth, ed., *The Messiah* (Minneapolis: Fortress, 1992), 386–87, 400–401. Speaking of ancient Jewish Messianic expectations, Dahl notes (386), "The expectation of another such person [in addition to a royal Messianic figure and an eschatological priestly figure], that of a prophet like Moses, was based upon Deut 18:15–19 and/or upon the expanded text of Ex 20:19–22 in the Samaritan Pentateuch and 4QBibParaph (= 4Q158)." For a more comprehensive study, cf. John J. Collins, *The Scepter and the Star: The Messiahs of the Dead Sea Scrolls and Other Ancient Literature* (New York: Doubleday, 1995), 116–22. According to Collins (116), "The eschatological prophet is a shadowy figure, not only in the Scrolls, but generally in the Judaism of the time," with reference to H. M. Teeple, *The Mosaic Eschatological Prophet,* Society of Biblical Literature Monograph Series, 10 (Philadelphia: Society of Biblical Literature, 1957). Collins suggests, however, that according to some key texts from the Dead Sea Scrolls, "the Messiah, whom heaven and earth will obey, is an anointed eschatological prophet, either Elijah or a prophet like Elijah" (120). See further Peter C. Craigie, *Deuteronomy,* New International Commentary on the Old Testament (Grand Rapids: Eerdmans, 1976), 263, n. 20, with reference to R. M. Grant, *Gnosticism and Early Christianity,* 2d ed. (New York: Columbia Univ. Press, 1966), 91, for Samaritan speculation about the identity of "the prophet."

14. Some irenic Jewish scholars (such as Pinchas Lapide) have suggested that if Jesus actually does return as Messianic King, then at that time the Jewish people will know that he was truly the Messiah. (For a relevant study by Lapide, cf. idem, *The Resurrection of Jesus: A Jewish Perspective* [Minneapolis: Augsburg, 1983]; see also idem, *Israeli Jews and Jesus,* trans. Peter Heinegg [Garden City, N.Y.: Doubleday, 1979].) But does Scripture give us the right—let alone the leisure—to simply wait and see? Is this God's primary way of calling his people to obedience? And who says that you or I will be alive when Yeshua returns? What if we pass away first? It is in this life that we must make up our minds about what we will do with this one called Jesus.

15. For representative Rabbinic discussion on the concept that there has never been another prophet like Moses, cf. Abraham Hirsch Rabinowitz, *The Study of Talmud: Understanding the Halachic Mind* (Northvale, N.J.: Aronson, 1996), 91.

16. Cf. further Michael Rydelnik, "Inner-Biblical Perspectives on Messianic Prophecy," in *Mishkan* 27 (1997): 43–57.

17. For an excellent treatment of Genesis 49:10, see Walter Riggans, *Yeshua ben David: Why Do the Jewish People Reject Jesus as Their Messiah?* (Crowborough, England: Marc, 1995), 308–30.

18. Genesis 3:15 has often been pointed to as the first Messianic prophecy in the Bible (thus, it is called the protoevangelium) and has an interpretive history dating back to the second century (see Claus Westermann, *Genesis 1–11*, trans. J. J. Scullion, S.J. [Minneapolis: Augsburg, 1984], 260–61, for details). Some Jewish traditions also speak of an ultimate fulfillment of this passage in Messianic times (see the Targums). However, I do not see this as a direct prophecy of Yeshua; rather, I understand it on two levels: (1) the immediate, contextual—and wholly natural—level (enmity between humans and snakes; humans killing the snakes, and snakes biting their heels); and (2) the larger, contextual—and more spiritual—level, reflected in Romans 16:20 (mankind's ultimate, but costly, triumph over Satan; this, of course, comes through the cross but cannot be limited to a prophecy of the cross); cf. further Joseph Shulam with Hilary LeCornu, *A Commentary on the Jewish Roots of Romans* (Baltimore: Messianic Jewish Publishers, 1998), 522–23. For a defense of the Messianic interpretation with reference to the Rabbinic sources, cf. Santala, *The Messiah in the Old Testament in the Light of Rabbinical Writings*, trans. William Kinnaird (Jerusalem: Keren Ahvah Meshihit, 1992), 37–42; see also Walter C. Kaiser Jr., *The Messiah in the Old Testament* (Grand Rapids: Zondervan, 1995), 37–42; Arnold G. Fruchtenbaum, *Messianic Christology* (Tustin, Calif.: Ariel, 1998), 14–15. For a fair discussion of the Messianic use (and abuse) of Genesis 3:15, cf. Riggans, *Yeshua ben David*, 287–307.

19. The NIV text notes offer the following alternative translations: "until Shiloh comes"; "until he comes to whom tribute belongs."

20. The footnote to this passage reads, "Shiloh, understood as *shai loh*, 'tribute to him,' following Midrash; cf. Isa. 18:7. Meaning of Heb. uncertain; lit., 'Until he comes to Shiloh.'"

21. Note that only the Stone edition, reflecting exclusively Orthodox Jewish scholarship, renders Hebrew *mehoqeq* ("lawgiver" or "ruler's staff") as "scholar." However, the translators indicate in the brief commentary included in the footnotes that Shiloh refers to the Messiah, and "all nations will acknowledge him and pay homage to him." For more detailed discussion of some of the history of these varied interpretations, cf. Riggans, *Yeshua ben David*, 311–14.

22. Ibid., 330.

23. Generally speaking, Numbers 24:17–18 is the primary passage pointed to by later Jewish tradition (see above, n. 1). I would point out again that the oral law—*the* foundation of traditional Judaism—is not explicitly mentioned once in the entire Torah. See vol. 4, 6.1–4.

24. My translation; the NIV renders, "Open my eyes that I may see wonderful things in your law."

25. Rabbi Shmuel Boteach, *The Wolf Shall Lie with the Lamb: The Messiah in Hasidic Thought* (Northvale, N.J.: Aronson, 1993), 7.

26. Ibid., 4, his emphasis. Rabbi Boteach also emphasizes the need to long for the Messiah's arrival (ibid.).

27. For background on this movement and for further information on the Lubavitcher Hasidim, see vol. 1, 1.6 and 2.2. See further the eye-opening volume of Professor David Berger, *The Rebbe, the Messiah, and the Scandal of Orthodox Indifference* (Oxford: Oxford University Press, 2001). In light of the principle of redemptive analogies, presented in vol. 2, 3.15, the very facts that cause professor Berger such alarm are the same facts that greatly encourage me. Romans 11:26!

28. "All About Moshiach: Questions and Answers (XI)," *The Jewish Press*, 15 January 1993, 19. It is also important to remember that Rambam (Maimonides), whose teaching on the Messiah is accepted without question by most traditional Jews, lists progressive signs through which one can identify the Messiah. As translated by Touger, *Laws of Kings and Their Wars*, 232, rendering Law of Kings 11:4, "If a king will arise from the House of David who is learned in Torah and observant of the mitzvoth, as prescribed by the written law and the oral law, as David his ancestor was, and will compel all of Israel to walk in [the way of the Torah] and reinforce the breaches [in its observance]; and fight the wars of God, we may, with assurance, consider him the Messiah [or, we may presume him to be the Messiah]. If he succeeds in the above, builds the Temple in its place, and gathers the dispersed of Israel, he is definitely the Messiah." The point is simple: The notion that one fine day you will be able to open the window, look at the world, and say, "What do you know! The Messiah has come!" is not even in accord with Jewish tradition, let alone biblical truth.

29. Cf. similarly Eliyahu Touger, *When Moshiach Comes* (Jerusalem and New York: Feldheim, 1997).

30. I find it interesting that all over Israel large billboards proclaim the Lubavitcher Rebbe as Messiah, years after his death in 1994 (without a resurrection). His followers are still calling for Jews to believe in him.

31. Matthew 1:23 agrees with the Septuagint here, reading, "will be with child" (Greek, *en gastri exei*); other translations understand the text to say, "The *'almah* is pregnant and about to give birth to a son." Both views are supportable by the grammar and context, the primary question being how one renders the participial *harah* ("is pregnant" versus "will conceive"). Delitzsch recognizes the grammatical issues but argues for a future understanding of the prophecy (the virgin conceives and bears a son) because, he claims, the Hebrew word *hinneh*, "behold," "is always used by Isaiah [seventy-eight times in total] to introduce a future occurrence." See F. Delitzsch, *Isaiah*, in C. F. Keil and F. Delitzsch, *Commentary on the Old Testament*, trans. James Martin and others, CD ROM ed. (Albany, Ore.: AGES Software, 1997), 183. Note that the Orthodox Jewish Stone edition renders the verbs as future: "Therefore, my Lord Himself will give you a sign: Behold, the maiden will become pregnant and bear a son, and she will name him Immanuel." The grammatical explanation for this rendering is that a predicate adjective and/or participle derives its tense from the surrounding verbal context, and in this verse, that context seems to be future (the Lord *will give* you a sign). See further Hans Wildberger, *Isaiah 1–12*, trans. Thomas H. Trapp (Minneapolis: Fortress, 1991), 286, n. 14d, where Wildberger notes, "Whether the participle is to be translated in a present or a future sense can be determined only on the basis of a full treatment of the entire section" (referring to the Septuagint and other Greek recensions). G. B. Gray, *The Book of Isaiah, 1–27*, International Critical Commentary (Edinburgh: T. & T. Clark, 1912), 127, presents both translations ("is with child and shall bear" and "shall be with child and bring forth") as possible.

32. There is dispute whether either or both of these occurrences are proper names ("Immanuel") or rather the words "God is with us"; for discussion, see the standard

commentaries and cf. Jacob Licht, "Immanuel," *Encyclopedia Miqra'it* (in Hebrew), (Jerusalem: Bialik Institute, 1950–82), 6:292, where it is pointed out that the name Immanuel is unique, found only here in the Scriptures, and otherwise unattested in ancient Near Eastern sources.

33. It is interesting to note that the Haftorah (or Haphtarah) selection from these chapters (meaning the weekly reading in the synagogues from the prophetic Scriptures) links chapters 7 and 9 together with the Torah portion called Yitro (i.e., Jethro, consisting of Exodus 18:1–20:26). The specific passages from Isaiah are 6:1–7:6; 9:5–6[6–7]. A cursory reading of these verses would indicate that God's answer to the threat to remove the Davidic king in Isaiah 7 is the birth oracle in Isaiah 9. How interesting! I would only add that God's *first* answer to the threat is found in Isaiah 7 itself, the Immanuel prophecy, which then ties in with the birth oracle in chapter 9. We will take this up in more detail in our ongoing discussion.

34. According to Delitzsch (*Isaiah*, 179–80, on Isa. 7:10–12), "A sign . . . was something, some occurrence, or some action, which served as a pledge of the divine certainty of something else. This was secured sometimes by visible miracles performed at once (Ex 4:8–9), or by appointed symbols of future events (Isa 8:18; 20:3); sometimes by predicted occurrences, which, whether miraculous or natural, could not possibly be foreseen by human capacities, and therefore, if they actually took place, were a proof either retrospectively of the divine causality of other events (Ex 3:12), or prospectively of their divine certainty (Isa 37:30; Jer 44:29–30). The thing to be confirmed on the present occasion was what the prophet had just predicted in so definite a manner, viz., the maintenance of Judah with its monarchy, and the failure of the wicked enterprise of the two allied kingdoms. If this was to be attested to Ahaz in such a way as to demolish his unbelief, it could only be effected by a miraculous sign."

35. This, of course, represents the traditional Christian view. For statements to this effect from early Christian leaders, see David W. Bercot, ed., *A Dictionary of Early Christian Belief: A Reference Guide to More Than 700 Topics Discussed by the Early Church* (Peabody, Mass.: Hendrickson, 1998).

36. One of the most respected Jewish scholars of the last generation, H. L. Ginsberg, longtime professor of Bible at the Jewish Theological Seminary, actually questioned the Hebrew text in its current form, since in his judgment there was no real sign recorded. "Immanuel," in the *Encyclopedia Judaica*, CD ROM ed. (Israel: Judaica Multimedia, 1997), states Ginsberg's views as follows: "It will become obvious, on reflection, that where the sign stands in the received text, between verses 10–14a and 17, it is inapposite, for two reasons: first, verse 11 leads us to expect here a sign 'down in Sheol or up in the sky'; and second, the tone of verses 13–14a and verse 17 leads us to expect an omen that bodes ill for Judah, not for Aram and Israel. The [Talmudic sage] R. Johanan (Sanh. 96a) rightly inferred from Isaiah 38:8 that prior to abruptly receding ten steps in the reign of Hezekiah the shadow has abruptly advanced ten steps in the reign of Ahaz (for us that involves regarding *be-ma'alot*, 'on the steps of' before Ahaz as a contamination, due to the four other occurrences of *ma'alot* in the same verse, of an original *bi-Yme*, 'in the days of'). Taking a hint from R. Johanan, Ginsberg inferred that this is the 'sign' that was originally related between 7:14a and 7:17. In summary, Ginsberg claims "the Immanuel sign is unhistorical." This again indicates the thorny problems of interpretation that surround Isaiah 7:14.

37. For a scholarly evangelical perspective on the evidence, cf. John H. Walton, "Isaiah 7:14: What's in a Name?" *Journal of the Evangelical Theological Society* 30 (1987): 289–306; idem, "*'alûmîm,*" *New International Dictionary of Old Testament Theology and*

Exegesis, ed. Willem VanGemeren (Grand Rapids: Zondervan, 1997), 3:415–419 (henceforth cited as *NIDOTTE*). For full citations from lexical and theological articles, arguing for the meaning of "virgin," cf. Glen Miller, "Response to 'The Fabulous Prophecies of the Messiah,' part 2, The Isaiah 7:14 Passage," <http://www.christian-thinktank.com/fabprof2.html>.

38. The masculine noun is also common in various Semitic languages; cf. B. Dohmen, *"'almâ,"* in *Theological Dictionary of the Old Testament*, ed. G. Johannes Botterweck and Helmer Ringgren, trans. David E. Green and others (Grand Rapids: Eerdmans, 1974), 11:155–56 (henceforth cited as *TDOT*). Referring primarily to evangelical writing on this subject, Walton rightly asks, "Why is it never mentioned that there are two masculine occurrences of this noun *('elem)*? In 1 Sam 17:56 David is described as an *'elem*, and the same term is applied to Jonathan's servant in 20:22. In neither of these cases is the sexual chastity of the individual a viable issue" ("Isaiah 7:14," 292). Walton, however, may have overlooked the fairly thorough 1980 article by Richard Niessen, "The Virginity of the *'Almah* in Isaiah 7:14," *Biblotheca Sacra* 137 (1980): 133–50 (see 135, where he notes that "the masculine derivative *'elem* 'young man,' is used in 1 Samuel 17:42, 56, and possibly 16:12. . . . First Samuel 20:22 uses *'elem* to describe the servant whom Jonathan sent out to chase arrows").

39. The derivation from the root *'-l-m*, "to hide, be hidden," has been suggested for centuries and remains popular to this day. However, there is no compelling reason to connect the concept of "being hidden" with that of being a virgin, especially since some of the *'almah*s referred to in the Tanakh went about freely in public and were anything but hidden (see, e.g., Gen. 24:43 and esp. Ps. 68:25[26]; I am aware, of course, that there were other alleged aspects of the *'almah*'s "hiddenness," but none are worthy of serious consideration). More importantly, there is a strong reason to connect Hebrew *'elem/'almah* with the Arabic root *ġ-l-m*, since both the verbal and nominal forms occur there (relating to coming into puberty and/or adolescence; or for animals, being in heat), and the nominal forms correspond to this root in Ugaritic (a Northern Canaanite language very close to Hebrew), in which the noun *ġlmt* (probably pronounced *ġalmatu*) occurs in the context of a goddess giving birth to a son (see below, n. 62, for further discussion), as well as in the context of the marriage of a king (the masculine form of this noun, *ġlm*, occurs frequently and simply means "young man"). Readers who have studied the Semitic languages know that in ancient Hebrew, the letter *'ayin* (which is the first letter of the words *'elem/'almah*) represented two distinct phonemes, namely, *'ayin* and *ġayin*, just as several letters in our English alphabet represent two distinct phonemes (e.g., the letter *c* can be pronounced as *s* or *k* even in the same word, like "circus," while the letter *g* can be pronounced *g* or *j* as in the word "garage"). So, e.g., the Philistine city of Gaza is spelled *'azzah* in Hebrew and would be pronounced *azzah*, not *gazzah*, by any Hebrew reader today. However, we know that it was originally pronounced *ġazzah*, as evidenced by its transliteration in the Septuagint as *gazza* (the Greek *gamma* being the closest sound available to represent Semitic *ġ*). So, based on the fairly clear evidence of the Semitic languages, we should recognize that the Hebrew *'ayin* in *'almah* was originally a *ġayin*, and is to be derived from the root *ġ-l-m* rather than *'-l-m*, ruling out even the possibility of a connection between *'almah* and the root *'-l-m*, "to hide, be hidden" (although, as stated, there is no good semantic reason to connect *'almah* to *'-l-m*). According to G. B. Gray, a careful Semitic scholar writing before the discovery of Ugaritic (*The Book of Isaiah*, 126–27), *'almah* means "a girl, or young woman, above the age of childhood and sexual immaturity . . . , a person of the age at which sexual emotion awakens and becomes potent; it asserts neither virginity nor the lack of it; it is naturally in actual

usage often applied to women who were as a matter of fact certainly (Gn 24[43], Ex 2[8]), or probably (Ca 1[3], Ps 68[26]), virgins. On the other hand, it is also used in Pr 30[19] where the marvels of procreation and embryology (cp. Ps 139[13–16], Ec 11[5]) seem to be alluded to, and the corresponding term (or terms) is used in Aramaic of persons certainly not virgin, as, *e.g.*, in [Targum] Jg 19[5] of a concubine who had proved unfaithful; in Palmyrene [an Aramaic dialect] it is used of harlots, and in a bi-lingual inscription *'lwmt'* [Aramaic for the *'almah*] apparently corresponds to [Greek] *[hē]tairo[n]."* Despite this detailed analysis, however, Gray oversimplifies his next statement by claiming, "The Hebrew word for *virgin* is *btwlh.* . . ." (ibid., 127). For further treatment of *betulah,* see nn. 47–59, below. The section on the etymology of *'almah* by Dohmen, *TDOT,* 11:158–59, is supplemented and rightly corrected by H. Ringgren, ibid., 11:159.

40. Of relevance is the fact that ancient Semitic legal documents never use the equivalent of *'almah* for "virgin."

41. Note the use of *'almah* in these verses: "See, I am standing beside this spring; if a maiden *('almah)* comes out to draw water . . . " (Gen. 24:43); "'Yes, go,' she answered. And the girl *('almah)* went and got the baby's mother" (Exod. 2:8); "In front are the singers, after them the musicians; with them are the maidens *('alamot)* playing tambourines" (Ps. 68:25[26]); "There are three things that are too amazing for me, four that I do not understand: the way of an eagle in the sky, the way of a snake on a rock, the way of a ship on the high seas, and the way of a man with a maiden *('almah)"* (Prov. 30:18–19); "Pleasing is the fragrance of your perfumes; your name is like perfume poured out. No wonder the maidens *('alamot)* love you!" (Song of Songs 1:3); "Sixty queens there may be, and eighty concubines, and virgins *('alamot)* beyond number" (Song of Songs 6:8). Could *'almah* mean virgin in each of these verses? Quite possibly (in some cases, quite certainly, although there is much dispute about Proverbs 30:19), and the fine Messianic scholar Walter Riggans expresses the predominant evangelical view in his *Yeshua ben David* (349–62), also noting, "In Hebrew legal documents and contracts . . . the term *'almah* is never used of married women." He argues, "If we cannot find any places in the Hebrew Bible where this term is used of non-virgins, then we have a very strong case for arguing that indeed a virgin birth is being prophesied by Isaiah" (356–57). However, John Walton points out, "In English a fiancée is often also a virgin (though the percent of semantic overlapping of these two words is in sad decline). That does not mean that the word 'fiancée' means 'virgin.' Someone could show me a thousand passages where 'fiancée' was used to refer to a virgin, but that would not change the meaning. It is the same with *'almah:* The word primarily describes an adolescent, or a young woman of marriageable age, who is presumably a virgin, but who is not *by semantic definition* a virgin" ("Isaiah 7:14," 292).

42. According to Walton, "Isaiah 7:14," 292, *'almah* in Isaiah 54:4 "is used to describe a rejected barren wife." Niessen, however, comes to the opposite conclusion, stating that the "most significant and illuminating usage" of *'almah* "is in Isaiah 54:4–5 where the word essentially means to be 'unmarried' and 'without children'. The term *'alûmîm* is placed in a position of contrasting parallelism with *'almanût,* 'widowhood,' so that it can only mean 'maidenhood,' and is further opposed to 'marriage' and 'many children' in the preceding context of 53:1–3" ("The Virginity of the *'Almah,"* 135). Both arguments, however, may be overstated, since *'almah* in Isaiah 54:4 simply means "youth, youthfulness," referring back to the widow's younger years, but without specifying whether or not she was married and therefore not proving or disproving virginity.

43. See the discussion of Gray, above, n. 39; cf. further the comments of Harry Orlinsky, below, n. 47.

44. It is often argued that in the culture of that time, a woman who was an *'almah*—in particular one who was the subject of a prophecy concerning a significant child she was to bear—was presumed to be a virgin, since, it is argued, there is no record of a married *'almah* in the Bible. There are, however, several problems with this argument, including: (1) If the goal of the prophecy was to clearly and unambiguously declare that there would be a virgin birth, a qualifying statement would need to be made (see the comments of J. A. Alexander, n. 46, below); (2) The cognate evidence (i.e., the word *'almah* in other Semitic languages) does not support this premise (see below, n. 39); (3) Many scholars believe that Proverbs 30:19 speaks of an *'almah* having sexual intercourse (although this interpretation is disputed; cf. Niessen, "The Virginity of the *'Almah*," and Miller, "The Isaiah 7:14 Passage," for good arguments to the contrary; see also above, n. 41).

45. This is the standard anti-missionary position, raised almost without exception when Isaiah 7:14 and the virgin birth of Yeshua are being discussed.

46. More than 150 years ago, Joseph Addison Alexander, one of the leading Christian scholars of his day, expressed the possibility that in Hebrew "the idea of a virgin could not be expressed except by a periphrasis" (J. A. Alexander, *Isaiah* [repr., Grand Rapids: Zondervan, 1974], 1:168). According to the Israeli biblical scholar Matityahu Tsevat ("*betûlâ*," *TDOT*, 2:340), in the ancient Near Eastern and Mediterranean world, "in early linguistic stages the concept of virginity, with all the meaning that belongs to it in early linguistic associations, can frequently be expressed only negatively," hence, "it is best to conjecture that there was an original common Semitic word *batul(t)*, and that it meant a young girl at the age of puberty and the age just after puberty. Then very gradually this word assumed the meaning 'virgo intacta' in Hebrew and Aramaic, a development that ended in Middle Hebrew, to which the German 'Jungfrau' offers an instructive parallel. It is not surprising that this process of narrowing the meaning and of making it more precise is discernible in legal language."

47. In the words of the respected Jewish biblical scholar Harry M. Orlinsky, "Although the term *btwlh* basically means 'maiden,' it is often used in contexts whose intent is to specify virginity," see "Virgin," in Keith R. Crim, ed., *Interpreter's Dictionary of the Bible*, supp. vol. (Nashville: Abingdon, 1976), 939. Orlinsky concurs with the observation of the Assyriological scholar J. J. Finkelstein, namely, that the Akkadian term *batultu* (equivalent to Hebrew *betulah*) denotes "an age distinction . . . and only implicitly, therefore, untouched. She is then more explicitly described as not yet having been deflowered, nor taken in marriage." In other words, in the ancient Near Eastern culture, it would be expected that a maiden would be a virgin simply because of her age. But this observation would also apply to Hebrew usage of *'almah*. According to Orlinsky, *'almah* "means simply 'young woman, girl, maiden'" (ibid., 940).

48. In the NJPSV, *betulah* is translated as "maiden" in Deut. 32:25; Isa. 23:4; 62:5; Jer. 31:13; 51:22; Ezek. 9:6; Amos 8:13; Zech. 9:17; Ps. 78:63; 148:12; Lam. 1:18; 2 Chron. 36:17 (all the previous verses contain *bahur*, "young man, youth"); 2 Kings 19:21 (= Isa. 37:22); Isa. 23:12; 47:1; Jer. 14:17 (fn.); 18:13; 31:4; 31:21; 46:11; Amos 5:2; Lam. 1:15; 2:13 (the preceding twelve verses contain *betulat bat*, "Fair Maiden"; or simply *betulat*, "Maiden"); Jer. 2:32; Joel 1:8; Ps. 45:15; Job 31:1; Lam. 1:4; 2:10; 5:11.

49. Note that virtually all of the translations of *betulah* as "virgin" in the NJPSV occur in (1) specific legal contexts (e.g., Exod. 22:15–16), (2) verses with explanatory comments (e.g., Gen. 24:16), or (3) contexts in which the meaning is certain because of the nature of the narrative in question (e.g., Esther 2:2–3, 17, 19). According to Tsevat ("*betûlâ*," *TDOT*, 2:341), "Out of the 51 times that *bethulah* occurs in the OT, 3 times

it clearly means 'virgin' (Lev. 21:13f.; Dt. 22:19; Ezk. 44:22), and once it certainly does not [referring to Joel 1:8]. . . . In 12 passages, almost all of which are poetic, it is connected (both in the sing. and in the pl.) with *bachur(im)*, and the two expressions together mean the same thing as 'young people'; here virginity plays no discernible role."

50. Cf., e.g., Isa. 23:4; 62:5; Jer. 2:32; 31:12; 51:22; Ezek. 9:6; Joel 1:8; Zech. 9:17; Pss. 78:63; 148:12; Job 31:1; Lam. 1:4, 18; 2:10; 5:11.

51. Messianic Jewish scholar Daniel Gruber notes that even in Talmudic language and law, there are discussions about the precise meaning of *betulah*. See his *God, the Rabbis, and the Virgin Birth* (Hanover, N.H.: Elijah Publishing, n.d.), 8–16, for extensive references. In keeping with this, classical scholar Adam Kamesar pointed out that "the possibility that a woman might conceive with her virginity intact, though by means of normal fertilization, is an occurrence which is conceded in the Talmud" (quotation is taken from <http://www.jfjonline.org/apol/qa/almah.htm>). See Kamesar's important article, especially in terms of ancient Christian polemics, "The Virgin of Isaiah 7:14: The Philological Argument from the Second to the Fifth Century," *Journal of Theological Studies*, n.s., 41, part 1 (1990): 51.

52. The rendering of the English Standard Version (Wheaton: Crossway, 2001) is therefore an improvement on most other English versions: "The young woman was very attractive in appearance, a maiden [the footnote reads, "or *a woman of marriageable age*"] whom no man had known. She went down to the spring and filled her jar and came up" (Gen. 24:16).

53. Some commentators have suggested that Job pledged never to gaze at one particular virgin, meaning "the virgin Anat" (a Canaanite goddess), thus he was committing himself to never engage in idolatry; see, e.g., Norman C. Habel, *The Book of Job*, Old Testament Library (Philadelphia: Westminster, 1985), 431–32, for discussion and refutation of this view.

54. Some have argued that the *betulah* spoken of here was only espoused to be married, and thus there would have been no sexual consummation of the marriage (cf., e.g., Radak; see further John H. Walton, "*bᵉtûlâ*," *NIDOTTE*, 1:782–83). But this argument, which is purely speculative, is only necessary if one first assumes that a *betulah* cannot be married. Tsevat, *TDOT*, 2:341, correctly notes that "this interpretation [namely, that *betulah* does not mean "virgin" at Joel 1:8] can be avoided only by the singular assumption that *ba'al* means not only 'husband,' but also 'fiancé.'"

55. As for using epithets such as "Daughter of Babylon" or "Fair Maiden Zion" to prove a semantic point, I accept the cautions of Walton, *NIDOTTE*, 1:783 (his comments also apply to the term "Maiden Anat"; see n. 56, below). My point, however, is simply that *betulah* in and of itself does not mean "virgin" in biblical Hebrew.

56. As is commonly noted, in the Ugaritic language (closely related to biblical Hebrew), the goddess known as Betulat Anat, "the Maiden Anat," is infamous for her promiscuity. Her description as "Betulah" hardly signifies a virgin.

57. The text comes from Nippur and was originally published by James A. Montgomery (*Aramaic Incantation Texts from Nippur* [Philadelphia: University Museum, 1913]). This text is discussed by Shalom Paul, the highly respected Israeli scholar of Semitics and the Bible, in his article on "Virgin" in the *Encyclopedia Judaica*. He makes a number of important observations, including the fact that "the biblical *betulah* . . . usually rendered 'virgin,' is in fact an ambiguous term which in nonlegal contexts may denote an age of life rather than a physical state. Cognate Akkadian *batultu* (masculine, *batulu*) and Ugaritic *btlt* refer to 'an adolescent, nubile, girl.' That the woman who

is so called need not necessarily be a *virgo intacta* is shown by the graphic account in a Ugaritic myth of the sexual relations of Baal with the goddess Anath, who bears the honorific epithet *btlt* (see Pritchard, *Texts*, 142). Moreover, in an Aramaic incantation text from Nippur there is a reference to a *betulta'* who is 'pregnant but cannot bear' (Montgomery, *Aramaic Incantation Texts*, in bibl. 13:9, 178). The male counterpart to *betulah* in the Bible is often *bahur*. . . . 'young man,' e.g., Jeremiah 31:12[13] and Amos 8:13 (cf. Joel 1:8, where a *betulah* moans for her bridegroom); and the word *betulah* interchanges with the somewhat synonymous age term *'almah* . . . which also describes a young woman. Thus, in Genesis 24:16, 43, Rebekah is first called a *betulah* and then an *'almah*. (Exactly the same interchange of the two words appears in a Ugaritic text.)" Paul also discusses the usage of *'almah*, noting that "despite a two-millennium misunderstanding of Isaiah 7:14, 'Behold a young woman [LXX: *parthenos*, "virgin"] shall conceive and bear a son,' indicates nothing concerning the chastity of the woman in question. The only way that the term 'virgin' can be unambiguously expressed is in the negative: thus, Sumerian and Akkadian, 'undeflowered,' and Akkadian, 'not experienced,' 'unopened,' and 'who has not known a male.' The description of Rebekah (Gen. 24:16), who is first called a *betulah*, 'young woman,' and then 'whom no man had known' (cf. Judg. 21:12), is similar. In legal contexts, however, *betulah* denotes a virgin in the strict sense (as does *batultu* in certain Akkadian legal contexts)." See further Walton, *NIDOTTE*, 1:781–84 (who defines *betulah* as a "girl under the guardianship of her father"; note also the oft-cited article of Gordon J. Wenham, *"Bᵉtulah, 'A Girl of Marriageable Age,' " Vetus Testamentum* 22 (1972): 326–48. Wenham points out, among other things, that in Esther 2:17–19, the young women who are chosen to spend the night with the king are referred to as *betulah* both before and after they have sexual relations with the king.

58. On the flip side—actually, the exact opposite of the anti-missionary view—I find insupportable the common evangelical argument that if Isaiah intended to prophesy a virgin birth in clear and unambiguous terms, he would have used *'almah* rather than *betulah*. A simple reading of the relevant verses in the Tanakh (see above, n. 41)—as translated in leading Christian versions—demonstrates that *'almah* did not clearly and unequivocally mean "virgin."

59. Walton, *NIDOTTE*, 1:783, makes the following distinctions between the two words: "The lexical relationship between *bᵉtûlâ* and *'almâ* is that the former is a social status indicating that a young girl is under the guardianship of her father, with all the age and sexual references that accompany that status. The latter is to be understood with regard to fertility and childbearing potential. Obviously there are many occasions where both terms apply to the same girl. A girl ceases to be a *bᵉtûlâ* when she becomes a wife; she ceases to be an *'almâ* when she becomes a mother." As nuanced as his argument is, in my opinion some of the biblical evidence would seem to challenge his conclusions. According to Delitzsch (*Isaiah*, 184), "The two terms could both be applied to persons who were betrothed, and even to such as were married (Joel 2:16; Prov. 30:19: see Hitzig on these passages). It is also admitted that the idea of spotless virginity was not necessarily connected with *'almâh* (as in Gen 24:43, cf., 16), since there are passages—such, for example, as Song of Sol. 6:8—where it can hardly be distinguished from the Arabic *surrîje;* and a person who had a very young-looking wife might be said to have an *'almah* for his wife. But it is inconceivable that in a well-considered style, and one of religious earnestness, a woman who had been long married, like the prophet's own wife, could be called *hâ'almâh* without any reserve. . . . On the other hand, the expression itself warrants the assumption that by *hâ'almâh* the prophet meant

one of the *'alâmoth* of the king's harem (Luzzatto); and if we consider that the birth of the child was to take place, as the prophet foresaw, in the immediate future, his thoughts might very well have been fixed upon Abijah (Abi) bath-Zechariah (2 Kings 18:2; 2 Chron. 29:1), who became the mother of King Hezekiah, to whom apparently the virtues of the mother descended, in marked contrast with the vices of his father. This is certainly possible." The next comments of Delitzsch (*Isaiah*, 184–85), turning to the Messianic significance of Isaiah 7:14, should also be cited: "At the same time, it is also certain that the child who was to be born was the Messiah, and not a new Israel (Hofmann, Schriftbeweis, ii. 1, 87, 88); that is to say, that he was no other than that 'wonderful' heir of the throne of David, whose birth is hailed with joy in ch. 9, where even commentators like Knobel are obliged to admit that the Messiah is meant. It was the Messiah whom the prophet saw here as about to be born, then again in ch. 9 as actually born, and again in ch. 11 as reigning—an indivisible triad of consolatory images in three distinct states, interwoven with the three stages into which the future history of the nation unfolded itself in the prophet's view. If, therefore, his eye was directed toward the Abijah mentioned, he must have regarded her as the future mother of the Messiah, and her son as the future Messiah. Now it is no doubt true, that in the course of the sacred history Messianic expectations were often associated with individuals who did not answer to them, so that the Messianic prospect was moved further into the future; and it is not only possible, but even probable, and according to many indications an actual fact, that the believing portion of the nation did concentrate their Messianic wishes and hopes for a long time upon Hezekiah; but even if Isaiah's prophecy may have evoked such human conjectures and expectations, through the measure of time which it laid down, it would not be a prophecy at all, if it rested upon no better foundation than this, which would be the case if Isaiah had a particular maiden of his own day in his mind at the time."

60. For good bibliographies on Isaiah 7:14, cf. the Isaiah commentaries of Wildberger, Watts, Blenkinsopp, Childs, and Oswalt, along with the works cited in the article of Niessen. Cf. also Tan Kim Huat, "Christmas in Isaiah 7:14—*Sensus Literalis, Sensus Plenior aut Felix Culpa?" Trinity Theological Journal* 9 (2000): 5–33, arguing for the *sensus plenior* approach, which is similar to, although not identical with, the approach that I advocate here.

61. Cf. Riggans, *Yeshua ben David*, 337. Wildberger, *Isaiah 1–12*, 310, notes that while the prophecy may be obscure to our ears, it was probably not obscure to the original hearers (although Martin Buber called Isaiah 7:14 the "most controversial passage in the Bible," cited in ibid., 307). This, of course, is presumably correct, since as Wildberger states (310), "it is not normal for prophetic oracles that they would not have an understandable meaning." The issue, however, is whether there is a purpose to the Immanuel prophecy as part of Scripture. If so, what is that purpose? Also, if it is an oracle concerning a child born to the house of David, then by its very nature, it takes on greater meaning in the larger picture of the Messianic hope.

62. When this Ugaritic text was first discovered, there was a misreading of this line due to its poor preservation, and it was thought that for the first time, the Semitic equivalents of *betulah* and *'almah* occurred in parallelism. This was then taken as evidence that *'almah* meant "virgin," and Christian and Messianic Jewish writers have often pointed to an article of the influential Semitic scholar, Cyrus H. Gordon, "Almah in Isaiah 7:14," *Journal of Bible and Religion* 21 (1953): 106, to buttress this view (see, e.g., <http://www.christiancourier.com/questions/virginProphecyQuestion.htm> [15 January 2002]). A more careful analysis of the Ugaritic tablets, however, indicated that

this reading was clearly in error, and scholars since then have transcribed the lines as *hl ǵlmt tld bn*, the translation of which I have cited in the text. For examples of scholars who pointed to Gordon's article in defense of the virgin birth interpretation of Isaiah 7:14, cf. Edward E. Hindson, *Isaiah's Immanuel: A Sign of His Times or the Sign of the Ages* (Grand Rapids: Baker, 1979); David H. Stern, *Jewish New Testament Commentary* 7 (henceforth cited as *JNTC*) in editions up to 1996; Stern subsequently corrected his discussion as soon as the matter was brought to his attention; Riggans, *Yeshua ben David*, 356–57, although, as expected, his conclusions are sober. For discussion of the Ugaritic text, see Wolframm von Hermann, *Yariḫ und Nikkal und der Preis der Kutarāt-Göttinen, ein Kultisch-Magischer Text aus Ras Schamra*, Beihefte zur Zeitschrift für die alttestamentliche Wissenschaft, 106 (Berlin: A. Topelman, 1968).

63. Gruber points out that "the ancient Rabbis found at least 16 Messianic prophecies in chapters 7 to 12 of the book of Isaiah. Some of these are transparently Messianic, others are embedded in the context. All of these rabbinically acknowledged Messianic references are part of the scriptural context of Is. 7:14" (*God, the Rabbis, and the Virgin Birth*, 23–24). He adds, quite tellingly, that the ancient rabbis "considered this a very Messianic portion. In fact, the only portion of Scripture in which the ancient Rabbis found more Messianic prophecies is Isaiah chapters 49–54" (ibid., 24). For all who know the content of those chapters in Isaiah, this is a highly significant observation.

64. I should emphasize here that *it is possible* that Isaiah's sign was understood by the original hearers as a prophetic announcement of a virgin birth, however: (1) The word *'almah* in and of itself does not prove that point, even if it was argued that an *'almah*, by presumption, was a virgin (being unmarried) and that it is certain God would not give a sign through an illegitimate birth (i.e., an unmarried *'almah* being pregnant). While that reasoning is logical, we simply do not have sufficient textual or linguistic evidence to argue that an *'almah* had to be an unmarried, never pregnant, young woman. (2) If, in fact, Isaiah indisputably prophesied a virgin birth, would that not mean that a virgin birth was expected *at that time*? (Kaiser, *The Messiah in the Old Testament*, counters this argument by suggesting that the first fulfillment—in Isaiah's day—was a partial one, meaning a child who was not truly Immanuel born to a non-virgin, whereas the true fulfillment—the birth of Jesus—was the complete one. But this is hardly compelling.) If so, were there *two* virgin births? The only way around this is to understand the Hebrew grammatical structure (predicate adjective + participle) in light of an apparently still-future sign, hence, "The *'almah* will conceive and give birth to a son," as reflected in the (Jewish) Septuagint and many translations, both Christian and Jewish. While this is possible (see above, n. 31, with the observation of Delitzsch, that *hinneh*, "behold," in Isaiah always introduces a *future* event), a strong argument can be made that the words announce an imminent birth.

65. According to John D. W. Watts, *Isaiah 1–33*, Word Biblical Commentary (Dallas: Word, 1985), 102, who interprets the sign with reference to the days of Ahaz (i.e., not with future reference to Jesus), "The entire setting shows a positive attitude toward the House of David. *h'lmh* must be someone in sight to whom Isaiah points. The most likely women to have been present with the King would have been the Queen and her escort. If this is true, the son that is to be born would be the heir apparent to the throne, i.e., the Anointed One. *In this sense, at least, the passage is 'messianic.'* It related to the fulfillment of God's promises to David and his dynasty. . . . It is significant that all the passages that explicitly deal with messianic themes related to the Davidic dynasty occur in the Ahaz section of the Vision (7:1–16; 9:5–6[6–7]; and 11:1–5, 10)" (my emphasis).

Note also that Dohmen, whose attempt to define *'almah* in the Hebrew Bible as an "alien woman" is quite forced, is still able to observe that with a reinterpretation of this prophetic oracle beginning in the days of Hezekiah, "the sign described in v. 14 becomes a symbol, and Immanuel becomes a savior figure expected in this sense. In the postexilic period Isaiah 7:14 was interpreted messianically in this sense" (*TDOT*, 11:162; the entire article, with a massive bibliography, runs from 11:154–63).

66. Note again Delitzsch on the progression from Isaiah 7–11: "The Messianic prophecy, which turns its darker side towards unbelief in ch. 7, and whose promising aspect burst like a great light through the darkness in Isa 8:5–9:6, is standing now upon its third and highest stage. In ch. 7 it is like a star in the night; in Isa 8:5–9:6, like the morning dawn; and now [approaching Isa 11] the sky is perfectly cloudless, and it appears like the noonday sun" (*Isaiah*, 235).

67. Joseph Blenkinsopp, *Isaiah 1–39: A New Translation with Introduction and Commentary*, Anchor Bible (New York: Doubleday, 2000), 238–39. According to Orlinsky (speaking of Isaiah 7:14), the text indicates that "before the baby that the pregnant woman will soon bear has grown significantly [7:16] the invaders will themselves be invaded. This is related to what the prophet says in the next chapter (8:1–4)," see "Virgin," in Crim, ed., *Interpreter's Dictionary of the Bible*, supp. vol., 940.

68. "Immanuel," *Encyclopedia Judaica;* the force of this is recognized by Alexander, *Isaiah*, 166–73.

69. According to Delitzsch (*Isaiah*, 187), "the sign in question was, on the one hand, a mystery glaring in the most threatening manner upon the house of David; and, on the other hand, a mystery smiling with which consolation upon the prophet and all believers, and couched in these enigmatical terms, in order that those who hardened themselves might not understand it, and that believers might increasingly long to comprehend its meaning."

70. Cf. the standard work of Robert H. Gundry, *The Use of the Old Testament in St. Matthew's Gospel, with Special Reference to the Messianic Hope*, Supplements to *Novum Testamentum*, vol. 18 (Leiden: E. J. Brill, 1967); more broadly, cf. Richard N. Longenecker, *Biblical Exegesis in the Apostolic Period*, 2d ed. (Grand Rapids: Eerdmans, 1999); see also the comments throughout Stern's *JNTC* on Matthew; and cf. further Craig S. Keener, *A Commentary on the Gospel of Matthew* (Grand Rapids: Eerdmans, 1999), which contains extensive references to the primary sources.

71. It is also possible that Matthew considered the fact that the prophecies contained in Isaiah 7:14–25 were also fulfilled (namely, that *before* Immanuel reached a certain age, the lands of those who were attacking Ahaz and Judah would be abandoned), and since he read the prophecy as future (the virgin *will* conceive . . .), and since the Maher-Shalah-Hash-Baz sign took the place of the Immanuel sign as a time setter, he might well have felt fully justified in citing Isaiah's prophecy with reference to Yeshua. It is also fair to ask why Isaiah declared that "within sixty-five years Ephraim will be too shattered to be a people" (7:8) if the sign later given by God was to be *immediate*, reaching total fulfillment just a few years later ("before the boy knows enough to reject the wrong and choose the right, the land of the two kings you dread will be laid waste" [Isa. 7:16]). Cf. J. Barton Payne, "Right Questions about Isaiah 7:14," in Morris Inch and Ronald Youngblood, eds., *The Living and Active Word of God: Studies in Honor of Samuel H. Schultz* (Winona Lake, Ind.: Eisenbrauns, 1983), 74–85.

72. According to Greek scholar Gerhard Delling, "In a special instance *parthenos* can even be a girl who has been raped, Gn. 34:3 for *na'arah* [Hebrew]," Delling, *"parthenos,"* in *Theological Dictionary of the New Testament*, ed. Gerhard Kittel for Ger-

hard Friedrich, trans. Geoffrey W. Bromiley (Grand Rapids: Eerdmans, 1976), 5:833 (henceforth cited as *TDNT*). Note also that the Septuagint renders *'almah* with *parthenos* at Genesis 24:43.

73. It could be argued that the meaning of *parthenos* was developing and becoming more narrow, so that when the Torah was translated into Greek, the word still carried meanings beyond that of virgin, but by the time Isaiah was translated—several decades later—the meaning had become more narrow. This, however, is somewhat tenuous (although anti-missionaries would certainly argue that by Matthew's day, *parthenos* meant "virgin"—otherwise, where is the controversy about Matthew's alleged misinterpretation of *'almah* if *parthenos* did not clearly mean "virgin" even in his day? Another possibility is that Genesis 34:3 is making reference to the situation before the rape recorded in 34:2, but this is certainly not the most natural reading of the text. Also, it fails to explain why the Septuagint would translate the Hebrew *na'arah*, "girl, young woman"—with no reference to virginity—as *parthenos*. Most interesting is the statement of Bruce Chilton, a New Testament and Aramaic scholar, who claimed that *neither* the Hebrew *'almah* (in Isa. 7:14) nor the Greek *parthenos* (in the Septuagint to Isa. 7:14 and in Matt. 1:23) meant "virgin"! See his *Rabbi Jesus: An Intimate Biography* (New York: Doubleday, 2000), 23. If that is the case, then most of this objection, along with some of my answer, has no relevance at all!

74. Tovia Singer, <http://www.outreachjudaism.org/rashi.html>.

75. Stern, *JNTC*, 7.

76. Ibid., 929–30. He further notes (930), "A friend says that Rashi did write the paragraph as quoted, but it is not in *Mikra'ot G'dolot*. However, until someone directs me to a genuine Rashi source for it, the matter remains as I have left it in this Appendix note." This speaks volumes for the integrity of Dr. Stern as both a scholar and a Messianic Jew, and one can only ask why Rabbi Singer still claims Stern deliberately misrepresented Rashi. Since Stern made his corrections in 1996, what else but a deliberate attempt to misrepresent Stern would motivate Singer to fail to update the discussion on his web site?

77. Unless otherwise noted, all quotes from Rashi's Bible commentary are from Rabbi A. J. Rosenberg, *Judaica Press Complete Tanach with Rashi*, CD ROM ed. (New York: Davka Corporation and Judaica Press, 1999). Stern, *JNTC*, 930, is actually more conservative in his translation of Rashi, translating the key word *r'uyah* as "appropriate": "she was an *'almah* for whom it was inappropriate that she give birth," noting that "some interpret this to mean either that it was improper for her to give birth (presumably because she was unmarried, in which case what would be proper is that she would be a virgin), or that she was too young to be physically capable of giving birth (in which case, unless she had been abused, she would be a virgin)."

78. When Rashi simply says, "Some say" (literally, "some interpret," *potrin*), he is citing a possible interpretation, otherwise he would not quote it at all (or he would quote it to refute it). In this case, he offers no refutation, but rather closes with this comment. For more on Rashi's methodology, see the series by Avigdor Bonchek, *What's Bothering Rashi?* 5 vols. to date (Jerusalem and New York: Feldheim, 1997–).

79. Delling, *"parthenos," TDNT*, 5:833. The discussion concludes with, "Historically, even in his narrow circle [i.e., the narrow circle of the Septuagint translator of Isaiah], this might arise if historical value can be accorded to the stricter statements of [Plutarch] . . . about Egypt."

80. Riggans, *Yeshua ben David,* 355, is correct in rejecting Fruchtenbaum's argument here, namely, that the reference to *the 'almah* in Isaiah's prophecy specifically had in mind Genesis 3:15.

81. Cf. Riggans, ibid., 339.

82. The words were originally composed in Latin by an unknown author in the ninth century *("Veni Emmanuel");* the first English translation was by John M. Neale in 1851. The words of the first stanza are: "O come, O come, Emmanuel / And ransom captive Israel / That mourns in lonely exile here / Until the Son of God appear," followed by the refrain, "Rejoice! Rejoice! / Emmanuel shall come to thee, O Israel."

83. According to Dohmen, a critical—as opposed to evangelical—Old Testament scholar, "The NT taking up of Isa. 7:14 . . . is not a piece of theologizing inspired by the LXX translation of the verse; on the contrary, it stands solidly in the tradition of the uses made of this verse within the OT itself, which lead up to a messianic interpretation" *(TDOT,* 11:163).

84. As translated by Sir Lancelot C. L. Brenton, *The Septuagint with Apocrypha: Greek and English* (repr., Peabody, Mass.: Hendrickson, 1986), 844.

85. *Origen Against Celsus,* in A. Roberts and J. Donaldson, eds., *The Ante-Nicene Fathers,* CD ROM ed. (Albany, Ore.: AGES Software, 1997), 5:218.

86. Cf. the following Rabbinic statements: "R. Yose the Galilean said: 'The name of the Messiah is Peace, for it is said, *Everlasting Father, Prince Peace'"* (Midrash Pereq Shalom, p. 101); "The Messiah is called by eight names: Yinnon [see Ps. 72:17], Tzemach [e.g., Jer. 23:5]; Pele' [Wonderful, Isa. 9:6(5)], Yo'etz [Counselor, Isa. 9:6(5)], Mashiach [Messiah], El [God, Isa. 9:6(5)], Gibbor [Hero, Isa. 9:6(5)], and Avi' Ad Shalom [Eternal Father of Peace, Isa. 9:6(5)]; see Deuteronomy Rabbah 1:20.

87. The entire verse is rendered there: "For a child is born unto us, A son is given unto us; And the government is upon his shoulder; And his name is called Pele-joezel-gibbor-Abi-ad-sar shalom." A footnote adds, "That is, Wonderful in counsel is God the mighty, the everlasting Father, the Ruler of peace." Similar to this is the rendering of the English text in the Jerusalem Bible, Koren Edition. The translation is a revision by Harold Fisch of the Michael Friedlander version.

88. A footnote supports the rendering of "grace" with reference to Isaiah 25:1.

89. I would gladly stand corrected on this should evidence to the contrary be forthcoming. To date, however, I have seen no evidence that the rendering of the NJPSV was clearly anticipated by previous Rabbinic literature.

90. Perhaps the rendering of Luzatto was closest to that of the NJPSV; see Delitzsch, *Isaiah,* 218. His comments on Luzatto's translation are worth noting: "The motive which prompted Luzzatto to adopt this original interpretation is worthy of notice. He had formerly endeavoured, like other commentators, to explain the passage by taking the words from 'Wonderful' to 'Prince of Peace' as the name of the child; and in doing this he rendered *pl' y'ts* 'one counselling wonderful things,' thus inverting the object, and regarded 'mighty God' as well as 'eternal Father' as hyperbolical expressions, like the words applied to the King in Ps 45:7a. But now he cannot help regarding it as absolutely impossible for a human child to be called *'el gibbor,* like God Himself in Isa 10:21." The careful reader will note the importance of the remarks of Delitzsch; see further vol. 2, 3.3 (for Talmudic treatment of this verse and the hyberbolic expressions).

91. See the Isaiah commentaries cited in the previous notes.

92. According to Delitzsch *(Isaiah,* 218), such a translation renders the name "sesquipedalian."

93. For a discussion of the Masoretic accents (which are *not* part of the original text), cf. ibid., 219–20.

94. Brevard S. Childs, *Isaiah,* Old Testament Library (Louisville: Westminster/John Knox, 2001), 78, note esp. n. c.

95. Blenkinsopp, *Isaiah 1–39,* 246. He notes that "Hero Warrior" is "literally, 'God warrior,'" and "is a divine title applied to the ruler, as can be seen from its reuse by a later interpreter in 10:21" (ibid., 250).

96. Delitzsch, *Isaiah,* 220; 223–24. The statement in the Talmud is found in b. Sanhedrin 94a, from the lips of Bar Kapparah. Contrast this with the sentiment of a certain Rabbi Hillel in b. Sanhedrin 98a (namely, that Israel would have no Messiah because they already enjoyed him in the days of Hezekiah), also cited in Delitzsch, *Isaiah,* 224. Regarding the comment of Bar Kapparah, Delitzsch states (*Isaiah,* 223–24), "There is so far some sense in this, that the Messianic hopes really could centre for a certain time in Hezekiah." Interestingly, the Hebrew text of Isaiah 9:6[5] contains an anomaly, as the letter *mem* in the word *lemarbeh* is written in its final (i.e., word ending) form (which is closed) even though in this case, it is found toward the beginning of the word. According to the Talmud (in the comment of Bar Kapparah), it was because Hezekiah fell short of his Messianic calling that the *mem* was closed. On a related note, cf. the recent study of Marvin A. Sweeney, *King Josiah of Judah: The Lost Messiah of Israel* (New York: Oxford Univ. Press, 2001).

97. Isaac Troki, *Hizzuk Emunah: Faith Strengthened,* trans. Moses Mocatta (repr., New York: Sefer Hermon, 1970), 106–7, his emphasis.

98. Ibid., 107.

99. Because the incarnation of the Son of God has often been thought of in crass terms by the anti-missionaries (see vol. 2, 3.2), with little effort to understand the lofty spiritual truths involved in that incredible divine act, the parallels with Jewish mystical thought have often been missed. For the contemplative reader, however, verses such as John 1:14, 18; Colossians 2:9; and 1 Timothy 3:16 relate well to Hasidic teachings on divine "contraction" and the mystical teaching that God must "adorn himself in a garb that conceals his true nature" (as quoted by Boteach, *The Wolf Shall Lie with the Lamb,* 24).

100. Interestingly, of the twelve times the noun *'amit* occurs in the Hebrew Bible, eleven are found in Leviticus in legal contexts (e.g., Lev. 5:21; 18:20; 19:11; 25:14), leaving Zechariah 13:7 as the only nonlegal occurrence.

101. For Messianic insights into the relevant texts in Zechariah, cf. David Baron, *Commentary on Zechariah: His Visions and Prophecies* (repr., Grand Rapids: Kregel, 1988).

102. In Psalm 90:2, the Stone edition renders this phrase as, "from the remotest past to the most distant future," which actually understates the Hebrew.

103. Note that Psalm 72 is widely recognized as a Messianic psalm (at the least, based on principle 2 in the appendix), giving added weight to the fact that Rashi cites it here, especially since verse 17 seems to speak of eternal origins ("before the sun," meaning either literal preexistence or conceptual preexistence). Interestingly, Rashi's actual comment on Psalm 72:17 in his commentary on the Psalms seems to contradict his application of that verse in his commentary on Micah, since he applies it to Solomon and explains, "**before the sun, his name will be magnified** All the days of the sun, his name will be magnified." See also above, n. 86, where it is noted that Yinnon is recognized as a name of the Messiah in the Rabbinic writings.

104. Francis I. Anderson and David Noel Freedman, *Micah: A New Translation with Introduction and Commentary*, Anchor Bible (New York: Doubleday, 2000), 468. Interestingly, Santala points out that David Kimchi actually states that the Messiah is *'el—*God!—in his comments on Micah 5:2[1]. However, since Kimchi did not believe in the Messiah's divinity, one must wonder what point he was trying to make; see Santala, *The Messiah in the Old Testament in Light of Rabbinical Writings*, 115. There is also some fascinating, relevant speculation in *Pirkey HaMashiach* (in *Midreshei Ge'ulah*) on the new Messiah of God and on the Messiah as Yahweh. Most scholars believe that 4 Ezra 7:29, where God says, "My son the Messiah will die," is probably a later Christian interpolation into an (originally) pre-Christian work. Thus, the text is not germane to our point.

105. As we will see in 4.8, the Christian scholar Origen in the second century made reference to Jewish leaders who interpreted Isaiah 53 with regard to the people of Israel as a whole, and there is one midrashic reference to Isaiah 53:10 being applied to the righteous in general.

106. Regarding Isaiah 42:1–7, note that the servant is given as a covenant *to/for the people* (meaning the people of Israel) and as a light *for the nations* (meaning the Gentiles). This would clearly point to the servant *as an individual*. A further "servant" reference is found in Isaiah 44:26, which seems to refer to God's prophetic servants in general, not to one particular servant or to the nation of Israel as a whole.

107. The Aramaic reads, "Behold my servant the Messiah."

108. Note also that Metsudat David interprets Isaiah 42:1 with reference to King Messiah.

109. Craig Keener's comments on Mark 10:45 ("For even the Son of Man did not come to be served, but to serve, and to give his life as a ransom for many") are simple, to the point, and relevant to our discussion: "By calling himself a 'servant' and defining his mission as 'giving his life a ransom for the many,' Jesus identifies himself with the suffering servant of Isaiah 53:10–12 (despite the contrary view of some interpreters today). Although the servant's mission had been given to Israel as a whole (Isaiah 41:8; 43:10; 44:2, 21; 49:3), Israel through disobedience could not fulfill it (42:19), so that the one who would fulfill it had to restore Israel as well as bring light to the Gentiles (49:5–7; 52:13–53:12). Because hardly anyone else had yet applied this passage to the Messiah, Jesus is trying to redefine their expectation about his messianic mission." See Craig S. Keener, *IVP Bible Background Commentary* (Downers Grove, Ill.: InterVarsity Press, 1993), 163–64.

110. According to Rashi, Ibn Ezra, Radak, and some of the other classic commentaries, the servant here is the prophet, rather than the Messiah or Israel. This means that these important Rabbinic commentaries do *not* interpret this passage in a national sense, recognizing the individual nature of the servant. This *completely* undercuts the whole anti-missionary argument—a *major* argument of the anti-missionaries, given the importance of Isaiah 53—that the servant in Isaiah 40–55 is always Israel. This is simply not so!

111. The marginal rendering suggested in the NJPSV footnotes is possible but highly unlikely.

112. Cf. Klaus Baltzer, *Deutero–Isaiah: A Commentary on Isaiah 40–55*, trans. Margaret Kohl, Hermeneia (Philadelphia: Fortress, 2001).

113. See Samson H. Levey, *The Messiah, an Aramaic Interpretation: The Messianic Exegesis of the Targum* (Cincinnati: Hebrew Union College/Jewish Institute of Religion, 1974), 63–67.

114. Note also Rashi's comment on Isaiah 53:8: "For because of the transgression of my people [this is allegedly a Gentile king speaking] this plague came to the righteous among them."

115. It is clear that the text cannot be speaking of a *still future* deliverance from exile, since, in particular, masses of Jews are not in exile in Babylon today.

116. Rashi interprets the clear, noncollective language of Isaiah 50:4–8 with reference to Isaiah himself (he explains verses 10–11 with reference to the prophets in general—specifically, the reference to "the word of his servant" in verse 10—and therefore not as pertaining to the nation as a whole). Joseph Blenkinsopp, *Isaiah 40–55: A New Translation with Introduction and Commentary,* Anchor Bible (New York: Doubleday, 2002), 82, commenting on the Septuagint's translation of some key servant passages in Isaiah 40–55, noted that "maintaining the collective interpretation of the Servant became more difficult with the detailed allusions to rejection, physical abuse, disfigurement, and eventually death, in 50:4–9 and 52:13–53:12."

117. See above, n. 113 (Levey); cf. further vol. 2, 3.23.

118. See Origen, *Contra Celsum,* bk. 1, chap. 55, cited in 4.8.

119. It is for this very reason that followers of Jesus are promised persecution, namely, suffering for righteousness in the midst of an unrighteous world, living as strangers and pilgrims in an often hostile environment (see, e.g., Matt 5:10–12; 10:16ff.; John 15:18ff.; Acts 5:41; Phil 1:29, among many references); see further vol. 1, 2.6, and cf. Joseph Ton (Tson), *Suffering, Martyrdom, and Rewards in Heaven* (Lanham, Md.: Univ. Press of America, 1997).

120. Ibn Ezra, in harmony with other classical Jewish commentaries, claims that Isaiah 49:7 ("This is what the LORD says—the Redeemer and Holy One of Israel—to him who was despised and abhorred by the nation, to the servant of rulers: 'Kings will see you and rise up, princes will see and bow down, because of the LORD, who is faithful, the Holy One of Israel, who has chosen you.'") refers to *the prophet himself* rather than to the nation. But this passage clearly parallels the promise to the servant of the Lord in Isaiah 52:13–15, a passage interpreted by Ibn Ezra with reference to the nation of Israel as a whole.

121. According to Delitzsch (*Isaiah,* 772), *be'ephes* in this context means, "'for nothing,' i.e., without having acquired any right to it, but rather serving in its unrighteousness simply as the blind instrument of the righteousness of Jehovah, who through the instrumentality of Asshur put an end first of all to the kingdom of Israel, and then to the kingdom of Judah." The NIV renders this as "lately," a translation rightly rejected in its day by Delitzsch (ibid.). The Stone edition appropriately renders *hinam* as "for naught" in Isaiah 52:3, 5 but then translates *be'ephes* as "without justification"—a rendering that is without justification. For other usages of *'ephes* (related to the meanings of "end, extremity, nonexistence"), see further D. J. A. Clines, *Dictionary of Classical Hebrew* (Sheffield, England: Sheffield Academic Press, 1993–), 1:359.

122. A number of Christian translations (such as the NLT and NRSV) render some of these terms with "without justification" or "without cause." See, e.g., the NLT's rendering of v. 4a, "Now they have been oppressed without cause by Assyria"), apparently overlooking the teaching of Isaiah and the other prophets that God used Assyria to judge Israel and Judah *because of sin* (see, e.g., Isa. 10:5ff.).

123. As rendered by Asher Finkel, *Ein Yaakov,* CD Rom ed. (Northvale, N.J.: Aronson).

124. Isaiah 57:1 is no exception. Rather, it says that the reason righteous individuals sometimes die before their time is to spare them from a greater calamity that is about to befall the sinning nation; cf. 1 Kings 14:1–13.

125. Cf. Ezek. 22:30–31; also 13:4–5; Ps. 106:23; cf. further Yohanan Muffs, "Who Will Stand in the Breach?: A Study of Prophetic Intercession," in idem, *Love and Joy: Law, Language and Religion in Ancient Israel* (New York: Jewish Theological Seminary, 1992), 9–48. Cf. also Moshe Greenberg, *Ezekiel 1–20: A New Translation with Introduction and Commentary*, Anchor Bible (New York: Doubleday, 1983), 236; and idem, *Ezekiel 21–37: A New Translation with Introduction and Commentary*, Anchor Bible (New York: Doubleday, 1997), 463.

126. Cf. the standard study of Gerhard Hasel, *The Remnant: The History and Theology of the Remnant Idea from Genesis to Isaiah*, Andrews University Monographs, 5 (Berrien Springs: Andrews Univ. Press, 1974).

127. Audio copies of the debate (including a recap with Sid Roth) are available through ICN Ministries, 4000 West Fairfield Drive, Pensacola, FL 32506; www.icnministries.org.

128. See S. R. Driver and Adolph Neubauer, eds. and trans., *The Fifty-Third Chapter of Isaiah according to the Jewish Interpreters*, 2 vols. (New York: Ktav, 1969), 2:78.

129. For a more extended quote from Ibn Krispin on this subject, see vol. 2, pp. 215–16.

130. Driver and Neubauer, *Fifty-Third Chapter of Isaiah*, 2:259.

131. Cf. the discussion in Levey, *The Messiah, an Aramaic Interpretation;* see further Pinkhos Churgin, *Targum Jonathan to the Prophets*, repr. with Leivy Smolar and Moses Aberbach as *Studies in Targum Jonathan to the Prophets* (New York: Ktav, 1983).

132. The question raised by the Ethiopian eunuch in Acts 8:34 (while reading Isaiah 53:7–8)—"Tell me, please, who is the prophet talking about, himself or someone else?"—is in keeping with this line of reasoning and is completely consistent with the most obvious meaning of the text.

133. This interpretation is in the midrash to Psalm 2:6, dealing with the Hebrew word *nasakti*, interpreted here to mean, "I have woven him," with reference to Judges 16:14, i.e., "I have drawn him out of the chastisements." R. Huna, on the authority of R. Aha, says, "The chastisements are divided into three parts: one for David and the fathers, one for our own generation, and one for the King Messiah; and this is that which is written, 'He was wounded for our transgressions, etc.'" See Driver and Neubauer, *Fifty-Third Chapter of Isaiah*, 2:10, for the translation.

134. Origen, *Contra Celsum* (i.e., *Origen Against Celsus*), bk. 1, chap. 55 (5:218).

135. Allan A. MacRae, a staunch evangelical Old Testament scholar, believed that the Gentile kings spoke the opening verses of Isaiah 53. However, in his view, this actually enhanced, not detracted from, the Messianic application of this chapter to Jesus. See his study on Isaiah 40–55, *The Gospel of Isaiah* (Chicago: Moody Press, 1977).

136. According to Ibn Ezra, the Jewish people brought healing to the nations in which they were scattered by praying for the peace and prosperity of those nations (as per Jer. 29:7). While this is certainly a noble thought, and while it is no doubt true that Jews have, at times, prayed for the welfare of the nations among whom they were scattered, this is not what Isaiah 53 states. Rather, it is the servant of the Lord's actual *suffering* that brings healing (see esp. vv. 4–6; only v. 12 partially supports Ibn Ezra's view). Does anyone imagine that during the horrors of the Holocaust, our people were praying for God's blessings on Germany, Poland, Ukraine, and the other nations that were slaughtering them? This is not meant to criticize the actions or reactions of our people toward their persecutors and oppressors; it is simply to say that the picture painted in Isaiah 53 did not accurately apply to them.

137. It is interesting to note that in the first edition of the NJPSV *Isaiah* (1972; the translation was attributed to H. L. Ginsberg), Isaiah 53:8 was rendered with "My people," the uppercase *M* indicating that deity was speaking. In the second edition (1986 or later), this phrase is changed to "my people," lowercase, indicating that the prophet was speaking. In either case, whether the Lord or the prophet is speaking, it is clear that this is not the voice of the Gentile kings.

138. I would encourage you to read through the Book of Lamentations and ask these two questions: For whose sins were the people of Israel suffering? Does the author of Lamentations fully acknowledge his people's guilt? The answers are self-evident.

139. Cf. the position of MacRae, cited above, n. 135.

140. The Dead Sea Scroll of Isaiah reads *nwg' lmw*, taken by Semitic scholar Mitchell Dahood to be a passive form (a Qal passive, to be exact), hence, "smitten for them" (see his article, "Phoenician Elements in Isaiah 52:13–53:12," in Hans Goedicke, ed., *Near Eastern Studies in Honor of William Foxwell Albright* [Baltimore: Johns Hopkins, 1971], 69–70). This reading completely removes the very basis of this part of the "plural servant" objection. Note, however, that the passive meaning is not assured, according to the scholar of Hebrew and Aramaic Edward Yechezkel Kutscher, *The Language and Linguistic Background of the Dead Sea Isaiah Scroll*, trans. Elisha Qimron (Leiden: E. J. Brill, 1979). Kutscher explains the anomalous form as a phonetic variation.

141. For the emendation of the text from *bemotayw* ("in his deaths") to *bamato* ("his burial mound"), cf. Blenkinsopp, *Isaiah 40–55*, 348; see further W. Boyd Barrick, "The Rich Man from Arimathea (Matt. 27:57–60) and 1QIsaᵃ," *Journal of Biblical Literature* 96 (1977): 235–39, following Ibn Ezra. This, of course, would completely remove the very objection being raised, since the noun would no longer be read as plural.

142. These arguments were already refuted in the nineteenth century by the Oxford Hebrew scholar Eberhard Pusey (see his preface to Driver and Neubauer, *Fifty-Third Chapter of Isaiah;* this two-volume project was actually Pusey's idea; see Raphael Loewe's fascinating prolegomenon to this book for further background). For a popular study, cf. Judy Conaway, *The Rejected Cornerstone: Does Yeshua Fulfill the Prophecy of Isaiah 33?* (n.p.: n.p., 2001).

143. Cf. Luke 2:22–24 with Leviticus 12:8.

144. The original source of this quote is unknown to me.

145. It is fair to ask a follower of the late Lubavitcher Rebbe, Menchaem Schneerson, hailed by many of his followers as the Messiah, how the picture of Isaiah 53 correlates with his life, since his disciples pointed to this very passage of Scripture when he suffered a debilitating stroke in 1992 at the age of ninety. He had several hundred thousand devotees around the world and was considered by his people to be the most influential Jewish leader of the twentieth century. Can't the same objection raised here against Jesus—incorrectly so, as we have seen—also be raised against the Rebbe? Yet anti-missionaries in his camp use this objection against Yeshua!

146. Different translations of the Hebrew in this passage of Isaiah are possible, none of which greatly affect the overall meaning, despite the specious arguments set forth in Gerald Sigal, *The Jew and the Christian Missionary: A Jewish Response to Missionary Christianity* (New York: Ktav, 1981), 50–53.

147. A working definition, then, for the root would be, "to be weak, debilitated; to be sick, suffer." For discussion of the relevant lexical data by a leading authority in the field, cf. Klaus Seybold, *"chalah, etc.," TDOT*, 4:399–409; see further the references in Michael L. Brown, *Israel's Divine Healer*, Studies in Old Testament Biblical Theology (Grand Rapids: Zondervan, 1995), 36–37, with nn. on 265.

148. D. Winton Thomas, a leading Hebrew and Old Testament scholar, devoted a number of studies to the root *yd'* (normally translated "to know"), arguing that in some instances it actually masked a different root meaning "to be humbled." For references, and for a translation of Isaiah 53 incorporating these insights, cf. Loewe, prolegomenon to Driver and Neubauer, *Fifty-Third Chapter of Isaiah*.

149. The New Testament portrays Jesus as being intimately involved with human sickness and pain—to the point of causing him grief and anguish—yet full of divine joy (Heb. 1:9, citing Ps. 45:7[8]; see also Luke 10:21). Such a picture is psychologically consistent, given the dual realities with which Yeshua lived: great intimacy with his heavenly Father—producing boundless joy—and great intimacy with the human race—producing boundless pain.

150. The portion of the Talmudic text in question is dealing with Rabbinic speculation about the name of the Messiah. One opinion of the sages is that "his name is the leprous one [Aramaic, *hiwwra'*] of the house of Rabbi"; Isaiah 53:4 is quoted as support.

151. For further discussion of the root *ng'* with bibliographical references, cf. Brown, *Israel's Divine Healer*, 317, n. 160. See also *Rejected Cornerstone*, 166–68, with reference to Delitzsch's treatment of *ng'*.

152. As rendered in Driver and Neubauer, *Fifty-Third Chapter of Isaiah*, 2:53–54.

153. See the relevant discussion about Messiah son of Joseph in vol. 2, 3.23.

154. David Flusser, *Judaism and the Origins of Christianity* (Jerusalem: Magnes, 1988), 423.

155. For discussion of the various Gospel accounts of this incident (whether there was one cleansing of the Temple or two), cf. the standard evangelical commentaries on the Synoptics and John.

156. The account of Jesus' trial before Pilate is most fully related in John 18:28–40, and at no time in that account does Jesus seek to defend himself, protest, or resist the sentence of death. Rather, he accepts it as his destiny.

157. As explained in John 19:28a, Jesus uttered these words ". . . knowing that all was now completed, and so that the Scripture would be fulfilled," with apparent reference to verses such as Psalm 22:15[16], "My strength is dried up like a potsherd, and my tongue sticks to the roof of my mouth; you lay me in the dust of death."

158. Francis Brown, S. Driver, and C. Briggs, *The Brown-Driver-Briggs Hebrew and English Lexicon* (repr., New York: Oxford Univ. Press, 1959), 283.

159. The KJV renders Psalm 22:30a[31a] as, "A seed shall serve him," bringing out clearly the Hebrew usage and indicating that it does not refer to specific offspring, but posterity in general.

160. Geza Vermes, "The Decalogue and the Minim," in his *Post-Biblical Jewish Studies*, Studies in Judaism in Late Antiquity, vol. 8 (Leiden: E. J. Brill, 1975), 169–77.

161. Loewe, prolegomenon to Driver and Neubauer, *Fifty-Third Chapter of Isaiah*, 20–22.

162. John E. Goldingay, *Daniel*, Word Biblical Commentary (Dallas: Word, 1989), 258, understates the significance of the prophecy, claiming that the prophecy "does not have a worldwide perspective; it is not speaking of the end of all history, or of the sin of the whole world."

163. Cf. Michael L. Brown, "Lamentations, Theology of," *NIDOTTE*, 4:884–93, and see the discussion in vol. 2, 3.13, regarding the significance of the rebuilding of the Temple.

164. For questions regarding the exact translation of some of the verbs in verse 24, see pp. 95–98.

165. Interestingly, based on Torah principles, it can be argued that God sent the people of Judah into exile for 70 years because the land had not enjoyed its Sabbaths for a period of *490 years*—the very same period spoken of by the angel Gabriel in the revelation of the 70 weeks of years. For the principle, see Lev. 26:2, 14–35. See further Bible commentaries on Dan. 9:24.

166. It should be noted that the traditional Jewish chronology followed by Rashi contains a significant error, since the Second Temple actually stood for roughly 600 years rather than 420 years. See vol. 1, 2.1.

167. This is partially confirmed by Heinrich W. Guggenheimer, *Seder Olam: The Rabbinic View of Biblical Chronology* (Northvale, N.J.: Aronson, 1998). See below, n. 169.

168. Ibid., 245.

169. Interestingly, Guggenheimer (ibid., 246) finds Rashi's approach to Daniel 8 and 9 to be "somewhat inconsistent in that in *Daniel* Chapter 8, whose vision is not treated in *Seder 'Olam* [the standard Rabbinic chronology], he refers that vision to Antiochus and the situation before the Maccabean revolt." Guggenheimer also points out (244) that in Rashi's comments on Daniel 9:24–27, Rashi "follows *Seder 'Olam* strictly in the interpretation of times and terms but superimposes references to messianic times that come from later medieval sources and are inconsistent with the interpretation of *Seder 'Olam* that the end of the vision is the destruction of the second Temple." This last observation is especially significant for our present discussion.

170. Frydland's autobiographical story is told in Rachmiel Frydland, *When Being Jewish Was a Crime* (repr.; Columbus, Md.: Messianic Publishing, 1998). To read his testimony of faith in Yeshua, along with the testimonies of other Jews—some of whom were ordained rabbis before coming to faith in the Messiah—see <http://www.menorah.org/salv.html>.

171. Note also that John J. Collins, a historical-critical commentator who rejects the Messianic interpretation, also translates *mashiach* as "the anointed one." *Daniel: A Commentary on the Book of Daniel* (Philadelphia: Fortress, 1994), 346.

172. In verses 25–26 the NIV renders *mashiach* as "the Anointed One," with "an anointed one" listed in the margin as an alternative rendering. This indicates that even conservative Christian translations recognize the validity of the points we are discussing in this objection. Note also that if the *mashiach nagid* of Daniel 9:25 is the same as the *mashiach* in 9:26 (a position that I do not find essential to embrace as a follower of Jesus; see below, 4.21), then it could be argued based on the unusual grammatical structure of *mashiach nagid* (an anointed one, a ruler, meaning "an anointed ruler") that the right interpretation would be "*the* anointed one." Gleason Archer ("Daniel," *EBC*, 7:119–20), notes that the words *ad mashiach nagid* "(. . . 'till an Anointed One, Ruler') could be translated 'till an anointed one, a ruler.' But since this pair of titles is hopelessly vague and indefinite, applying to almost any governor or priest-king in Israel's subsequent history, it could scarcely have furnished the definite *terminus ad quem* the context obviously demands. It is therefore necessary to understand each of these terms as exalted titles applying to some definite personage in future history. In Hebrew, proper names do not take the definite article, neither do titles that have become virtually proper nouns by usage. GKC (pars. 125 f-g) cites many examples of these: e.g., *shaday* (. . . 'the Almighty'), *satan* (. . . 'the Adversary'), *tebhel* (. . . 'the world'), *'elyon* (. . . 'the Most High'). We therefore conclude that 'Messiah the Ruler' was the meaning intended by the author. The word order precludes construing it as 'an [or "the"] anointed ruler,' which would have to be *nagid mashiah*."

173. Gerald Sigal also objects strongly to other aspects of the KJV rendering of Daniel 9:26, stating that "the words v'ayn lo (9:26) are incorrectly translated by the King James Version as 'but not for himself.' They should be translated as 'he has nothing' or 'he shall have nothing.' There are Christian commentators who maintain this phrase has both meanings, but that claim cannot be supported grammatically" (<http://www.jewsforjudaism.org/j4j-2000/index.html>). In point of fact, the NKJV is one of the only modern Christian versions that perpetuates this translation, so Sigal's argument is really beating a dead horse. Not only so, but when translations in his own Orthodox Jewish tradition exhibit similar faults, he chooses not to criticize them, let alone attack them with such antagonism and disdain.

174. As noted in the NIV and most modern versions, the Masoretic manuscripts offer variant readings for several of these verbs. The overall sense of the verse is not affected, however. See the commentaries for discussion.

175. Kaiser, *The Messiah in the Old Testament*, 202, his emphasis.

176. See James E. Smith, *What the Bible Teaches about the Promised Messiah* (Nashville: Nelson, 1993), 384. For refutation of the allegation that verses such as Matthew 23:32 are anti-Semitic, cf. vol. 1, 2.8.

177. I have changed Smith's reference to "the obtuseness of the Jews" to "the obtuseness of [his fellow] Jews" to remind the reader that Yeshua, the Jewish Messiah and the last (and greatest) national prophet, spoke to his own people as an in-house, family member. This was not an anti-Semitic criticism coming from the outside. See again vol. 1, 2.8.

178. Smith, *The Promised Messiah*, 385, supports this view with reference to 1 Chronicles 23:13, where, according to a minority of interpreters, the high priest is set aside as "most holy" (cf. the rendering in the Stone edition, "Aaron was set apart, to sanctify him as holy of holies"), using the same Hebrew phrase *(qodesh qodashim)* that elsewhere is used with reference to the most holy place in the Temple, or to the holiest items in the Temple. According to Gleason Archer ("Daniel," *EBC*, 7:119), "Twice qodhesh qadhashim (. . . 'the most holy') refers to the altar—Exod 29:37; 30:10; four times to the holy objects of the Holy Place or temple—Num 18:10; Ezek 43:12; 45:3; 48:12. Gesenius-Buhl (*Handwörterbuch*, p. 704) suggests that in Dan 9:24 *qodeš qadašî* refers to the temple. In Exod 30:36 it is used of holy incense; in Lev 24:9 of the memorial bread (showbread). Or it refers to the priestly portion of peace offerings ('fellowship offerings,' NIV)—Lev 2:3, 10; 6:10; 10:12. In Lev 6:18, 22 it is used of sin offerings; in Num 18:9; Ezra 2:63; Neh 7:65 of offerings in general; likewise in Lev 21:22; 2 Chronicles 31:14; Ezek 42:13; 44:13. Ten times it is used of the Holy Place of the tabernacle or temple—Exod 26:33–34 *(bis)*; 1 Kings 6:16; 7:50; 8:6; 2 Chronicles 3:8, 10; 4:22; 5:7; Ezek 41:4."

179. Smith, *The Promised Messiah*, 384–85.

180. Collins, *Daniel*, 345. Interestingly, Collins does not directly explain the phrase "to bring in everlasting righteousness." Jewish scholars tend to follow either the standard, historical-critical interpretation articulated here by Collins or the interpretation espoused by Rashi and Seder Olam Rabbah, who understand Daniel 9:24–27 to culminate with the destruction of the Second Temple in 70 C.E.

181. Thus, James A. Montgomery, a respected Semitic and biblical scholar, was forced to acknowledge that this interpretation "would then take us down some 65 years too far. We can meet this objection only by surmising a chronological miscalculation on the part of the writer" (*Daniel*, International Critical Commentary [Edinburgh: T. & T. Clark, 1927], 393). Montgomery, however, claims that the author of Daniel "was

not embarrassed, in the absence of a known chronology, in squeezing these 434 years [i.e., the 62 weeks of years] between the Return and the Antiochian persecution" (ibid.).

182. Goldingay, *Daniel*, 257, citing N. W. Porteous at the end of the quote. This really is quite fascinating: Critical scholars determine that Daniel is speaking of a period of seventy sevens ending in the time of Antiochus but then turn around and state that Daniel was way off in his chronology, since the seventy sevens don't end at that time. What makes this all the more unfortunate is that many critics arrive at this conclusion because they refuse to believe that Daniel could have actually been predicting future events under the inspiration of the Holy Spirit. Thus, they not only shoot themselves in the foot with their faulty reasoning, but they miss one of the greatest predictive prophecies contained in the Scriptures.

183. As stated by Archer, "It is axiomatic among critics who rule out supernaturalism that Daniel's successful predictions of events leading up to the reign of Antiochus Epiphanes (175–164 B.C.) can be accounted for only by assuming that some unknown pseudepigrapher wrote this book so as to make it seem an authentic sixth-century prophecy" ("Daniel," *EBC*; Archer notes that this view goes back to the third-century philosopher Porphyry). Archer has also argued that dating Daniel to the second or third century B.C.E. goes against the linguistic evidence; cf. idem, "The Aramaic of the Genesis Apocryphon Compared with the Aramaic of Daniel," in J. Barton Payne, ed., *New Perspectives on the Old Testament* (Waco: Word, 1970), 160–69; idem, "The Hebrew of Daniel Compared with the Qumran Sectarian Documents," in John H. Skilton, ed., *The Law and the Prophets* (Nutley, N.J.: Presbyterian and Reformed, 1974), 470–81. Cf. also Zdravko Stefanovic, *The Aramaic of Daniel in the Light of Old Aramaic* (Sheffield, England: Sheffield Academic Press, 1992); more broadly, see Edward M. Cook, *Word Order in the Aramaic of Daniel* (Malibu, Calif.: Undena, 1986).

184. Archer, "Daniel," 7:112.

185. Cf. also 1 Thessalonians 2:16, along with the notes and explanations provided in vol. 1, 2.8.

186. Archer, "Daniel," 7:113; Archer adds, "The Crucifixion was the atonement that made possible the establishment of the new order, the church of the redeemed, and the establishment of the coming millennial kingdom." I would suggest that similar statements could be made for the first two phrases as well, thus removing the need to point to a still-future fulfillment.

187. Montgomery (*Daniel*, 398) makes reference to a fascinating Rabbinic interpretation of this phrase, noting that according to C. Schöttgen in *Horae hebraicae*, Rabbi Moses Haddarshan "is reported to have said: 'The eternal righteousness, that is King Messiah,' which interestingly enough agrees with [Jerome's] statement [fifth century C.E.] that the Jews of his day made the same equation."

188. Cf. the usage of Isaiah 6:9–10 in the Gospels (e.g., Mark 4:1–12); cf. further the discussion in Romans 9–11 and 2 Corinthians 3. Once again, I see no reason to follow Archer here when he states, "This fulfillment surely goes beyond the suffering, death, and resurrection of Christ; it must include his enthronement on the throne of David—as supreme Ruler over all the earth" ("Daniel," 7:113).

189. Ibid.; cf. further my discussion in vol. 2, 3.17.

190. Ludwig Köhler and Walter Baumgartner, *Hebräisches und aramäisches Lexikon zun Alten Testament* (Leiden: E. J. Brill, 1967–96), 2:1078 (henceforth cited as *HALAT*), cites Daniel 9:24 and 1 Chronicles 23:13 under the heading of "meaning the temple." Interestingly, these are the only references cited under this heading.

191. Before Jesus was conceived, the angel Gabriel announced to the virgin Miriam, "The Holy Spirit will come upon you, and the power of the Most High will overshadow you. So the holy one to be born will be called the Son of God" (Luke 1:35). NIV also offers the alternative rendering, "so the child to be born will be called holy," in the text notes.

192. C. Schöttgen, as cited in Montgomery, *Daniel*, 398.

193. Cf. Keil, *Daniel*, in C. F. Keil and F. Delitzsch, *Commentary on the Old Testament*, 1028–33. Keil also discusses 1 Chronicles 23:13.

194. Some believe that "the most holy" refers to the Messiah's coming to the Temple in Jerusalem, but most scholars do not consider this interpretation worthy of serious discussion.

195. Cf. further b. Avodah Zarah 2b.

196. The Talmud itself cites Daniel 9:24–27 as setting the time for the destruction of the Second Temple; see b. Nazir 32b.

197. The reason there are only 483 years from 457 B.C.E. to 27 C.E. (instead of 484 years) is because there is no "zero year." In other words, we count directly from 1 B.C.E. to 1 C.E.

198. This is recognized even by Jewish tradition itself; see the discussion of Harry. M. Orlinsky, prolegomenon to Christian D. Ginsburg, *Introduction to the Masoretico-Christian of the Hebrew Bible* (New York: Ktav, 1966), i–xlv.

199. Archer, "Daniel," 7:114.

200. Ibid.

201. Sigal seriously misrepresents the Christian position when he writes, "By creating a sixty-nine week period, which is not divided into two separate periods of seven weeks and sixty-two weeks respectively, Christians reach an incorrect conclusion, i.e., that the Messiah will come 483 years after the destruction of the First Temple" (<http://www.jewsforjudaism.org/j4j-2000/index.html>). His error, of course, is not in claiming that Christians believe the Messiah would come after this 483-year period but rather in stating that Christians believe "the Messiah will come 483 years *after the destruction of the First Temple*" (my emphasis). Who holds *that* position? We date the beginning of the 483 period to the command to *restore and rebuild Jerusalem*, as per Daniel 9:25, not to the *destruction of the First Temple*. Moreover, that Temple was destroyed in 587 or 586 B.C.E. (according to all chronologies except the Rabbinic chronology; see vol. 1, 2.1). Deducting 483 years from this date brings us to 104/103 B.C.E., one century *before* Yeshua's birth. What Bible-believing Christian or Messianic Jew argues that Daniel's prophecy was more than one hundred years off?

202. Albert Barnes, *Barnes' Notes on the Old Testament*, commenting on Dan. 9:24.

203. My position here is in contrast to the position of Archer and other Christian scholars who point to an end-of-the-age (= "Great Tribulation") fulfillment of the seventieth week, with the Antichrist as the main figure involved.

204. For details on which scholars have followed which views, see the standard commentaries on Daniel.

205. Scholars today—almost without exception and with complete justification—reject the view that Daniel's seventy weeks of years are to be calculated based on an alleged 360-day prophetic year.

206. The footnote to verse 27a explains that, "The Roman emperor would make a treaty with the Jewish nation for seven years; but for the second half of that term the Romans would violate that covenant and impede the Temple service. The 'mute abomination,' i.e., a temple of idolatry, was erected by the emperor Hadrian on the Temple

Mount *(Rashi)*." I should point out that the Stone edition's rendering of the words *we'en lo* (v. 26a) as stating that the anointed one will be cut "and *will exist no longer*" (my emphasis) is not representative of the majority of translations, Christian or Jewish.

207. Another problem with the critical interpretation of the seventy weeks is that only the destruction of Jerusalem in 70 C.E., rather than the defiling of the Temple by Antiochus IV in the 160s B.C.E., would live up to the description that "devastation will continue to overwhelm desolate Jerusalem until what God has decreed is exhausted" (to use Goldingay's words, *Daniel,* 263).

208. Kaiser, *The Messiah in the Old Testament,* 203.

209. The Talmudic interpretation found in b. Sanhedrin 97a points us in the same general direction, stating that the seventy weeks are divided into seven parts, after which the Messiah will come.

210. A potential candidate such as Cyrus, who was a key *mashiach* in biblical Jewish history, is disqualified because of chronological issues, since there is no valid way to begin the *terminus a quo* of Daniel 9:25 (received by revelation from the angel Gabriel somewhere around 539 B.C.E.) with a date 49 years *before* Cyrus (who issued his decree to rebuild the Temple in the year 539 B.C.E.)!

211. Gerald Sigal also makes the odd claim that the second anointed one mentioned in the text is Alexander Yannai, the ruthless high priest who led Israel from 103 to 76 B.C.E. There are, however, insuperable difficulties with this interpretation: (1) Since Cyrus cannot be the *mashiach* mentioned in Daniel 9:25, Alexander cannot be the *mashiach* who is cut off 434 years after Cyrus. (2) Even using Sigal's dating ("The first seven weeks ends in 537 B.C.E. The second segment of the Seventy Weeks period, sixty-two weeks in length, covered by verse 26, culminates in 103 B.C.E."), why does this period culminate with the *beginning* of Yannai's reign rather than the end of his reign, his alleged "cutting off"? (3) Aside from the fact that the identification of Alexander Yannai is quite tenuous (why single him out, and why point to someone in whose lifetime what was written in Daniel 9:24–27 did *not* take place?), Sigal's explanation of being cut off and having nothing is bizarre, since nothing unusual is recorded about Yannai's death. Thus, he must argue that the verb *yikkaret* here means "suffer the penalty of excision" (as in "being cut off" for certain sins in the Torah), claiming that, "The penalty accompanying karet is here aptly described as 'to have nothing,' or 'be no more.'" This is impossibly forced, since being cut off and having nothing (or being no more) unquestionably speaks of *death* (as widely recognized by Jewish commentators and translators). Not only so, but the only definitive evidence that Alexander Yannai suffered this alleged penalty of excision is that Sigal says he did! See concisely <http://www.jewsforjudaism.org/j4j-2000/html/reflib/dan9120.html>.

212. Similarly, Ibn Ezra, commenting on Psalm 45:16[17], sees his interpretation as fitting both David and the Messiah.

213. I cite the Stone edition here to emphasize that even through traditional Jewish eyes, the Hebrew *yelidtika* is rightly rendered, "I have begotten you." See further vol. 2, 3.3.

214. The Syriac Peshitta understood *bar* as "son"; other ancient versions (Greek, Aramaic, Latin) understood the meaning to be "purity," "chastity," "discipline," "pure," "unmixed" (reading the Hebrew as either *bar* or *bor*).

215. Among these translations are the KJV, NKJV, NIV, and NASB.

216. A. Sh. Hartom, *The Book of Psalms* (in Hebrew) (Tel Aviv: Yavneh, 1972), 12: "It is possible that the word *bar* occurs here according to its meaning in Aramaic, 'son', in which case it should be interpreted: kiss the son, that is, the king (v. 7), as if to say,

give him glory (2 Sam. 10:1; 1 Kin. 19:18; Hos. 13:2)." Hartom's volume belongs to a commentary series that was edited by the respected Orthodox scholar M. D. (Umberto) Cassuto.

217. Samuel Loewenstamm and Joshua Blau, eds., *Thesaurus of the Language of the Bible*, vol. 2 (in Hebrew and English) (Jerusalem: The Bible Concordance Press, 1959), 146–47. Blau and Loewenstamm also mention kissing "the soil (before the king's feet)" as a possibility.

218. Cf. A. A. Macintosh, "A consideration of the problems presented by Psalm ii. 11 and 12," *Journal of Theological Studies*, n.s., 27 (1976): 138ff. for translations of both Ibn Ezra as well as Radak (the latter understanding *br* as "elect, chosen," from a putative root *brr*, "to choose, select"); Arnold B. Ehrlich, *Die Psalmen*, Hüldiget dem Sohne (Berlin: M. Poppelauer, 1905), 4; A. Sh. Hartom, *The Book of Psalms*, 12; Loewenstamm and Blau, *Thesaurus*, 2:147–48. Moreover, it can be argued that some Christian scholars have unconsciously steered *away* from such a translation for fear of seeming partial and biased. In any case, from the viewpoint of a contextual and philological study of Psalm 2, what does *any* rendering of verse 12 have to do with later Jewish or Christian interpretations, especially in light of the fact that in spite of the popularity of Psalm 2 in the New Testament (esp. v. 7; cf. Donald Juel, *Messianic Exegesis* [Philadelphia: Fortress, 1988], 62), verse 12 is never quoted? For an interesting study of the affect of medieval Jewish-Christian polemics on the concept of Israel as God's "son", see V. Huonder, *Israel Sohn Gottes. Zur Deutung eines alttestamentlichen Themas in der judischen Exegese des Mittelalters* (Göttingen: Vandenhoeck & Ruprecht, 1975).

219. Of minor grammatical importance is the question of why there is no definite article before *bar* (in other words, why the word "the" is not found), but in poetic contexts such as Psalm 2, the definite article would not be necessary; cf. Delitzsch, *Psalms*, in Keil and Delitzsch, *Commentary on the Old Testament*, 847.

220. As cited in Santala, *The Messiah in the Old Testament in the Light of Rabbinical Writings*, 121, from the Amsterdam edition, part 3, 307a. Another citation of this passage in the Zohar (vol. 1, 267a), adds the words, "It is also said about the Messiah son of Joseph," possibly referring to b. Sukkah 52a, cited above.

221. Joseph Addison Alexander, *The Psalms Translated and Explained* (repr; Grand Rapids, Baker, 1977), 68. This agrees with the rendering of the NJPSV, as cited: "For You will not abandon me to Sheol."

222. For the meaning and etymology of *shahat*, also rendered "pit" (cf. Isa 38:17, with *shahat beli*), see M. Held, "Pits and Pitfalls in Akkadian and Biblical Hebrew," *Journal for the Ancient Near Eastern Society of Columbia University* 5 (1973): 173–90; cf. further N. J. Tromp, *Primitive Conceptions of Death and the Netherworld in the Old Testament* (Rome: Pontifical Biblical Institute Press, 1969), 19, 33, 67, 69–71; *HALAT*, 4:1365–66; and the articles on Sheol in *NIDOTTE* (see the index vol., 5:724, s.v. "sheol," for references); cf. also *HALAT* 4:1274–75. More broadly, cf. Tromp, *Primitive Conceptions*, with Assyriological strictures from W. von Soden, "Assyriologische Erwägungen zu einem neuen Buch über die Totenreichvorstellungen im Alten Testament," *Ugarit Forsehungen* 2 (1970): 331–32.

223. Old Testament scholar A. A. Anderson presents both views, suggesting that verse 10 "probably" means that "God will deliver his servant from an untimely death, or from the danger of death during his allotted span of life," but also states that "it is just possible that the Psalmist may have hoped that, in some way or other, his fellowship with God would not come to an end," even suggesting that the text contains an "allusion . . . to the belief of the resurrection of the body." Anderson, *The Book of Psalms*

(1–72): The New Century Bible Commentary (Grand Rapids: Eerdmans, 1972), 1:145–46. It seems that the reason Anderson is uncertain about this psalm expressing a hope in the resurrection from the dead is not primarily the simple meaning of the text but rather the larger question of whether such a belief was known at that time.

224. Martin S. Rozenberg and Bernard M. Zlotowitz, *The Book of Psalms: A New Translation and Commentary* (Northvale, N.J.: Aronson, 1999), 79.

225. Ibid. The abbreviation B.B. refers to the Talmudic tractate b. Baba Bathra.

226. Ibid. The authors, however, claim that "there is, however, no hard evidence that immortality as understood later on was a living concept in biblical times" (ibid.), also claiming that it is "anachronistic" to assign this psalm "to David's time and contend that he was expressing a belief in resurrection" (ibid., 75). Other biblical and ancient Near Eastern scholars differ with this; cf. Willem VanGemeren, "Psalms," *EBC*, 5:158–59.

227. Rosenberg notes that this explanation is only found in some Rashi manuscripts, meaning that Rashi himself or an editor of his works wrote it. Either way, this explanation derives from a traditional Jewish source.

228. According to Delitzsch (*Psalms*, 1666), such "Messianic Psalms of David are reflections of his radical, ideal contemplation of himself, reflected images of his own typical history; they contain prophetic elements, because David there too speaks *en pneumati* [Greek for "in the Spirit"] but elements that are not solved by the person of David."

229. In fact, the Hebrew word *'aharit*, which means "the end, the final consequences" (see Prov. 23:17–18; 24:19–20), and other times refers to physical offspring (see Ps. 109:13 in NRSV). For the spiritual implications of this concept, cf. Michael L. Brown, *Go and Sin No More: A Call to Holiness* (Ventura, Calif.: Regal, 1999), 76–89.

230. Tovia Singer, <http://www.outreachjudaism.org/like-a-lion.htm#1ret>.

231. My emphasis. Remember that David was recognized as a prophet in the Scriptures and in Jewish tradition; see, e.g., 2 Samuel 23:1 with Rashi's commentary.

232. After reviewing the various suggestions offered by Jewish scholars as to the identity of the sufferer in Psalm 22, Rozenberg and Zlotovitz then note, "Traditional Jewish scholarship sees this psalm as foretelling of the coming events surrounding Purim. The anguished cry, 'My God, my God why have You abandoned me?,' is ascribed to Esther. . . . Christian scholars *have also understood* this psalm as being predictive but have connected the psalm to the events surrounding their Messiah" (*The Book of Psalms*, 120–21, my emphasis).

233. I have observed through the years that anti-missionaries often ignore or betray ignorance of normative, traditional Jewish interpretations when those interpretations contradict the polemical point they are making, as is the case here. It is therefore fair to ask what their primary motivation is. Is it faithfulness to (traditional) Judaism, or is it pulling Jews away from other beliefs? If it is the former, why then contradict or ignore the very men whose teachings form the core of traditional Judaism?

234. As noted by Charles A. Briggs (*Messianic Prophecy* [New York: Scribner's, 1889], 326), cited in Kaiser, *The Messiah in the Old Testament*, 112–13, the sufferings described in Psalm 22 "find their exact counterpart in the sufferings on the cross. They are more vivid in their realization of that dreadful scene than the story of the Gospels. The most striking features of these sufferings are seen there, in the piercing of the hands and feet, the body stretched upon the cross, the intense thirst, and the division of the garments."

235. Rashi explains this phrase to mean "to the crushing of death."

236. On the crucifixion imagery in this psalm, see 4.25.

237. Again, one need not raise the question of whether or not the psalmist actually spoke of his own *death* and resurrection; it is sufficient that he spoke of his own extreme sufferings and deliverance in graphic, poetic terms that quite literally foreshadowed the Messiah's death and subsequent deliverance from the grave.

238. Smith, *The Promised Messiah,* 146, cited in Kaiser, *The Messiah in the Old Testament,* 113.

239. From the standard translation of William G. Braude, *Pesikta Rabbati: Homiletical Discourses for Festal Days and Special Sabbaths,* 2 vols. (New Haven: Yale, 1968), 680–81.

240. Ibid., 685–86.

241. Ibid., 686–87. All of these citations can be found in the useful Internet article on Psalm 22 found on <http://www.messianicart.com/chazak/ps22.htm>.

242. Singer, <http://www.outreachjudaism.org/like-a-lion.htm#4ret>.

243. Ibid.

244. As pointed out in the very useful Internet article mentioned in n. 241, above, Singer is especially vitriolic in his attacks. The following verbiage is noted from Singer's article on Psalm 22 (there is some overlap here with my citations in the text, but I list them again in full for impact: "1. Christian translators rewrote the words of King David; 2. The insertion of the word 'pierced' into the last clause of this verse is a not-too-ingenious Christian interpolation that was created by deliberately mistranslating the Hebrew word *kaari* as 'pierced'; 3. the phrase 'they pierced my hands and my feet' is a Christian contrivance that appears nowhere in the Jewish scriptures. 4. . . . this stunning mistranslation in the 22nd Psalm . . . 5. This verse was undoubtedly tampered with years after the Christian canon was completed. 6. The Bible tampering . . . 7. Why then did [the Christian translators] specifically target Psalm 22 for such Bible tampering? 8. This church revision of the 22nd Psalm . . . 9. The church, therefore, did not hesitate to tamper with the words of the 22nd Psalm. . . . 10. . . . the stunning mistranslation in this chapter . . ." Sadly, such charges expose the serious lack of scholarship that is rampant in Rabbi Singer's articles and tapes, as can be readily seen by comparing his comments with those of contemporary Jewish and Christian scholars who have written commentaries on Psalm 22.

245. It should be noted that the reading *ka'ari,* "like a lion," is not without problems, since there is no verb in this clause. In other words, the Hebrew literally reads, "like a lion my hands and feet," necessitating the addition of the words "they are at" in most contemporary Jewish translations. Thus, the NJPSV translates, "Like lions [they maul] my hands and feet" (with reference to Rashi and Isaiah 38:13 in the footnote). Cf. Rozenberg and Zlotowitz, *The Book of Psalms,* 122, 127. *Stone* translates, "Like [the prey of] a lion are my hands and my feet."

246. This observation undermines the claim of Rabbi Singer that "when the original words of the Psalmist are read, any allusion to a crucifixion disappears" (<http://www.outreachjudaism.org/like-a-lion.htm#4ret>).

247. Cf. Martin Abegg Jr., Peter Flint, and Eugene Ulrich, eds. and trans., *The Dead Sea Scrolls Bible: The Oldest Known Bible* (San Francisco: HarperSan Francisco, 1999), 519: "Psalm 22 is a favorite among Christians since it is often linked in the New Testament with the suffering and death of Jesus. A well-known and controversial reading is found in verse 16, where the Masoretic text has 'Like a lion are my hands and feet,' whereas the Septuagint has 'They have pierced my hands and

feet.' Among the scrolls the reading in question is found only in the Psalms scroll found at Nahal Hever (abbreviated 5/6HevPs), which reads, 'They have pierced my hands and my feet'!"

248. In contrast with this, only one Masoretic manuscript reads *ka'aryeh* ("like a lion"; *'aryeh* is a variant spelling for *'ari*, "lion"). Delitzsch (*Psalms*, 1039) points out that the Masoretic scholars were aware of a textual variation in two occurrences of this same form, and he notes that "perceiving this [difficulty of the translation 'like a lion' in the context], the Masora on Isa xxxviii. 13 observes, that *k'ari* in the two passages in which it occurs (Ps. xxii. 17, Isa. xxxviii. 13), occurs in two different meanings, just as the Midrash then also undestands *k'ri* in the Psalm as a verb used of marking with conjuring, magic characters."

249. The exact evidence as documented in the standard edition of Kennicot and de Rossi lists seven Masoretic manuscripts *reading k'rw*, while three other manuscripts have the *reading krw* in the margins. It has also been pointed out by some scholars that the Hebrew word used for "lion" in Psalm 22:13[14] is the more common *'aryeh*, making it more doubtful that a different form of the word, namely, *'ari*, would be used just two verses later. Yet this is what the normative reading in the Masoretic manuscripts would call for.

250. Note that Rashi pointed to this very verse in Isaiah to explain Psalm 22:17.

251. Delitzsch, *Psalms*, 1039; cf. also Glen Miller, "The Isaiah 7:14 Passage."

252. Singer, <http://www.outreachjudaism.org/like-a-lion.htm#4ret>, my emphasis. His attack on the Septuagint is perhaps even more remarkable. Cf. the following selections, which either completely contradict the verdict of modern scholarship or drastically overstate the evidence: "It is universally conceded and beyond any question that the rabbis who created the original *Septuagint* only translated the Five Books of Moses and nothing more" (actually, there was no such thing as a "rabbi" at the time the Torah was translated into Greek). "This undisputed point is well attested to by the Letter of Aristeas, the *Talmud*, Josephus, the church fathers, and numerous other critical sources" (he fails to note that some of these sources preserve the *legendary* account of the origins of the Septuagint!). ". . . even the current *Septuagint* covering the Five Books of Moses is an almost complete corruption of the original Greek translation that was compiled by the 72 rabbis more than 2,200 years ago for King Ptolemy II of Egypt. . . . The *Septuagint* that is currently in our hands—especially the sections that are of the Prophets and Writings—is a Christian work, amended and edited exclusively by Christian hands. There is therefore little wonder that the *Septuagint* is esteemed in Christendom alone. In fact, in the Greek Orthodox Church, the *Septuagint* is regarded as Sacred Scripture." (He closes by noting, "I have addressed the subject of the *Septuagint* more thoroughly in a previous article entitled **'A Christian Defends Matthew by Insisting That the Author of the First Gospel Used the *Septuagint* in His Quote of Isaiah to Support the Virgin Birth.'"**) For a detailed introduction to the whole issue of the text's critical use of the Septuagint and other ancient versions, written by a leading authority in the field (currently a professor at the Hebrew University in Jerusalem), cf. Emanuel Tov, *Textual Criticism of the Hebrew Bible*, rev. ed. (Philadelphia: Fortress, 2001).

253. See the references cited above, n. 70; note also the Romans commentary of Shulam and LeCornu, cited below, n. 356.

254. For a typical example, see, conveniently, the footnotes to the Stone edition of Proverbs 5, following Rashi's commentary.

255. For discussion of the translation of this phrase ("a body you prepared for me" in the Greek as opposed to the "my ears you have pierced, dug through" in the Hebrew) in Hebrews 10:5, see 5.5.

256. For an interesting midrashic interpretation, cf. Midrash Ruth 8:8, on Ruth 4:19.

257. See 4.28; note also principle 2 in the appendix, along with vol. 2, 3.2.

258. Santala, *The Messiah in Light of the Rabbinical Writings*, 111, his emphasis.

259. Ibid.

260. Ibid., 113. According to Edersheim, "*Ps. xlv.* is throughout regarded as Messianic. To begin with; the Targum renders *verse* 2 (3 in the Hebrew): 'Thy beauty, O King Messiah, is greater than that of the sons of men.'" See Alfred Edersheim, *Life and Times of Jesus the Messiah* (repr., Peabody, Mass.: Hendrickson, 1993), 918 (2.788 in other editions).

261. Actually, in Exodus 7:1, *'elohim* does *not* mean "judge" contrary to Rashi's explanation; rather, as indicated by the related passage in Exodus 4:16, and as rendered in the NJPSV, *'elohim* in these passages means "in the role of God." The Stone edition renders *'elohim* in Exodus 4:16 as "leader" and in 7:1 as "master," both of which fall short of the mark.

262. Cf. further vol. 2, 3.3, with special reference to the rendering of H. J. Kraus.

263. Rozenberg and Zlotowitz, *The Book of Psalms*, 274, 277.

264. Ibid., 277.

265. Singer, http://www.outreachjudaism.org/psalm110.html>.

266. Rabbi Singer also claims that "the original Hebrew text was masked" in Christian translations, ibid.

267. Ibid.

268. Singer, as posted on his web site (see n. 265, above).

269. Ibid.

270. This *(yhwh)* is the so-called tetragrammaton, which occurs more than six thousand times in the Tanakh.

271. Literally, "my lords"; see vol. 2, 2.1.

272. The Hebrew is literally, "The utterance of YHWH to my lord."

273. If Jesus quoted the verse in Aramaic, he could well have said *marya* (meaning Yahweh) said to *mari* ("my lord/Lord"), following the exact same custom as in Hebrew. The Targum to Psalm 110 is more paraphrastic and expansive.

274. Although anti-missionaries strenuously object to the translation of *'adoni* in Psalm 110:1 as "my Lord" instead of "my lord," this matter is actually of no importance at all in Yeshua's argument. He is simply stressing that David, the greatest king in Israel's history, calls the Messiah his lord.

275. Singer, as posted on his web site (see n. 265, above). Oddly enough, Rabbi Singer later reverses himself on this point, noting that "the King James Version and a few other Bibles still render the second 'Lord' as if it were sacred; however, they translate the first 'LORD' in upper case. This is a helpful hint to the keen observer that there is a distinction between them. Of course, it's up to the curious Bible student to then look up the second 'Lord' in a Hebrew Bible. Only such a deliberate and thorough investigation would uncover how the text was doctored." Needless to say, any biblical scholar—Jewish or Christian—could not countenance the possibility of intentionally mistranslating a text or "doctoring" it to hide its true meaning. Rather, different translations arise from different translational convictions.

276. Singer, ibid.

277. Genesis 18 provides the classic example of interpretive issues arising because of the varying Masoretic vocalizations for the two words *'adonai* (with the short vowel *patah*, which could mean "my lords") and *'adoni* (with the long vowel *qametz*, which refers to Yahweh), both of which are spelled with the identical consonants (see vol. 2, 3.1). Interestingly, *'adonai* (with *qametz*) in Judg. 6:15 is rendered with "my lord" in the LXX *(kyrie mou)* as opposed to simply Lord *(kyrie*, as it is usually rendered with reference to Yahweh), a rendering possibly reinforced by Judg. 6:13, with *'adoni*. This, then, could point to a change in the Masoretic vocalization of *'adoni*.

278. To repeat, there is no such ambiguity in English translations, since the English custom for more than five hundred years has been to render *yhwh* with LORD (all uppercase) and *'adon* with lord or Lord.

279. Once again, Rabbi Singer completely misses this point, claiming that it was the New Testament that started this translation custom: "If we look at the original Greek of Matthew 22:44 we find the same doctoring of the text in later Christian translations of the Book of Psalms. When Matthew has Jesus quote Psalm 110:1 to the Pharisees, the identical Greek word *kyrios* (pronounced koo-re-os) is used both times the word 'Lord' appears in Matthew 22:44" (as posted on his web site [see n. 265, above]).

280. Rashi's explanation here, following the midrash, is weak (namely, that "from Zion" means that Melchizedek came from Zion/Jerusalem with bread and wine for Abram and his men when they returned from battle).

281. Cf. Midrash Tehillim (Psalms) 18:29.

282. Cf. Hermann L. Strack and Paul Billerbeck, *Kommentar zum Neuen Testament aus Talmud und Midrasch* (München: C. H. Beck, 1922–1961), Vol. 4/1:452–465; see also David M. Hay, *Glory at the Right Hand: Psalm 110 in Early Christianity* (Nashville: Abingdon, 1973).

283. According to Ibn Ezra, it was written when David's men swore to him, "You will not go out with us in battle."

284. Both Ibn Ezra and Radak claim that *priest* here simply means "servant," pointing to 2 Samuel 8:18, where David's sons are called "priests." This strained interpretation (see vol. 1, 2.1), provides eloquent testimony to the difficulties presented by this verse when it is applied to David rather than the Messiah.

285. According to D. A. Carson, "Psalm 110 uses language so reckless and extravagant ("forever," v. 4; the mysterious Melchizedek reference, v. 4; the scope of the king's victory, v. 6) that one must either say the psalm is using hyperbole or that it points beyond David. That is exactly the sort of argument Peter uses in Acts 2:25–31 concerning another Davidic psalm (Ps 16)," "Matthew," *EBC*, 8:467.

286. Although some rabbinic commentaries dispute that David wrote this about the Messiah, other rabbinic sources (e.g., Midrash Tehillim 2:9; 18:29) follow the Messianic interpretation, indicating that they had no trouble with David calling the Messiah "lord" (this interpretation was so common that it is presupposed by the New Testament). There are also rabbinic traditions that speak of the Messiah's preexistence and his heavenly dialogs with God, indicating again that he was not merely a physical descendant of David. Cf. Patai, *Messiah Texts*, 17–22.

287. Delitzsch, *Psalms*, 1664–65.

288. Very farfetched is the view of Nachmanides (in his classic Barcelona debate of 1263), followed recently by Tovia Singer, namely, that David wrote this psalm for his court poets to recite *about him*. This not only sounds strange, it could well be called egotistical. Still, Singer argues, "King David composed Psalm 110 for liturgical recitation by the Levites in the Temple years after his death. Therefore, the Levites would

read this lyric, The Lord [God] said to my master [King David] 'Sit thou at my right hand. . . .' For the church, however, the Psalmist's original intent was superseded by its interest in Christianizing this verse. Thus, the opening verse in Psalm 110 was altered in order to paint Jesus into the Jewish scriptures," <http://www.outreachjudaism.org/psalm110.html>.

289. Carson, "Matthew," *EBC*, 8:468, makes a good point for the historicity of the New Testament interpretation: "Even the fact that Jesus' use of Psalm 110:1 was susceptible to an interpretation denying that the Messiah must be of Davidic descent argues strongly for the authenticity of this exegesis of the psalm, for it is unlikely that Christians would have placed this psalm on Jesus' lips when his Davidic sonship is taught throughout the NT (in addition to Matthew, cf. Mark 10:47–48; 11:10; Luke 1:32; 18:38–39; Rom 1:3; 2 Tim 2:8; Rev 3:7; 5:5; 22:16). Jesus' question (v. 45) is not a denial of Messiah's Davidic sonship but a demand for recognizing how Scripture itself teaches that Messiah is more than David's son."

290. For more on this, including the Talmudic explanation for these two apparently contradictory descriptions, see vol. 1, 2.1. The answer, of course, is that the prophecies are not either/or, but both/and. The Messiah first came riding on a donkey; he will return in the clouds of heaven.

291. Remember that Zerubbabel was of Davidic descent.

292. According to Kenneth L. Barker, "Zechariah," *EBC*, 7:639–40, this is Messianically applied in the Targum, the Jerusalem Talmud, and the Midrash.

293. Cf. the insightful comments of Barker (ibid., 7:638–39) on Zechariah 6:9–10: "The position of this actual ceremony after the eight visions is significant. The fourth and fifth visions, at the center of the series, were concerned with the high priest and the civil governor in the Davidic line. Zechariah here linked the message of those two visions to the messianic King-Priest. In the fourth vision (chap. 3), Joshua was priest; here (v. 13) the Branch was to officiate as priest. In the fifth vision (chap. 4), Zerubbabel was the governing civil official; here (v. 13) the Branch was to rule the government. In 4:9 Zerubbabel was to complete the rebuilding of the temple; here (v. 12) the Branch would build the temple. In 4:14 Zerubbabel and Joshua represented two separate offices; here the Branch was to hold both offices (v. 13). Thus restored Israel is seen in the future under the glorious reign of the messianic King Priest. The passage is typical-prophetical. Joshua served as a type of the Messiah, but at certain points the language transcends the experience of the type and becomes more directly prophetical of the antitype."

294. Commenting on Zechariah 6:12, Rashi states, "And some interpret [the passage] with reference to King Messiah, but all the content speaks [only] of the Second Temple."

295. Cf. Barker, "Zechariah,"*EBC*, 7:639, "Some interpreters argue that the original reading at the end of the verse was 'Zerubbabel son of Shealtiel' instead of 'Joshua son of Jehozadak.' But Eichrodt (*[Theology of the Old Testament]* 2:343, n.1) rightly considers 'that the interpretation of this passage in terms of Zerubbabel, which can only be secured at the cost of hazardous conjecture, is mistaken and that a reference to a hoped-for messianic ruler after Zerubbabel's disappearance is more in accordance with the evidence.' Furthermore, no Hebrew MSS or ancient versions have the Zerubbabel reading."

296. There are a number of relevant articles in John Day, ed., *King and Messiah in Israel and the Ancient Near East: Proceedings of the Oxford Old Testament Seminar* (JSOTSup 270; Sheffield, England: Sheffield Academic Press, 1998).

297. Another Rabbinic list omits the Shekhinah and separates the ark of the covenant from the mercy seat with the cherubim, thus making five missing items.

298. Troki, *Faith Strengthened*, 170. For the comparison between the First and Second Temples, cf. esp. b. Yoma 21b and 52b; see further H. N. Bilalik and Y. H. Ravnitzky, eds., *The Book of Legends: Sefer Ha-Aggadah*, trans. W. G. Braude (New York: Schocken, 1992), 161, #11; cf. also ibid., 165–66, #28, for b. Yoma 9b and Eyn Yaakov.

299. For Troki, this promise also excluded the possibility of fulfillment in the days of the Second Temple; see vol. 1, p, 223, nn. 12–13. Troki's own answer was a counsel of despair: The prophecy referred to the *Third Temple!* See vol. 1, ibid.

300. Cf. vol. 1, 2.6 (explaining Matt. 10:34); regarding the greater glory of the Second Temple, cf. *Batei Midrashot* 2, 24:11, listing the five elements missing from the Second Temple that will return to the *final* Temple, based on Haggai 2: the fire of the Shekhinah, the ark, the kapporet and cherubim, the Holy Spirit, and the Urim and Thummim.

301. The footnote to the translation reads, "The salvation will be so complete that people will be astonished if even one man is killed by the enemy (Radak)."

302. A note to the word "lament" states that the meaning of the Hebrew is uncertain, which is odd, since the Hebrew *wehibitu* simply means "they shall look." Apparently the translators saw something else in the text that made them think the Hebrew here was ambiguous.

303. Keil notes that "'*et-'asher* is chosen here, as in Jeremiah 38:9, in the place of the simple *'asher*, to mark *'asher* more clearly as an accusative, since the simple *'asher* might also be rendered 'who pierced (me)'," with ref. to the standard Hebrew grammar of Ges. §123, 2, Not. 1, *Zechariah*, in C. F. Keil and F. Delitzsch, *Commentary on the Old Testament*, 922. See further Clines, *Dictionary of Classical Hebrew*, 1:441, 1g.

304. This is why the translators of the Stone edition switched objects in the middle of the sentence, as observed.

305. It is actually so common that the preface to the NIV states that "the Hebrew writers often shifted back and forth between first, second and third personal pronouns without change of antecedent, this translation often makes them uniform, in accordance with English style and without the use of footnotes" (cited in the *EBC* endnote to Zech. 7:13, providing a case in point). Note also that in Zechariah 12 the Lord speaks in the first person a number of times, as cited above, but alternating with third-person language as well—in other words, going from "I" to "the Lord"; cf. verses 7–9.

306. The difference in the Hebrew is from *'elay* ("to me") to *'elayw* ("to him"). This reading is also supported in John 19:37. As to why this is quoted in John's Gospel as a *past* event ("These things happened [i.e., the Messiah's crucifixion] so that the scripture would be fulfilled: 'Not one of his bones will be broken,'" and, as another scripture says, "They will look on the one they have pierced."), cf. George R. Beasley-Murray, *John*, Word Biblical Commentary (Dallas: Word, 1987), 355.

307. Cf. Kaiser, *The Messiah in the Old Testament*, 224–25.

308. Or "to him whom they pierced."

309. Of course, I understand that my people did not actually crucify Yeshua, but it was our leadership who rejected him (something traditional Jews feel was a good decision!), handing him over to the Romans to be crucified. Thus, Peter was completely right in saying, "This man was handed over to you by God's set purpose and foreknowledge; and you, with the help of wicked men, put him to death by nailing him to the cross" (Acts 2:23); and again, "You disowned the Holy and Righteous One and asked that a murderer be released to you. You killed the author of life, but God raised

him from the dead. We are witnesses of this" (Acts 3:14–15). But he is quick to add, "Now, brothers, *I know that you acted in ignorance,* as did your leaders. But this is how God fulfilled what he had foretold through all the prophets, saying that his [Messiah] would suffer. Repent, then, and turn to God, so that your sins may be wiped out, that times of refreshing may come from the Lord" (Acts 3:17–19). For discussion and refutation of the anti-Semitic charge that "the Jews" are Christ-killers, see vol. 1, 2.7.

310. For more on this, see Michael L. Brown, *Our Hands Are Stained with Blood* (Shippensburg, Pa.: Destiny Image, 1992), 165–73.

311. For references to relevant discussion of the prophetic significance of the biblical feasts and holy days, see ibid., 39–41, 233–234, 81–84.

312. See further Baron, *Zechariah;* cf. also F. F. Bruce, *The New Testament Development of Old Testament Themes* (Grand Rapids: Eerdmans, 1968), 110–13.

313. It was in the popular study of Dennis Prager and Joseph Telushkin, *The Nine Questions People Ask about Judaism* (repr., New York: Simon and Schuster, 1986).

314. The absurdity of this argument is highlighted by the level of charges brought by anti-missionaries. Typical is the comment of Singer: "Missionaries manipulated, misquoted, mistranslated and even fabricated verses in Tanach in order to make Jesus' life fit traditional Jewish messianic parameters and to make traditional Jewish Messianic parameters fit the life of Jesus." See *A Lutheran Doesn't Understand Why Rabbi Singer Doesn't Believe in Jesus: A Closer Look at the "Crucifixion Psalm,"* Outreach Judaism, <http://outreachjudaism.org/like-a-lion.htm>.

315. As translated by Boteach, *The Wolf Shall Lie with the Lamb,* 3, my emphasis.

316. "Appendix VI, Messianic Prophecy Cited in the New Testament," in Smith, *The Promised Messiah,* 491–501. This useful appendix begins with the relevant New Testament text, followed by the Old Testament reference, the indication of fulfillment (i.e., how it was cited in the New Testament), the speaker, and the gist of the prophecy.

317. Herbert Lockyer, *All the Messianic Prophecies of the Bible* (Grand Rapids: Zondervan, 1973), 146–58.

318. See Edersheim, *Life and Times of Jesus the Messiah,* 2:980, appendix IX, "List of Old Testament Passages Messianically Applied in Ancient Rabbinic Writings." The examples in the following list are found on 2:980–1010. Despite its age, this remains the most complete and usable list of its kind, although the method of citing Rabbinic texts has since changed, and some of the citations may have been noted incorrectly in his discussion.

319. Ibid., 2:985. The only issue I would take with Edersheim's rendering is his use of uppercase pronouns (Him, His) when dealing with the Messiah, since this is not in keeping with Rabbinic practice.

320. The Schottenstein edition of the Talmud provides extensive discussion of this important Talmudic section; cf. also T. Leyishuah, ed. and trans., *The Chofetz Chaim on Awaiting Moshiach* (Jerusalem and New York: Feldheim, 1993).

321. Many scholars follow the view of C. H. Dodd in his classic study, *According to the Scriptures: The Sub-structure of the New Testament* (London: Nisbet, 1952), in which he argued that certain texts from the Hebrew Bible, joined primarily by theme, were grouped together as a collection of Messianic testimonia, drawn on throughout the New Testament writings. The origins of this collection would ultimately be in Yeshua's teachings as transmitted to his disciples.

322. Note also that Maimonides acknowledged that even the Talmudic sages differed in terms of some of the specific chronological details of the Messiah's advent, writing, "There are some Sages who say that Elijah's coming will precede the coming

of the Messiah. All these and similar matters cannot be [definitely] known by man until they occur, for these matters are undefined in the prophets' [words], and even the wise men have no established tradition regarding these matters, but only [their own] interpretation of the verses. Therefore, there is a controversy among them regarding these matters. Regardless [of the debate concerning these questions] neither the order of the occurrence of these events nor their precise details are among the fundamental principles of the faith." See Touger, *Laws of Kings and Their Wars*, 244–46, rendering Laws of Kings 12:2. It should also be pointed out that there was no standardized Jewish teaching on the Messiah until Maimonides wrote his famous Law Code almost seven hundred years after the completion of the Talmud—and even then, not all Jews accepted his rulings as binding.

323. See the discussion in Touger, *Laws of Kings and Their Wars*, 247.

324. Of course, someone might point out that the followers of Muhammad number more than one billion as well, and they too are monotheists. The fundamental difference, however, is that they do *not* regard the Tanakh (as we now have it) as the Word of God, and therefore the Koran does *not* quote the Hebrew Bible as sacred Scripture (in contrast with the New Testament, which does hundreds of times; see vol. 4, 5.1), nor is Allah, the God of the Muslims, the same as Yahweh, the God of the Tanakh (whereas Christians around the world worship the God of Israel as the one true God, revealed to us in and through the Messiah; see vol. 2, 3.1–3.4). Therefore, it is not fair to compare Jesus with Muhammad, since Jesus came in fulfillment of what was written in the Hebrew Scriptures, coming at the time he was required to come, whereas Muhammad simply founded a new religion.

325. Edersheim, *Life and Times of Jesus the Messiah*, 2:996, notes that, "*Is. xxxv*. 5, 6 is repeatedly applied to Messianic times. Thus, in Yalkut i. 78 *c*, and 157 *a*; in Ber. R. 95; and in Midrash on Ps. cxlvi. 8."

326. For studies on the veracity of the New Testament witness, cf. Craig L. Blomberg, *The Historical Reliability of the Gospels* (Downers Grove, Ill.: InterVarsity Press, 1987); J. P. Moreland, Scaling the Secular City: A Defense of Christianity (Grand Rapids: Baker, 1987); the older study of F. F. Bruce, The New Testament Documents: Are They Reliable? (repr., Downers Grove, Ill.: InterVarsity Press, 1994), is still valuable.

327. For further discussion, with reference to the relevant scholarly literature, cf. Brown, *Israel's Divine Healer*, 218–20; idem, *The Revival Answer Book: Rightly Discerning the Contemporary Revival Movements* (Ventura, Calif.: Renew, 2001), 138–61.

328. For representative testimonies, cf. the literature cited in vol. 1, p. 221, n. 56; see also above, n. 170.

329. This was the case in my own life: I first experienced the life-transforming power of the God of Israel through Jesus the Messiah, then began to study the Scriptures and learn of the Messianic prophecies, and then entered into dialogue with rabbis and anti-missionaries. Each stage of this process ultimately resulted in my faith growing stronger, not weaker.

330. For literature on the Messianic symbolism of the feasts, cf. vol. 1, 2.1 and p. 225, n. 22.

331. Michael O. Wise, The First Messiah: Investigating the Savior Before Jesus (San Francisco: HarperCollins, 1999); Israel Knohl, *The Messiah Before Jesus: The Suffering Servant of the Dead Sea Scrolls* (Berkley: Univ. of California Press, 2000); for a summary of research through the mid-1980s, see Emil Schürer, *The History of the Jewish People in the Age of Jesus Christ (175 b.c.–a.d. 135)*, rev. ed., ed. Geza Vermes, Fergus Millar, and Matthew Black (Edinburgh: T. & T. Clark, 1973–87), 2:547–49.

332. It is also correct to render this, "we may presume that he is the Messiah."

333. As rendered in Touger, *Laws of Kings and Their Wars*, 232, rendering Laws of Kings 11:4.

334. Ibid., 233.

335. Bear in mind that when Isaiah 2:1–4 was written, the Temple in Jerusalem was standing; thus, this prophecy cannot be pointed to as evidence that the Messiah would build a future Temple to the Lord. (In fact, the Messiah is not even mentioned in this passage.) What *is* prophesied is the extraordinary exaltation of the house of the Lord.

336. Note, however, that Rashi applies this title to Zerubbabel in Zechariah, finding no Messianic significance to it.

337. In Haggai 2:20–23, God speaks of Zerubbabel in almost Messianic terms for at least two reasons: First, it reaffirms the universal, royal promise to the Davidic line, despite the lack of a Davidic king at that time; second, it clearly reverses the curse that was spoken over Jehoiachin (also called Jeconiah or Coniah), son of Josiah, in Jeremiah 22:18–30. The curse in question is found in 22:30. For the restoring of favor to Jehoiachin's line—Zerubbabel was his grandson—cf. esp. Hag. 2:23 with Jer. 22:24; see also Jer. 52:31–34. It was recognized by both the Talmud and Rabbinic commentaries (cf. Radak) that the curse on Jehoiachin's line was, in fact, reversed; for further discussion of this in the context of Messianic polemics, cf. 5.12. For Zerubbabel as a Messianic figure in later Jewish literature (esp. in the medieval *Sefer Zerubbabel*), cf. Patai, *Messiah Texts*, 37–38, 110–11, 125–28, 251–52, 254.

338. Cf. Ralph L. Smith, *Micah-Malachi*, Word Biblical Commentary (Waco: Word, 1984), 218–19.

339. See vol. 2, 3.13, for information about the importance attached to the building of the Second Temple.

340. See the standard contemporary commentaries for details.

341. As noted by Old Testament commentator Joyce G. Baldwin (cited in Smith, *Micah-Malachi*, 219), "The building of Zerubbabel's Temple can hardly have been meant because it was already well on the way to completion, and those 'far off' are not necessarily confined to Jews of the dispersion (cf. 2:11; 8:22). The 'Book of Visions' [of which Zechariah 6 is a part] looked farther afield than the rebuilding in Jerusalem, and embraced all nations. Like many other prophetic passages it was concerned with the focal point of all history, the coming of the Davidic king, who would transform the concepts of Temple and of leadership."

342. Cf. also b. Sanhedrin 99a, "All the prophets, all of them, did not prophesy except of the days of the Messiah," quoted in the epigraph of this book along with Acts 3:24, "Indeed, all the prophets from Samuel on, as many as have spoken, have foretold these days."

343. Touger, *Laws of Kings and Their Wars*, 230, rendering Laws of Kings 11:3.

344. Ibid.

345. It is not surprising that traditional Jews believe that the Patriarchs, Moses, the prophets, and the kings and leaders of Judah observed the precepts of the oral Torah, since it is common for religious people to project their own beliefs back on their spiritual forefathers. Thus, Christians often see references to the cross in Old Testament passages where such a concept would have been completely unknown. All of these anachronistic retrojections, however, should be rejected. As to the Messiah's calling to lead all peoples, both Jew and Gentile, into the knowledge of God and observance of his laws (Hebrew, *torah*), see Isa. 42:1–4; Jer. 31:31–34.

346. For the Rabbinic recreation of the Messiah as a great Torah sage, cf. Jacob Neusner, *Messiah in Context: Israel's History and Destiny in Formative Judaism* (Philadelphia: Fortress, 1984).

347. Touger, *Laws of Kings and Their Wars*, 230, rendering Laws of Kings 11:3. For debate and discussion concerning the Rambam's view here, cf. ibid., 231–32.

348. Cf. Brown, *Israel's Divine Healer*, 215–222.

349. Interestingly, Touger, *Laws of Kings and Their Wars*, 233, notes that elsewhere in his Law Code (Hilchot Teshuvah 9:2), Maimonides "relates that the Messiah will possess prophetic powers that approach those of Moses. However, in the present context, the Rambam does not mention these abilities because he desires to emphasize the Messiah's achievements as a Torah leader and not his greatness as an individual." Again, this is quite telling. Cf. further the standard commentaries on Maimonides' Mishneh Torah for discussion of this section of his Law Code.

350. Ginsberg was one of the three primary translators of the New Jewish Publication Society Version of the Bible and a longtime professor at Jewish Theological Seminary. He was hailed by W. F. Albright, the brilliant biblical archaeologist, as the top scholar in Northwest Semitic languages of his day.

351. The explanatory footnotes to this verse give further background based on Ginsberg's article, "The Oldest Record of Hysteria with Physical Stigmata—Zechariah 13:2–6e," in Yitzchak Avishur and Joshua Blau, eds., *Studies in Bible and the Ancient Near East: Presented to Samuel E. Loewenstamm, on His Seventieth Birthday* (Jerusalem: E. Rubinstein's, 1978), 23–27. Note that the Stone edition reads, "scars between your arms."

352. Note that the Septuagint's rendering of Hosea 6:2 reads, "On the third day we shall be raised up and we shall live," while the Targum renders, "In the day of the resurrection of the dead he will raise us up that we may live," avoiding the issue of the third day entirely—possibly because of the use of the text by the early followers of Jesus. For discussion on the significance of these translations as related to the question of resurrection on the third day, see Anthony C. Thiselton, *The First Epistle to the Corinthians: A Commentary on the Greek Text* (Grand Rapids: Eerdmans, 2000), 1195–97, with reference to G. Delling, *"hemera," TDNT*, 2:949 (more broadly, 2:943–53).

353. Of less importance theologically, but still of some relevance, we should note that there are several occasions in which a destination was reached on the third day, indicating completion of a journey. (See, e.g., Josh. 9:17; 1 Sam. 30:1; 2 Sam. 1:2; see also 1 Kings 3:18, where the third day is significant for another reason.)

354. Roland Gradwohl, "Drei Tage und der dritte Tag," *Vetus Testamentum* 47 (1997): 373–78 (I cite the abstract published in *Old Testament Abstracts* 21.1, no. 139 [1998]). Note also that there are a number of passages in which three days signifies a period of trial (e.g., Gen. 42:17; Exod. 10:22–23; 15:22; Judg. 4:14) or deliberation, again with the concept of bringing something to climax or completion (e.g., 1 Kings 12:5, 12; Ezra 10:7–9).

355. K. Lehmann, *Auferweckt am dritten Tag nach der Schrift*, 2d ed. (Freiburg: Herder, 1969), 176–81, 262–90, with reference also to the midrashic material, cited in Thiselton, *First Epistle to the Corinthians*, 1197.

356. It should also be pointed out that Paul's interpretation is clearly within the bounds of accepted interpretative methods in early Judaism; those unfamiliar with modern scholarship on the Jewishness of Paul's thought and methodology should begin with the watershed study of W. D. Davies, *Paul and Rabbinic Judaism: Some Rabbinic Elements in Pauline Theology*, 4th ed. (Philadelphia: Fortress, 1980); on a less techni-

cal level, cf. Brad H. Young, *Paul the Jewish Theologian: A Pharisee among Christians, Jews, and Gentiles* (Peabody, Mass.: Hendrickson, 1998); for some novel—and challenging—approaches to Romans and Galatians, cf. Mark D. Nanos, *The Mystery of Romans: The Jewish Context of Paul's Letter* (Philadelphia: Fortress, 1996); idem, *The Irony of Galatians: Paul's Letter in First-Century Context* (Philadelphia: Fortress, 2001); cf. also Joseph Shulam and Hilary LeCornu, *A Commentary on the Jewish Roots of Romans* (Baltimore: Messianic Jewish Publishers, 1997), as well as Stern, *JNTC*, on Paul's epistles. Recent relevant surveys covering the wider issue of Paul and the law—massive amounts of scholarship have been devoted to this subject—include Stephen Westerholm, *Israel's Law and the Church's Faith: Paul and His Recent Interpreters* (Grand Rapids: Eerdmans, 1998); Frank Thielman, *Paul and the Law: A Contextual Approach* (Downers Grove, Ill.: InterVarsity Press, 1994).

Glossary

Babylonian Talmud. The foundational text for Jewish religious study, it consists of 2,500,000 words of Hebrew and Aramaic commentary and expansion on the **Mishnah.** It includes much **Halakha** as well as **Haggada,** and thus it touches on virtually every area of life, religion, custom, folklore, and law. It reached its final form between 500 and 600 C.E., and it is mainly the product of the Babylonian sages. *See also* **Palestinian Talmud.**

Five Scrolls. (Hebrew pronounced kha-MESH-me-gi-LOT) The biblical books of Song of Songs (Song of Solomon), Ruth, Lamentations, Ecclesiastes, and Esther. They were read in the synagogues on special holidays. *See also* **Ketuvim.**

Haggada. (sometimes spelled Aggada) Nonlegal (i.e., nonbinding) Rabbinic stories, sermons, and commentaries relating to the **Tanakh** and Jewish life. *See also* **Halakha** and **Midrash.**

Halakha. A specific legal ruling ("What is the Halakha in this case?") or Rabbinic legal material in general. The word Halakha is interpreted as meaning "the way to go." *See also* **Haggada.**

Humash. (pronounced KHU-mash) Another name for the Five Books of Moses. *See also* **Written Torah.**

Ibn Ezra. Abraham Ibn Ezra (1089–1164). One of the three greatest Jewish medieval biblical commentators, especially famous for his careful attention to Hebrew grammar. *See also* **Radak** and **Rashi.**

Jerusalem Talmud. *See* **Palestinian Talmud.**

Kabbalah. The general term for Jewish mystical writings and traditions. It literally means "that which has been received." *See also* **Zohar.**

Ketuvim. Writings. This refers to the third division of the Hebrew Bible (*see* **Tanakh**) and includes Psalms, Proverbs, Job, the **Five Scrolls,** Daniel, Ezra-Nehemiah, and 1 and 2 Chronicles.

Masoretic Text. The term for the closely related Hebrew text editions of the **Tanakh** transmitted by the Masoretes ("transmitters") from the sixth to the eleventh centuries. All translations of the **Tanakh** (including the King James and *all* modern versions) are primarily based on this text. (*Note:* There is not *one* Masoretic Bible; there are thousands of Masoretic manuscripts with almost identical texts.)

Midrash. Rabbinic commentaries on a verse, chapter, or entire book of the **Tanakh,** marked by creativity and interpretive skill. The best-known collection is called Midrash Rabbah, covering the Five Books of Moses as well as the **Five Scrolls.**

Mishnah. The first written collection of legal material relating to the laws of the **Torah** and the ordinances of the sages. It provides the starting point for all subsequent **Halakha.** It was compiled approximately 200 c.e. by Rabbi Judah HaNasi (the Prince) and especially emphasizes the traditions of the rabbis who flourished from 70 to 200 c.e. *See also* **Babylonian Talmud, Palestinian Talmud,** and **Halakha.**

Mishneh Torah. Systematic compilation of all Jewish law by Moses Maimonides (also called Rambam; 1135–1204). It remains a standard legal text to this day. *See also* **Shulkhan Arukh.**

Mitzvah. Commandment. The foundation of Jewish observance consists of keeping the so-called 613 commandments of the **Torah.**

Nevi'im. Prophets. This refers to the second division of the Hebrew Bible (*see* **Tanakh**) and consists of Joshua, Judges, 1 and 2 Samuel, 1 and 2 Kings (together called the Former Prophets), and Isaiah, Jeremiah, Ezekiel, and the Twelve Minor Prophets (together called the Latter Prophets).

Oral Torah. All Rabbinic traditions relating to the **Written Torah** and various legal aspects of Jewish life. The traditions were first passed on orally before they were written down.

Palestinian Talmud. Similar to the **Babylonian Talmud** but based primarily on the work of the sages in Israel. It is shorter in scope, less authoritative, and therefore, studied less than the **Babylonian Talmud.** It reached its final form in the Land of Israel approximately 400 c.e.

Radak. Acronym for *Rabbi David Kimchi* (pronounced kim-KHEE; 1160–1235). He wrote important commentaries on much of the **Tanakh.** *See also* **Ibn Ezra** and **Rashi.**

Rashi. Acronym for *Rabbi Shlomo Yitschaki* (pronounced yits-KHA-ki; 1040–1105), the foremost Jewish commentator on the **Tanakh** and **Babylonian Talmud.** Traditional Jews always begin their studies in Bible and **Talmud** with Rashi's commentaries as their main guide. *See also* **Ibn Ezra** and **Radak.**

Responsa Literature. (Hebrew pronounced she-ey-LOT u-te-shu-VOT, "Questions and Answers") A major source of **Halakha** from 600 C.E. until today, it consists of the answers to specific legal questions posed to leading Rabbinic authorities in every generation. *See also* **Oral Torah.**

Shulkhan Arukh. The standard and most authoritative Jewish law code, compiled by Rabbi Joseph Karo (1488–1575). *See also* **Mishneh Torah.**

Siddur. The traditional Jewish prayer book, containing selections from the **Tanakh** as well as prayers composed by the rabbis.

Talmud. *See* **Babylonian Talmud** and **Palestinian Talmud** (Jerusalem Talmud).

Tanakh. Acronym for *Torah, Nevi'im, Ketuvim,* the Jewish name for the Old Covenant in its entirety. Although the order of the books is different from that of the Christian Old Testament, the contents are the same.

Targum. Literally, "translation." This refers to the expansive Aramaic translations of the Hebrew Bible that were read in the synagogues where biblical Hebrew was no longer understood. They were put in written form between 300 and 1200 C.E. The most important Targums are Targum Onkelos to the Five Books of Moses, and Targum Jonathan to the **Nevi'im** (Prophets).

Torah. Literally, "teaching, instruction, law." It can refer to: (1) the **Written Torah** (the first division of the Hebrew Bible; *see* **Tanakh**); or (2) the **Oral Torah** in its entirety (this of course includes the **Written Torah** as well).

Torah She-be-al-peh. *See* **Oral Torah.**

Torah She-bikhtav. *See* **Written Torah.**

Tosephtah. An early collection of Rabbinic laws following the division and order of the **Mishnah** but containing parallel legal traditions not found in the **Mishnah.**

Written Torah. The Five Books of Moses (the Pentateuch). *See also* **Humash.**

Zohar. The foundational book of Jewish mysticism. It was composed in the thirteenth century, although mystical tradition dates it to the second century. *See also* **Kabbalah.**

Subject Index

Aaron, 15–17, 97, 115, 143, 190, 218 n. 178
Abijah (mother of Hezekiah), 206 n. 59
Abraham (Abram), 115, 133, 139–40
    Isaac, binding of (*See* Akedah)
    and Melchizedek, 139–40
    Messiah higher than, 59–60
    offspring blessed, 11, 42, 96
Adam, 96
'adonai, 135–38, 226 n. 274, 227 nn. 277–78
Agag, Amalekite king, 79
Agrippa, Judean king, 89–91, 100–101, 111
Ahab, king of Israel, 72
Ahaz, Davidic king, 18–20, 27, 36, 192, 200 nn. 34
Akedah (binding of Isaac), 3–5, 13, 182, 195–96 nn. 2–3
Akiva, Rabbi, 157, 179
almah, 20–25, 28–31, 199 n. 31, 201–3 nn. 38–47, 204–9 nn. 57–77
Alshech (El-Sheikh), Rabbi Moshe, 49–50, 58
Amos (prophet), 172
Ancient of Days, 143
Anderson, Francis, 40
angel(s), 169
    Gabriel, 88, 91, 220 n. 191
    Messiah loftier than, 59–60
Anointed One *(mashiach)*
    rulers gathering against, 112–13
    two anointed ones, 109–11
    See also mashiach; Messiah
Answering Jewish Objections to Jesus:

General and Historical Objections (Vol. 1), XIII
Objections to the New Testament (Vol. 4), XIII–XIV
Theological Objections (Vol. 2), XIII
See also specific topics
anti-missionaries, 223 n. 233
    on belief in Messiah, 13–14
    and Christianity, 7
    Sigal, Gerald (anti-missionary author), 86
    See also Singer, Tovia; specific topics
Aram, 18–20
Archer, Gleason, 95–99, 103–4
ark of the covenant, 147
Artaxerxes I, Persian king, 106–7
Assyria, 19, 26–27, 36, 53, 62–63, 191, 213 n. 122
atonement, 6–7
    of Jerusalem and Israel, 149–52
    Messiah's death as, 100, 111, 131

Babylon, Babylonian empire, 16, 36, 40–49, 62–63, 99, 170, 173
    Daniel in, 87, 99–100
Balaam, 63
Barnes, Albert, 104–5
belief. *See* faith
Benjamin, 115
Benjamites, 183
Bethlehem, 27, 38–39, 159
betulah, 21–23, 203–7 nn. 46–62
Blau, Joshua, 113–14
Blenkinsopp, Joseph, 26–27, 34
blood, in atonement, 6–7
Boteach, Rabbi Shmuley, 14

Index of Scripture and Other Ancient Writings

247

Apocrypha

New Testament